# Quiet Neighbors

Erick W. Miller

*AuthorHouse™*
*1663 Liberty Drive*
*Bloomington, IN 47403*
*www.authorhouse.com*
*Phone: 1-800-839-8640*



*First published by AuthorHouse 4/21/2011*

*ISBN: 978-1-4567-5377-1 (e)*
*ISBN: 978-1-4567-5375-7 (hc)*
*ISBN: 978-1-4567-5376-4 (sc)*

*Library of Congress Control Number: 2011905429*

*Printed in the United States of America*



*This book is printed on acid-free paper.*

I was divorced for the second time. The whole country was suffering the effects of a stagnated economy. A man couldn't buy a job. I was so far behind with child support and credit card debt that I became a homeless man wanted in two states. Both states had seemed like home for a long time. Now I had to become a non-person, someone that you could look right at and not really see. It was time for me, Derrick Johnson, to disappear.

My normally full money belt now only served to hold up my pants. I'd spent the last of its contents trying to make one last merry Christmas for my three precious children. Those were some difficult good-byes to say. I could only hope to find cash employment where I was headed. Maybe I could earn enough to get back into the good graces of the law and my two ex-wives.

My immediate problem was going south as quickly as possible since winter in Wisconsin is harsh. October is already too cold to sleep outside. Freights were my best bet. At night, the train wouldn't notice my extra one hundred and ninety pounds. My favorite saying used to be, "No matter what happens, I've been through worse." This was a factual statement for a Vietnam infantry veteran. Yeah, when it gets too tough for me, no one else will know because they'll all be dead!

That's what I was thinking as I rode south towards the Gulf of Mexico. Brave thoughts for a man with less than a hundred dollars, damn few clothes, a home made poncho and my thirty-eight special revolver. Since the war, I never left home without it. As a matter of fact, I carried it around my home, I took it in the bathroom and I slept with it. It had become my only friend, ferocious and dependable. The bottom line in any argument is a gun. People knew that I had it and no one doubted that I would use it. I'd reached the time when all of my friends had deserted me. That .38 was the only friend that I needed.

I was already missing my children, but that was all that really bothered me. I was young and strong and looking forward to my next adventure. I'd been in worse predicaments and had gotten used to thinking on my feet.

Women had always been my weakness and I admit that my thoughts were already drifting in that direction. I had a libido like King Kong. I always said that it took a two-hundred-pound nymphomaniac to keep me at home and didn't mind if they were a few pounds either way. Girls like that seldom took me seriously and became their own worst enemies. They couldn't believe that I found them attractive enough to remain faithful.

It was these fond memories of my Reubenesque sweeties that lulled me to sleep on the first leg of my journey. The dreams were interrupted when the train started slowing down. It already seemed warmer. I had slept for some time. I hadn't the faintest idea where I was, but hopefully out of Illinois.

It was starting to get light and the train appeared to be stopping. Time to be on my guard. The pistol gave me the edge. Still, I'd rather not be discovered. The freight dropped some cars, picked up others, and changed crews. After about an hour of banging and lurching, the old train headed south again. It seemed like I got on the right freight. Evidently the bulk of its cargo was southbound.

I was getting hungry but I put it out of my head. The trip was my first priority, one step at a time. As the sun got higher, the day got continually warmer. I peeked out the door to get some clue as to my whereabouts. One pine tree looks like another, but at least they were getting taller. The heat and hypnotic motion of the train soon had me sleepy again. Since there wasn't anything better to do, I succumbed to the drowsiness.

This time I awoke soaked with sweat. The train was slowing again. As it stopped, the door to my car slid open. The three faces in the door needed shaves and looked nearly as bad as they smelled. The bottom line in any argument filled my hand as if it had a life of it's own. The three fugitives from soap and water decided that this car was too crowded. They must have seen the hollow points in the exposed part of the cylinder and realized that I wasn't bluffing.

I was beginning to wonder if this was the end of the line when Mr. Train started rolling south again. At least I wouldn't be in danger of freezing for a couple of months. That should be enough time to get work and a place to stay.

Food! I wish that I'd thought of bringing food. At least I wasn't in a state where the law wanted me. At the next stop, I would have to hop off and do something about my hunger. I still had eighty-eight dollars and every stop was in or close to a town. My plan was to walk south looking for a store and hopefully catch the same train. This was a lot to hope for but it was my only plan.

I wrapped my clothes in my poncho as neatly as I could so as not to look too much like the hobo that I was. There wasn't too much that I could do to hide my two-day beard, but it was fashionable at the time anyway. My appearance was still fairly neat and I wasn't carrying the aroma of the three bums that wanted to share my first class berth, not yet anyway.

I managed to slip out undetected and even find a little store just south of the switching yard. I got some apples, bananas, sub-sandwiches, and a couple of ice-teas. I found out that I was in Mississippi, but the name of the town was a mystery. The clerk at the counter seemed to think that "Mississippi" was all the information that I required. I could tell that my accent annoyed him and I was trying to keep a low profile.

My grocery bag and bedroll made quite a load. I still had to slip back into my empty car unnoticed. Fortune smiled and I was able to find my former accommodations safely. The car was still empty which is good since I'm so territorial. My first wife said that I was like a mean dog on a chain that wouldn't allow anyone in the yard. That was a better analogy than she could have imagined. By then, my PTSD *had* made me like a mean dog. My friends had evaporated like rain on a summer sidewalk.

With the train rolling and some food to chew on, my spirits rose. I began running my former friends through my mental computer. The end result was that each man of them would only go so far in a real test. That is when I decided to go it alone. A partner is just a witness. It sure would have been nice to have some of the guys from the jungle to travel with. After a year in that Hellhole, you knew who was who.

One winter, when there was no work, I tried to get my roofing crew to go to South America looking for artifacts. These guys looked like gorillas. They were great in a bar fight and two of them were hunters. I guess that they were only good at shooting unarmed Disney characters. When it came to the possibility of running into other armed men, every one of them backed out. Deer, ducks and rabbits don't shoot back and that suited them just fine.

I'd have been wealthy or dead from trying if I'd have suggested that idea to my stalwart partners from my Platoon in Vietnam. None of us had ever shot a woman or a kid or a water buffalo. I'm sure that there were a few cowards who had. They and the bunch at My Lai ruined the reputations of all of us.

Hell, a man could have been a Chaplain's assistant over there, but when you got home, you were labeled as a baby killer, period.

The food put me in a better mood. I had my roofing hatchet and a hook bladed knife wrapped in a cloth nail apron along with a chalk-line. All that I needed was work. I'd been working since I was nine years old. I got into construction when I was fourteen. Work held no fears for me. It kept me healthy and in shape. The roofers with the nail guns were always mad at me. At the end of the week, I always had just as many shingles installed as the best of them despite the fact that I nailed by hand.

What I needed now was a bath and a shave. It would feel good to brush my teeth too. I decided to get off at the next stop and take care of my problem. I knew that I would have to nurse my cash. I also knew that being filthy was no way to go job hunting. I wanted to keep my current living arrangements my little secret. Police like to check homeless men to see if they are wanted. (If he looks like a hobo and smells like a hobo, he's probably wanted somewhere.)

The train finally stopped and I made my move. We were very near the Gulf now. The pines were mixed with palmettos and there was a swamp at the bottom of every depression. I hiked into town with my head up and tried not to get near anyone, embarrassed to share my deteriorating fragrance with a soul.

The store that I chose was a Ma and Pa business. They were usually more sympathetic and less likely to tell the police about some smelly stranger. I bought soap, razors, a toothbrush and paste and even splurged on some after- shave. Now all that I needed was a stream and I could be human again.

I took my bag and bundle and headed into the woods as discretely as possible. Setting my sights on a clump of saw palmetto downhill from me, I went in search of the green bathroom. It turned out to be right where I thought it would be.

Between the rows of palmetto ran a clear, sandy stream. The first thing was to look around for snakes, fire ants, and the stray bear or cougar. Now at last I could get rid of that full feeling that was bordering on cramps. Everything came out O.K. and I could finally bathe.

• • •

Feeling and smelling like a new man, that King Kong inside me started to holler and scream. I wasn't prepared to turn him loose yet. "Miles to go before I sleep" was telling him to take a cold shower. Old Kong wasn't in charge here and common sense was conjuring intrusive thoughts to cover the hollering and screaming.

A tree branch provided a place to strengthen my muscles. Pull-ups and chin-ups followed by several push-ups to stay in shape. I liked to think of my pistol as a last resort. Usually people gave me room. When they crowded me, I could normally run them off with my abrasive manner and no nonsense appearance. My 190 pounds was solidly packed on a mere 5'6" frame. I looked like a large dwarf that spent too much time at the gym. There was always some fool half my age and twice my size that thought that I was over the hill. Occasionally I had to give lessons in respecting one's elders.

With all that said, this was to be my current plan. Looking like the rest of the Christian folks on the street, mingling was easier. I could therefore stroll about town to determine it's true size and how much building was going on. The stroll was a short one. The town was as small as it looked the first time. I was smart enough to realize that a Yankee stranger could starve to death here and not be mourned over.

Plan 'B' was as I suspected it might be. I would head west to Beaumont or Houston where there was more building going on. Wasting time is hard on a poor man's bankroll. Spending the night was not an option. I'm not a thief or robber. Working was the only way I would consider to improve my financial situation.

Back to the store for an over priced map. It was a necessary purchase if I wanted my plan to go well. It looked like my southbound tracks had crossed an east/west set about four or five miles north. I hated to retrace my steps, but I'm a realist and walking was something that I had to get used to. So walk I did and I even enjoyed the walk. The boxcar had me sort of down in the mouth. The fresh air and sun were good medicine for depression.

The hike went quickly. The tracks here were side by side which would double my chances of catching a west bound. I took that as a good omen. I hiked west to the first curve where the train would presumably slow down a little. Now I sat down in some cover on the outside of the curve. This was the blind side in case anyone decided to look.

I ate the last of my chow and drank my last ice tea. The part about the ice was in name only, and the food was so well on its way to the grave that I felt it necessary to ask the Lord to bless it for me. I had never been an angel and I didn't know if I'd be good at it.

The third train by was a freighter. The problem was that it was moving too fast. I realized that I would have to walk back to the beginning of the curve to have enough running room or this hop could be fatal. The first thing to do was rig my backpack so I would have two free hands. Removing my bootlaces, then cutting one in half to share between the boots did this. Their length was more than enough to do the job. I always carried a sharp knife on the premise that they don't run out of bullets. I also carried matches wrapped in plastic and tin foil. When I used to have a vehicle, I also carried a blanket, a shovel, a first aid kit, and a gallon of drinking water. Those were the days.

With my preparations complete, I continued my waiting game. There were a few more trains from each direction before I saw what I needed. The first open boxcar I saw had me up and running. I decided to throw my backpack in so I wouldn't be so heavy. This wasn't going to be easy, but I'd committed myself when I threw my pack. After a brief horrifying moment, I scrambled inside. Thank God it was empty.

...

Catching the westbound to Beaumont solved my most immediate problem. Now I had time for serious planning. I had my health, $62.00 and another clean set of clothes. I was still optimistic, but I knew that the freight yard in Beaumont would be busy even after dark. I still had to see if Beaumont was my kind of town and if it had enough building going on to share with a Yankee stranger. Even a town the size of Beaumont could be a hostile, closed community.

Just before sunset, we rolled into town. I exited the boxcar quickly and unceremoniously. I was sure to be spotted. I figured that if I hit the ground running, I'd be too hard to catch. The railroad bullies wanted slower, weaker prey. Besides, I no longer looked like a bum. I could have been anyone cutting through the yard.

I strolled into town like I was the mayor, well, maybe not quite so furtive. Anyway, I wanted to look like I fit in. This was a good-sized town. There was plenty of building to boot. I was getting tired of walking so I stopped at a fancy place with arches of gold. Besides, their Happy Meals were cheap.

I freshened up in the men's room before going to the counter. I wanted to look my best in case the opportunity to flirt myself into a place to stay should arise. Ordering the Happy Meal didn't raise as many eyebrows as my accent. That was a real attraction. Now if I could get one of the counter girls to think that my accent was as cute as I was trying to look. The only one taking the bait had a wedding band on, not my style. I'd made that mistake before and I'm still ashamed at the grief that I caused.

Taking my tray to the dining area, I hoped that my luck would improve. It didn't. That's where I met the counter girl's husband. I swear that I didn't throw the first punch, but I threw the next two, which may have been overkill. I just wanted it over quickly. Anyway, his wife hurt him more than I did.

Grabbing my Happy Meal, I made for the door with my head down. I just hate talking to police. They have a tough job and I respect them for it. I just didn't have any money for fines and there was no time allotted in my hectic schedule for jail. I had a train to catch, goodbye Beaumont.

Happy Meals taste good hot. Warm is OK too. That's how I ate mine when I quit running. I was lost now, but I wasn't deaf or stupid. Finding the freight yard would be as simple as listening for the trains. I found the tracks first and followed them to sanctuary.

I negotiated the yard unnoticed and found an empty labeled "Return to Houston Yard". Now all that remained was holding my breath until departure. Through all this, I managed to hold onto my bundle of clothes and tools. I hoped to catch some 'Z's before I got to Houston. The two cities weren't all that far apart.

. . .

I never did get that nap that I was hoping for. It's darn near all city between the two towns. It sure had grown since my last visit, and it was big in 1985. I was hoping that my journey would end in this neck of the woods. Here I knew people and had connections. I should have planned this from the start. It would be good to see old friends and find instant work.

I hopped out near I-45 and began what I hoped would be the final leg of my journey. Instantly I saw my predicament. There was a huge drainage ditch that Houstonians were fond of calling bayous. That's about what they are too. All they were are concrete lined natural washes or creeks. There was so much paved land in town that every rain filled them to near over flowing.

The last rain must have been recently. This one was just about full, and as far as I could see in either direction, there was no way around or over. Alligators are rare this close to town but not unheard of. Alligator gar and Cottonmouths are a little more common.

The water was moving fast. Crossing was going to be dangerous, but I had no choice. At least I had darkness working for me. I threw my bundle across and walked upstream to where I thought the current might carry me if I lived. Who said that hopping freights was scary?

I felt safer with my boots on. There was no way to avoid getting the pistol wet. I would need both hands and the grace of God for this. I realized that my imagination was going to be an enemy too. I'd long ago learned to face my fears. This was just another one of those times.

It wasn't very far straight across, but the current wouldn't allow me to go straight across. When I lowered myself into the water, I wasn't even sure that I would make it across. I kicked off the concrete bank as hard as I could and started swimming madly. I tried to ignore the things bumping into me in the black water. Did I forget to mention that I'm not a good swimmer? My body is so dense that I don't float. This means that I have to keep moving to stay above water. The current enhanced this handicap.

If anyone is a survivor, it's me. Besides, I had three children who would miss their father.

Pulling myself out on the other side used the bulk of my strength. I had just enough energy to finish the prayer that I'd started before the murky water interrupted me. The search for my belongings was a short one. Now I had to use my last set of dry clothes. I hated putting my wet boots over my dry socks. Having wrapped my gear back up, it was time to check my revolver. It was a good old Smith and Wesson. I emptied it and shook out the water. Dry firing it a few times assured me that its performance wasn't affected. I'd have to get some gun oil very soon. Now to get to a telephone and call some friends.

. . .

Those phone calls weren't going to be as easy as I first thought. My wallet got soaked and my phone numbers were destroyed. I should have thought to throw it across with my bundle. That mistake served as a wake up call. A phone book should remedy my new problem, now to find one.

My confidence was at it's usual high. I'd need a bite to eat, a roll of quarters, and a pay phone with a directory. I could see a truck stop on the other side of I-10. Crossing six lanes of 55 miles per hour traffic was my next challenge. That proved to be as dangerous as it sounded. After reaching the safety of the north side, I made up my mind that I wasn't going to be doing that very often.

The truck stop had everything that I needed, even good news. It seemed as if most of my old friends had moved or their phone numbers had been changed with no further information available. I was able to track down a contractor whose roofs I used to deck and shingle. He was forced to retire due to a back injury, and he didn't have any work. He did have an empty rental house north of Cut-n-Shoot. Yes folks, that's the town's real name. It is east of Conroe near the 336 Loop.

Old David turned out to be a friend. I guess that none of my roofs leaked. He made the trip down from River Plantation and refused to take any gas money. He said that the four-bedroom house was mine for $200 per month and he would wait until I was on my feet. When I asked him why it was so cheap, he said that no one wanted to rent it and he was afraid that it might get vandalized since it was at a dead end.

He forgot to mention the cemetery next door. I found that out when we got to the end of three miles of dirt road with woods on both sides. It was no real problem for me; dead people can't hurt anyone. He did warn me that the swamps behind the house had an unusually high population of cottonmouths. David knew that I wouldn't mind since I used to raise snakes. "Snake Man" had been my nickname when I lived down here before. I would just have to be careful in the yard until I got a lawnmower.

David remembered my earning potential and handed me an envelope with $500 in cash. All that he said was "I trust that you'll be staying here awhile." I shook his hand, which was as good as a contract among gentlemen.

"You'll never regret this," is what I told him.

He showed me how to turn on the electric outside and said that he'd have the bill switched to my name. While I watched his tail lights disappear, I realized what it was like to have a real friend for the first time in a long while.

Opening the screen door revealed a wasp nest. Thank god that it wasn't a cloudy night or I would have missed seeing the welcoming committee. The little buggers barely acknowledged the disturbance. They didn't enjoy the torch I used the next time I opened the door. Worked like a charm, it did. The matches from my plastic and foil packet were earning their keep.

With the wasps out of the way, my suite was ready to occupy. That dirt road seemed a lot longer when I entered the darkened kitchen. Turning on the light didn't do a lot to dispel the stark loneliness of the place. It certainly didn't make the neighbors anymore lively. That was fine with me, I liked it quiet. It looked like keeping up with the Jones's wouldn't be much of a problem. They did, however, have me beat in the "being deceased" department.

After turning on a few more lights, I decided to go pay my respects to the Jones's. It was a chilly night so snakes wouldn't be prowling about. I assumed that the Jones's would be asleep since they didn't have any lights on. I did check my pistol and reloaded it with dry ammo. My motto is "Be prepared". The bottom line and I took a stroll to see the neighbors. They weren't talking, but their home surely was. It told me that they had no living relatives to tend to their graves. It was either that, or no one cared. The grass was knee to waist deep with weeds being the predominant species of flora.

There were trails from small animals, but no sign of human disturbance. The cemetery was much larger than it first appeared. Most of the headstones were hidden by the weeds. The larger monuments on the high ground were all that showed from the road. I made a mental note to leave the wildflowers and hack down the weeds.

The sooner that I made it look like my neighbors had neighbors was the sooner this place would be removed from the list of illegal dumps and lover's lanes. I said goodnight to the Jones's and threaded my way through the markers back to my new home.

Before I could even dream of sacking out, I had to evict any and all bugs. The place must have had some tight screens because the few that I did find were just dead moths and flies on the windowsills. This was good news since there were two kinds of poisonous spiders plus a few rare scorpions in the area. After sleeping on the ground in the jungle for a year, bugs and I didn't get along.

There was an old metal spring bed sans mattress that I could rig a bunk on. The wire spring mesh of the bed would be kinder to my back than the floors of the boxcars had been. First, I had to light the propane space heater. Again I thanked my foresight to carry matches.

I don't know how long that David had owned this place, but it looked like it had been empty since Methuselah had been in diapers. All of that meant nothing to me. I was already bonding with my neighbors and the desolation was a perfect retreat when my PTSD reared its ugly head. I could barely wait to explore it all in the daylight.

Sleep was slow in coming. I had too much on my mind. Now that I'd thrown out the anchor, I was thinking about my three children. The youngest girl by my second wife was a very old seven. I thought that I had explained the situation well enough as to leave no doubts of my return. They all knew what their Moms had cooked up for me, yet naturally they still loved their mothers. I hoped that I'd made it clear that I'd see them as soon as possible.

My immediate problems were obvious. I finally put my worries in the Lord's hands and fell asleep.

. . .

Rain woke me at three-fifteen. It was ominously quiet despite the rain. I got up and looked out the windows starting with the side facing the Jones's. I don't know what I expected to see, maybe an army of slow moving zombies, like some old horror movie. The view wasn't too clear out of any of the windows. I've had insomnia since I left Vietnam. Often, I would have horrible dreams. Twisted versions of the war where the enemy wouldn't die no matter how many times I shot them. The worst ones were when I was out of ammunition. Those usually brought me awake with my heart racing.

Back in bed, I tried thinking happy thoughts to dream about. Women popped in my mind as they frequently did. From this category I tried to build a dream. Sometime later, my dream was interrupted by the sound of a vehicle coming up the road. Holy cow, it was nearly 9am. David's truck was approaching. David was alone and he got out smiling. "Did the neighbors give you any trouble last night?"

"Don't be picking on my new friends or I'll send some of them out to your house some night!" He didn't like that thought, but he got a kick when I referred to them as "The Jones's".

He got a bicycle out of the back of the truck. "My son got his license and he won't be caught dead on this anymore." He said that I could borrow it until I got some real wheels. David was a lifesaver. He also brought coffee and rolls, which we consumed while leaning on the hood of his truck.

His daughters were out of college and were both married. His son was a senior in high school. David did all the talking and was polite enough not to ask any questions.

He said that there was a housing development on the southbound 336 Loop on this end of 105 and he put in a good word for me. All that I had to do was mention his name and I could have a job as a carpenter or roofer, whichever I chose.

I told him about the PTSD and explained that it made me too irritable to work with others. The roofing job would suit me just fine because I could work alone and as late in the day as I wanted.

All of this was music to my ears. Soon I could pay David back and get a car. I asked him if he had a ladder that I could borrow. He said that he'd drop it off at the project and chain it up. I could get the key from the superintendent. Conroe was feeling like home again.

I thanked David and told him that I needed today off to do laundry and pick up some more clothes. He came inside and showed me how to prime the well and get the water running. Then he lit the hot water heater and reminded me not to let the propane run out. I waved goodbye and went around the house to check the gauge on the tank. It showed 60% of a 250-gallon capacity. The place felt like home already. My clothes from last night were fresh enough to wear today, as if I had a choice.

The shower and shave coupled with a full wallet put me in a good mood. Before I headed into town, I wanted to look around my yard and the immediate surroundings. I was curious to know if the Cottonmouth story was true or if the locally dominant species was just one of the large water snakes prevalent near the gulf. Hearing it from David, I tended to think that it was truly the highly irascible Cottonmouth. These evil creatures have two nasty secrets. The first being that their powerful bodies need not be coiled to strike in any direction. The second is that they will eat literally anything including other snakes. This allows them to eliminate their competition and reproduce (live birth) at alarming rates. King snakes and man are their chief enemies.

It was with these happy thoughts that I began my exploration. My front yard faced the southern sun, so I expected that the eastern side, near the propane tank and tower antenna, would be the best place to start. No luck there, but the tall grass could have hidden anything. Also, it was pretty chilly for snakes to be about this morning. On the north side, I made a discovery. There was a pair of cellar doors next to the back door. They were easily missed last night in the darkness and high weeds.

There was no lock. I opened one side. No one could have been prepared for what I saw next. There was about a dozen Cottonmouths on the steps and several more in sight on the dirt floor. They must have started gathering for the winter. The cemetery and the house were the only high ground in the area and the cellar was a perfect den site. I closed the door as quickly and gently as possible. This was a challenge that couldn't be ignored for long. David wasn't lying, but I'm sure that he had no idea of the scope of the problem. The snakes would only be down there for a little over four months out of the year. They must have been proliferating since the house's last occupation. Now they were a serious problem, my problem.

The snakes could stay where they were for now. They obviously couldn't get into the house. The cellar temperature and darkness were more suited to their den needs. I had to think about this problem for awhile. Basically, I liked snakes. These guys were minions of the devil, not to be confused with normal snakes.

I decided to wait for another month when all had surely congregated for the winter, then I could flood the cellar and electrocute them. This was no endangered species to be handled with kid gloves. This infestation was a menace to the environment akin to the plague. Destroying this one den would restore a natural balance to the swamp.

I'm sure that I know how this population got out of hand. Many people kill every snake that they see. The problem that this causes is that many beneficial species are killed, including king snakes and rat snakes. This leaves more food for the Cottonmouths who give live birth. The egg laying snakes are slower to proliferate because their eggs are threatened by raccoons and ants. The process of replacement is gradual, but inevitable. Now that the environment is saturated with the odor of the Cottonmouth, all but the King Snakes are reluctant to return. This creates another problem since many disease-carrying rodents are too large for anything but the Rat Snakes and Timber Rattlers. The rattlers in the area have been hunted to the brink of extinction.

In the spring, I could gather some of the beneficial snakes to speed the process of restoration. Right now I had to pedal my way to a Laundromat or 'Washeteria' as the locals were fond of calling them.

The bike was in good shape and surely beat walking. Once again I thought of what a lifesaver David was. The sun came out as I was going up the road and I looked forward to a productive day. The first stop had to be the Goodwill store. I hoped for and found baskets for the front and rear of the bike. A cheap pair of pliers solved the installation problem. Next came my wardrobe. Mostly Jeans and T-shirts with some hooded sweatshirts for cooler days. I could buy a coat when the weather dictated it.

I also bought a small saucepan to heat soup or water for instant coffee. The rest of my kitchenware would have to wait until after work tomorrow. The baskets would only hold so much. Now, for the washeteria, and all those women! (How's my hair look?")

My hair must have looked just fine. She was my kind of girl, no wedding band, soft all over, and no men's clothes in her wash. She wasn't washing any children's clothes either, but she looked to be pregnant. She was only too happy to tell me that her jerk boyfriend was in jail and never called or answered any of her letters. He knew that she was pregnant because she'd written him the news. For all that she cared, he could go to hell in a hand-basket. He wouldn't be out for almost a year, and he'd most likely take off to avoid fatherhood.

I told her that I liked children and I liked her. She gave me her phone number and asked me to call her tonight. Oh happy day, King Kong would have to shower and shave. She was a brunette too. I had bad luck with the blondes in my life. I grabbed some bread, lunchmeat and vegetables on the way home.

Margaret was her name, and she had green eyes. She was 36 years old and her jail bird boyfriend had been her first lover. She didn't date much in high school and never did more than kiss those boys. My being 8 years older didn't bother her at all. She had two male friends that she had serious feelings for but both had died in Vietnam. She was intrigued with the fact that I'd lived through the infantry over there. She didn't smoke, drink, or use drugs. The more that I knew about her was the more that I realized that she was perfect for me. She was what I was looking for when the first two blue eyed mistakes took me off the streets.

When the conversation got around to my living quarters, she was horrified to know that I was living next to the Cut'n'Shoot cemetery. Now I was getting some background on my happy home. The last occupants had lived there in the mid 1970's, a family with seven children and the maternal grandmother. The cemetery grounds were well kept then.

Their dogs and regular lawn mowing kept the varmints in the swamp where the children were forbidden to play. The children were taught to fear all snakes, a good way to stay alive when you couldn't tell one from another.

One Saturday night, the family returned from the theater to find their Border Collies dead in the front yard. The dogs had been hacked to death. The front door was locked. The father sent the children and the mother to wait in their van. When he unlocked the front door, which had never been locked before, he found his headless mother-in-law sitting in her favorite chair with her head in her lap. There was a large, inverted cross, jammed down into her neck. The back door was locked too.

Dad went to the van and called the sheriff on the CB radio. Then he took his rifle out of the van and told his wife to take the young ones to her sister's while he waited for the police with his two oldest boys. He didn't tell his wife what he had found, but she must have guessed something because she started crying so violently that her oldest girl had to drive.

When the police arrived, the father and the two boys had been killed too. Their attention must have been on the two dead dogs for the killer to be able to sneak up. They were hacked as badly as the dogs. They had all been beheaded as well. Dad's head had been found much the same as grandma's, but the boy's heads had been carried off.

The police had never had to deal with anything like this before. It read like a horror movie. The Houston police had a squad who dealt with cult killings. They were summoned in to help. Even the cult squad had never seen anything this grisly including back when the Charles Manson killings sparked some copycats.

Margaret told me that the case was never solved. Fingerprints were taken from the cross in the old woman's neck, but a match was never found. The police thought that it was the work of one man since the only tracks not belonging to the family really stood out. They were the tracks of a very heavy man with size 16EE boots. Those tracks came out of the swamp and returned there too.

The only man in the area with feet that big was a black railroad worker who was in Navasota that night. There were too many witnesses for him to be a suspect. He was a family man and a churchgoer as well.

Naturally dogs were sent in and the swamp was searched as thoroughly as possible. Neither the giant nor the boy's heads were ever found.

Every time a tall heavy stranger came to town, people would alert the police. The man would be taken in for questioning, but either his feet were way too small or he had an iron clad alibi. Eventually the harassment of big strangers stopped, but people never forgot the grisly event. Even the local teenagers wouldn't drive to the dead end. The man who tended the cemetery quit and no one took his place. The few elderly people with relatives buried out there stopped visiting.

It wasn't until David moved down from Arkansas that the family found a buyer for the property. He was never told of the place's history. He would go there alone on weekends to clean and paint. The police had the blood scrubbed years earlier. Any remaining stains were unidentifiable. He tried to rent it out for years. Eventually he got the story of his 'impossible to rent' house from friends at church. Then, even David quit going out to cut the grass. The beautiful swamp lost its beauty.

I was surprised that I never heard the story when I was in Conroe earlier. I guess that it was so horrible that it was assumed to be common knowledge. I was disappointed that David never mentioned any of this to me. He probably thought that I knew. After all, it was an old story and I had spent a few years in town before. It wouldn't have altered my decision to move in. Being a light sleeper with a gun, I'd be proud to take out a genuine bogeyman. The town would consider me a hero.

Between the snakes and the bogeyman, I didn't invite Margaret out to my place. I didn't want to scare her off by asking to spend the night on our first date, so I kissed her and said goodnight. She begged me to be careful and said that she'd pray for me. I told her to pray for the other guy and that I'd call her tomorrow after work. I told her that a .38 special could kill a black bear and that she'd never meet a lighter sleeper than me. Then I hopped on the bicycle and rode off into the sunset. How embarrassing!

That three-mile long dirt road seemed a little longer and lonelier that night. I sure wish that I'd left a light on before I went to Margaret's. Oh well, the lights weren't on in the Vietnamese jungle either.

Before I was halfway up the road, I remembered that I hadn't gotten any coffee. I wasn't sure that I could survive without it, so I reluctantly turned around and pedaled to the 7-11. Maybe I could find some Cream of Wheat or Oatmeal for breakfast too.

The 24-hour store had what I needed plus some fresh fruit. Always health conscious, I got some apples, bananas, and grapefruit. The clerk asked me if I was new in town. When I said yes and mentioned where I lived, he started to tell me the story all over again. I stopped him the first time that he paused for breath and told him that I'd heard the whole story.

He said, "And you're going to stay? Man, you're crazy! I won't even go down there in the daylight."

Now to face that long dark road again. The only streetlight was at the highway end. Now I was glad that my bike didn't have a light. Such a little beacon would surely hail my approach, something that I'd rather keep a surprise. Past experience and the revolver gave me the courage and confidence to ride up to the dark house. A small deer walked out of the woods in front of me and aged me a few years. That was all that I encountered on the way in. Leaving the bike out front, I circled the house with drawn pistol. I gave the cellar doors a wide berth and completed my rounds without incident. Now to enter the scene of the crime and continue the search.

I was a Point Man in the war and always hated night moves. At least back then I had a machine gunner behind me along with the rest of the squad. I was feeling very alone when I put the key into the lock. With the kitchen light on, it looked a little more like the place that I slept in last night. The big difference was psychological. Now I knew something that I didn't know last night. I also knew that I would have to explore the entire house and attic every night or I would never be able to sleep.

The bedroom doors were all closed to save on propane. Why heat the whole house when my bunk was in the dining room? Opening each door was an adventure by itself. Turn on the light, and each closet was a separate adventure. My instincts told me that I was the sole occupant, but prudence guided me on. Eight doors and eight adventures later, I still had to check the attic. There I would be the most vulnerable. My head would be the first thing above the floor and I didn't want to end up like Grandma, Dad, and the boys.

I closed the door to the master bedroom and turned off the light. I needed my eyes to adjust to the dark. Now, it was time for the big moment. Before, I had thought that swimming bayous at night and crossing interstate highways was scary. That was child's play compared to this.

Folks, here is where I'm going to make a few of you mad. I was as serious as a heart attack when I said that no matter what happens, I've been through worse. Vietnam was one of those places where you just had to be there. Here I would probably be facing only one man whose MO seemed to be a machete. So what if he was a foot and a half taller and had a 150 pound advantage? I'd learned that guns make everyone the same size. Some were bigger when their opponent was slow to react or just couldn't bring themselves to shoot their fellow man. Anything or anybody that tries to kill me is in trouble. I loved life and I don't freeze.

I flung open the attic door. I didn't want to appear timid. I was the hunter here. My eyes were thoroughly adjusted to the dark when I jumped up to squat on the attic floor. Spinning rapidly, I could see that it was empty. The pull chain light had no bulb. Light from gable and roof vents allowed better vision than I had hoped for. The only blind spot was behind the chimney. Checking it was only a matter of ceremony since there was no sign of disturbance in the carpet of dust on the floor. As expected, the bogeyman wasn't behind the chimney.

The first thing that I needed to do was buy extra bulbs and install yard lights. A big dog would help too. First the Cottonmouths had to go. Dogs don't usually know enough to leave them alone. I wasn't looking forward to doing this search every night. I also knew that if it became too routine, that I might grow careless or skip it some night that I was tired from working late.

I left the lights on, locked the door and went to say hi to the Jones's. Looking at the dark mound full of headstones and tall grass was like the attic all over again. A man in camouflage could be lying out there and you wouldn't know it unless you stepped on him, which is exactly what happened. I stepped on someone in the grass. The body must have been thrown here, because the weeds seemed undisturbed. At first, I thought that it was a log because he was so stiff. I didn't remember any logs last night so I knelt to explore.

I'd seen plenty of death before. I'd seen cargo nets full of bodies and decapitated men and stacks of body bags. That was something that you expected and accepted in war. Finding a man without his head next to your home in the good old U. S. of A. was another thing altogether. I couldn't call the police and I couldn't use my neighbor's phone. My only choice was to hop on the bike and go to the 7-11's pay phone.

On the way out, I decided to call David first. He could help smooth things between the cops and me. It had been a long time since I'd lived around here. That made me a stranger and a suspect.

After calling David, I called 911. There might not be anything to be done for the dead man, but clues get old fast in the damp climate this time of year. Unless that body was dumped, it was less than 24 hours old. I wondered if it was the work of a copycat or if old Big Foot was back. I had a feeling that he never left.

I told the police that I'd wait by the streetlight at the end of the road. David showed up moments before three squads pulled up. Each car had two men. At least they were taking it seriously. Maybe they knew something that I didn't. I put the bike in David's truck and we took the lead.

I felt much safer than the last time I came up the dirt road. As we got closer to the house, I noticed two more sets of headlights join the parade. When we pulled in, I discovered that the last two units were K-9 Patrols.

I led them to the body and they used the dogs and their five-cell torch lights to search the area. There was another body, headless like the first. The police said that they were probably two hunters missing since yesterday. Fingerprints would have to make the ID's positive since the dogs couldn't find the heads to check dental records.

Once again the trail led to the swamp. There was no mistaking the huge boot prints leading into the shallow, murky water. If this was the work of a copycat, he sure had some big feet of his own. The dogs wanted to go into the swamp, but the common sense of the matter was that German Shepherds hunt by sight more than smell and the bodies were about ten hours old. My kitchen and dining room were filled, but not before I showed a pair of policemen my problem in the cellar. I didn't want any innocent people getting killed while searching for clues. By the light of the torch, it looked as if the number of snakes had grown significantly. Upstairs, I told them of my plan to electrocute them. All agreed that it was a brilliant solution.

A lot of good ideas were tossed around the table including a check on boot sales in a fifty-mile radius. Those may have been a custom made pair. God forbid if they were home made. That would make them all but untraceable. I told them to put leather shops at the head of their list since that's where the bikers got custom gear made.

This suggestion got the Sergeants attention. "Have you any military experience?" he asked.

When I told him that I was a point man in the 101st Airborne/ Airmobile Infantry, he really took notice.

He said, "You may be the best man here qualified for the job of leading the search. Would you consider being deputized?"

At 44 years old, I didn't feel outclassed by the group in my home. "Does this include a sidearm and an M-16?" He assured me that we'd all be outfitted exactly that way. Then I asked him, "Is there any chance of a permanent job from this?"

He said, "That depends on how well that you handle yourself. At the very least, there was a sixty-thousand dollar reward put up by the family of the first victims and area banks for the death or capture of the murderer."

The Sergeant's words were music to my ears. I wasn't in the least worried about handling myself. I was, however, worried about the strangers that I would be working with handling *them*selves.

I told him that I'd probably killed more people than anyone in the room, maybe even put together and none of them had been women or children. I told him that with an M-16 and his two dogs that I'd take off tonight alone.

He was the boss and he said that he didn't want to lose his dogs and have to look for another body. Tomorrow he'd have some bloodhounds here and we'd get on line for a proper search. Then he went outside to radio his plan and needs. I went out with him as an extra set of eyes and ears for which he expressed his appreciation.

He sent for several pair of waders, six bloodhounds and a sharpshooter. He also requested an extra badge, M-16 and .357 magnum revolver.

When we re-entered the kitchen it got quiet. One of the older cops who'd been an MP in Vietnam just finished explaining the duties of a Point Man and had the rest convinced that I'd have gone it alone tonight as I had boasted.

Now that I'd gained minor celebrity status, the sergeant swore me in and everyone shook my hand like they were proud to share this adventure with me. That was the first time since I left the Army that I felt like I belonged anywhere. I could sense that they expected results with me along, I hoped that I wouldn't let anyone down.

David said goodnight and left with the bulk of the police. The sergeant and his partner insisted on staying the night. I told them that their company was more than welcome. We agreed on pulling guard in shifts with everyone awake at 4:30 AM. Tomorrow would be a rough day even if we weren't successful.

...

All of us wanted first guard since we were too excited to sleep. We decided to kill the lights and wait until 10 O'clock to draw straws. I lit the range and made some instant coffee. We had to pass the pan around since I still hadn't gotten dishes. 10:00 came and went. It was unanimously agreed that we would all stay awake and watch the rear and two sides of the house, hoping that the yard light and the presence of the squad would keep that side psychologically off limits to our bogeyman.

With the light from the space heaters casting shadows, we watched from our individual guard posts. It was so dark, and we had so many blind spots, that watching from the windows was a wasted effort. Exhaustion finally set in for all of us, and we gave up on the guard idea altogether. I promised them that I was a light enough sleeper to be sufficient guard.

I wondered if they had nightmares too. The dreams couldn't be any worse than the reality surrounding the events in and around this house. I wondered if Big Foot knew about the den in the cellar. I wondered if I was going to get any sleep before 4:30. I finally did fall back to sleep. More nightmares, what else?

4:30 AM came way too soon. We made a half-hearted attempt at washing up and passed around the coffee pan again. Full daylight didn't come until nearly seven O'clock. The rest of the crew started showing up at about six. A couple of the guys even brought real coffee and sandwiches. By seven, everyone was there with bells on. By the time that we moved out at 7:30, we were all armed to the teeth with bloodhounds in the center and regular K-9's on the flanks. I was given center stage where the boot prints entered the water. Any time that he stepped on solid ground or a patch of roots, he left mud. I kept watching for signs that he might have doubled back. I didn't want to be embarrassed by this psycho.

For the longest time he went in a straight line like he had a specific destination in mind. We came to a stream of water that should have been clear but was rather murky instead. It occurred to me that our quarry was walking up the stream, stirring up the bottom. We sent one K-9 and one bloodhound with their handlers and some backup to track upstream on this shore. The rest of us, and the other two dogs, crossed over to keep an eye on the other shore.

Our boy never left the water. To make matters worse, the stream split into two narrow streams that rapidly spread apart. This meant that we'd have to split into four groups that would quickly lose sight of each other. It occurred to me that our prey might incite our groups to shoot at one another. I shared my thoughts with the Sergeant who agreed with my reasoning.

I suggested that half of the party hang back at the stream junction while the other half went upstream for fifteen minutes. Upon their return, group two could repeat the process up the other stream. If neither team produced results, we'd have to head back or spend the night in the swamp.

As it turned out, neither team produced results. We had a decision to agonize. Both teams had murky water in the streams that they followed. Had our prey gone up one side, crossed over and doubled back? He had plenty of time to have done just that and then simply swam downstream. We couldn't know how intelligent this guy was. Many of us assume that big people are stupid. To underestimate one's enemy is to increase their arsenal.

I laid my thoughts out to the posse. They were all stunned at the possibilities. "Mr. Big Foot could lead us in circles out here. He could even be back at the cemetery." I reminded them that none of the dogs ever alerted so it was probably a cold trail. "So far, he hasn't used a gun which is not to say that he doesn't have one. He might be as good of a shot as our sharpshooter. The possibilities are endless and many are in his favor," I said.

We decided to retrace our steps with me in the lead and dogs at front and rear. To everyone's amazement, I lead them right back to where we entered the swamp. Our man had given us the slip. They would have to check shoe stores and leather works. We could only hope to catch the headhunter before he struck again.

Now I made a strange request to the Sergeant. I gave him the names of three men that I'd served with in Vietnam and asked him to trace them for me. I gave him the towns and states where he might begin the search. I told him that those men and I would be more than enough to get this job done. He agreed on the condition that he and one other man be allowed to join the hunt. I had no problem with the extra firepower and was ecstatic that he had accepted my plan at all.

I warned him that we would be sleeping out there and might be out for days. I told him that we'd be living out of backpacks and would have to drink iodized stream water.

That's when he interrupted me. " I graduated from Ranger School and served in Grenada and Desert Storm. My friend from SWAT has similar credentials. We both have personal body counts from the military as well as with the police force."

I said, "Welcome home and thank you for your service. Sergeant, I'll be proud to have you both with us. I have another request and that is for a machine gun. Two of my friends were gunners in Vietnam. One, for a very long time."

"We'll be outfitted as you requested and dressed in camouflage," he said. "You'll be proud of the team that we field."

The Sergeant was complying with most of my requests. I still think I could have shortened the search by going after the man at night with a dog. He thought he was saving my life, but my ego wouldn't allow me to entertain that thought.

...

I bummed a ride to the 7-11 and called Margaret. She was glad to hear from me but broken hearted to find out that I wouldn't be seeing her for about a week. I promised her that this wasn't goodbye. I told her that I'd been deputized and would be working with the police. I told her to save all of her love for me. That cheered her up and I could sense her anticipation through the telephone.

My home would be the patrol base. There would be a decoy family of undercover police living there. Two of the younger members of the force would pose as the two sons. The parents would be chosen from more senior officers.

The house was furnished and the telephone was hooked up. We in the field would communicate with the house through the use of PRC-77 military radios. That would put 911 and back up a phone call away. The decoy family would have a nervous little beagle for a burglar alarm.

Our instructions were to treat anyone caught in our net as innocent until proven guilty. Other than that, we were authorized to use deadly force against any hostile attack.

They found my army friends even though two of them had re-located, one of them several times. They were flown in at federal expense. Our headhunter had captured national attention. A month or so ago, there were similar killings in Louisiana. Most law enforcement officials who were familiar with the case had assumed that the killer had died in the swamps. When similar cases showed up in a neighboring state, the FBI got involved. They were understandably excited about our two recent slayings.

The FBI would pick up the tab for the entire operation. They approved of our plan, but expressed concern over the ability of us older members of the squad being able to keep up. When we introduced ourselves to their rather soft looking field rep., he changed his attitude. We all had the thousand-yard stare and I was the midget of the group. Barry was 6'0" with ten months in a Tiger Platoon and many years as a Fireman. Edwin was 6'2" with 32 months in Vietnam, most of that Infantry, plus time as an MP. Travis was 6'0", and a former prizefighter with at least one charge of attempted murder on his rap sheet.

I think that after the introductions, he was feeling sorry for the machete killer. Be that as it may, we were determined to find our man if he was still in Texas. We were all pretty sure that it was indeed him who traveled from Louisiana last month. This guy had as many facets as a well-cut diamond. He may even have a support network of people as dangerous as he was. We, on the swamp squad, had the experience and determination to do whatever was necessary to bring in or kill this animal.

I convinced them that we should move out at night. Ed and I would move out on a two-man point, five meters apart. Travis would carry the machine gun. Barry would carry the PRC-77 and be assistant gunner to Travis. He had been a Gunner *and* Point Man before too. They would be 1 meter apart and 5 meters behind Ed and me. The two ex-rangers would be 5 meters behind them carrying fully automatic M-14's with starlight scopes, which were night vision devices. They would be both flank and rear security with 10 meters between each other. They would be very vulnerable, hence very alert. Johnny was left flank and the Sergeant (Don) was on right flank. Ed, Barry, and I carried M-16's. Everyone had side arms. We also had an army scout dog for the operation. Its training was more suited for this mission.

All of the excess personnel left when the decoy family showed up with their dog. They were in a used car modified for police use. We could never be sure if the whole operation hadn't been compromised but the plan was already in motion. Now the swamp team could sleep until dark.

Ed, Travis, Barry and I had a lot to catch up on. Stories would have to be short with the details saved for after the mission. It was sure good to see them all alive and in good health. Right now, sleep was a must.

...

The decoys woke us at 9PM. We loaded our systems with coffee and ate what was our last hot meal for a long time. Our backpacks were loaded with army chow. Canned C-rations to be eaten cold. We would be on strict noise, light, and smoke discipline from the moment that we left the house.

The dining room light was off and the double doors closed. Soon, we'd be going out the back. Our cue would be the car door slamming around front. One of the decoy sons was supposed to drive to the 7-11 as a distraction, just a quick trip for minimal security breach. Darkness was the ocean that our monster swam in.

We heard our cue and stepped out into eternity. We each carried a .357 magnum and a boot knife. I wish that we could have checked the cellar, but I figured that the Cottonmouths would have taken care of the headhunter. With the last man out the door, we formed up in our order of march. Our flanks were out and each of them looked around the corners of the house. I felt like I was among invincible company.

I had no qualms about the mission. I was, however, worried about the decoy family. The Beagle was an excellent watchdog, but they only had two seasoned officers in their group.

With the scout dog in the middle, Ed and I moved out into the dark drizzle. All of this was reminiscent of a very bad adventure from a long time ago. There was excitement and dread in me, probably in all of us.

The rangers may have felt it differently than us older men, but I was sure that they would hold up their end.

I was familiar with the path out so I whispered to Ed to follow my lead. First, I wanted to check on the Jones's. I had the other four wait, as Ed and I took the dog to the cemetery. The wind was at our back, so we circled the cemetery to maximize the dog's effectiveness. Ed was five yards to my right on the swamp side. At night in the high grass, he was practically invisible. I made the mental note to bring the flanks in closer. We swept the ground with the dog roaming freely. Glad not to have found anything, we rejoined the group. They said that we didn't flush so much as a raccoon.

Back to the swamp. We were wet and cold already, just like home (Vietnam). Our plan was to go to the stream and head the other way. We would adhere to this plan unless the dog alerted at which time we could adjust accordingly. The four of us in the middle had seen scout dogs killed before and knew that they weren't infallible. We intended to protect this one like one of us.

We had a dilemma when we reached the forty foot wide stream. We would have to split up to cover both sides. We left the dog with the gun team along with one flanker. Ed, Sergeant Donald and I waded across. We were about ten feet apart, on line so we hit the shore at the same time. Then we executed a right face and both groups moved out in unison. We did our best to stay parallel to the group across the stream. The vegetation was sparse along the stream's edge. I guessed that frequent flooding kept the shores barren.

I was shorter and had better night vision than Ed, so I went first. Donald brought up the rear. Johnny was on point on the far bank with Barry and Travis walking side by side about five yards to his rear. The trees were mostly barren. We were close enough to town to have some light reflected down from the clouds and back up from the stream. The effect was rather spooky. It was brighter than I had hoped so we could at least see each other across the stream.

At 10 O'clock, Barry had to call in a situation report. He did this walking. The code was to break squelch twice if all was fine, once for a hot trail. We would go vocal if we made contact.

Shortly after ten, the dog stopped and did some serious sniffing. It looked like Big Foot had finally left the water. The three of us were waved back across. We waited to break squelch to see if this was truly a fresh trail.

We followed the dog back south into the brush. He led us to a gruesome sight. The missing heads of the two hunters, most likely, were propped upside down in a fire pit. The brains had been scooped out. Now we knew what the machete man ate. The monster was a cannibal too. Next question was, had he ever carted off any whole bodies? Don said that it was a definite possibility. There were always unsolved missing person reports, way too many at that. Up until now, he'd figured that most had just moved on without telling anyone to avoid paying debts, escape jail time, or to leave a bad relationship or marriage. Our latest discovery put a grisly twist on the missing-persons file.

We poked around long enough to decide that our evil giant was long gone. We took a chance and radioed our findings to the house. They said that an armed team would come out with bloodhounds to retrieve the heads. We reminded them that this guy was famous for doubling back.

We picked up the trail again farther downstream when the dog left the brush. I think that the dog's keen eyes were following boot prints. There couldn't be much scent left after the rain. We pressed on at a quicker pace. Our man was walking boldly along the stream like he was confident that no one was following. I was hoping that he wouldn't double back, but rather lead us to a permanent camp or even a cabin.

We broke squelch negative at 11:00 PM, and again at midnight. The cannibal looked like he could walk forever. When I thought how far that he had walked and doubled back, and swam and walked to his first camp, burdened with the two heads, my hair stood up. I called a halt and we moved into the brush for a whispered meeting. I shared my thoughts and my concern that this bold trail could be leading to a trap. I suggested that we put men on the other bank again to watch for tracks over there. We went back to our earlier method of travel with three men on each bank. This time we walked abreast with our flank security well inside the brush line.

We were too far from town to get any reflected light off the clouds now. This meant that we were out of visual contact with the party on the other bank, which was now fifty feet away. I switched places with Don so he could keep an occasional watch with his starlight scope. It was past 1AM and all that I could do was assume that Barry had called in his situation report. He'd proven dependable under fire a long time ago. There was an island in the stream and we started towards it to find the other team approaching it as well. We met on the small island and saw the tracks right away. The other team was surprised. Johnny said that the tracks on their bank had kept going in a straight line. So our friend had doubled back! Was he behind us or ahead? We took a vote. We unanimously agreed that he was just checking his back. He would not have come all this way to turn around.

We covered the small island and discovered his second camp. He had skinned a catfish and eaten it raw. There was no sign of a fire and there were ominous bite marks on the scraps of skin. At the far end of the island, his tracks showed signs of coming and going. It looked like he headed to the shore that Ed and I had just left. We were right and picked up the trail immediately. Time for another strategy session. We all felt that we must be near his base camp. We all agreed that this man was as dangerous as he was evil.

I pointed out that he may not be alone, he may have dogs, guns, and even booby traps. I said, "This is time for us to make camp."

I got no argument from anyone in the face of all that logic. I didn't want to cross the river in daylight, so we moved inland fifty meters and set up in a perimeter. Everyone faced out and we broke out chow. No matter how hungry you are, cold C-rations still taste awful. The dog didn't mind them, but what does a dog know anyway?

We decided on 50% alert with every other man awake. The dog could have his nightmares in the center of the circle of cold, wet, miserable crazy people. He seemed to bond to Barry and slept by him. The rest of us were amazed since none of us felt the bond and wouldn't sleep next to Barry for all the tea in China. Oh well, if he liked cold C's, sleeping with Barry wasn't that far of a stretch.

...

Thank God that we had set up fifty meters inland or we may have never found the cannibal's base camp. We were on 100% alert since 6AM. We'd eaten breakfast in the dark and taken care of business in the brush. We were all nearly frozen except for Barry and Fido. Was it my imagination or had they gotten closer during the night? Naw, that dog would never do anything that disgusting.

All kidding aside, as it grew brighter, we could see a small hill a little farther inland. The brighter that it became, the less that it looked like a hill and the outlines took on a man-made quality. Soon, the cabin was plain to everyone. Once again, the questions about booby traps and dogs were on everyone's mind.

With Ed and me in front, we crept forward, looking for anything out of the ordinary. The dog would alert at the first sign of motion. Our two short columns continued without finding anything. We got right up to the back wall of the cabin. So far, there was no hint of any dogs. No dogs and no booby traps, I thought that this guy was supposed to be paranoid, back tracking all the time. Something was wrong here. The man that we were following wouldn't let anyone walk right up to his front door so easily. Right about then, I spotted the platform in the tree.

It had a little roof over it and it appeared as if Tiny was still asleep. That was one sturdy tree because he was truly a giant. Without speaking, I pointed to the platform. Everyone's eyes got big. He slept where he could watch the front door of his cabin.

We crouched down on the blind side of the cabin to formulate a plan. We felt sure that we had found our man. The unknowns were, was the cabin empty, and did the monster have a gun? Our first move was to radio in our find. We'd need two helicopters, one for the giant and one for us.

I volunteered to make my way around to a tree next to the sleeping giant and climb up to his level. Once there, I could pop him if necessary or demand his surrender. The gun team would cover the cabin door and the two rangers could support me from the ground. It sounded easy, but I was nervous just the same. There were still the unknowns to deal with.

Well, I volunteered, so off I went to make like a squirrel. I thought that I made too much noise climbing the adjacent tree. I was reminded of Jack and the Beanstalk and stifled a laugh. This is where your life is supposed to pass before your eyes. I took it as a good sign when that didn't happen to me. Finally at a level to see into nature-boy's bedroom, I saw what I should have expected. Both of the missing hunting rifles were in the bed. Thank God that he was a sound sleeper. I had a feeling that the report of a gun by his ear would have more of an impact than the foolish demands of a human squirrel. I took it upon myself to fire a shot into the air and yell “Freeze!”

When his eyes shot open, he was looking into the bore of a very large pistol ten feet from his face. “Throw down your weapons!” was the first time that I let the ground crew know that he was armed.

Taking their cue from me, the rangers each fired a round into the air. Then Tiny looked down and saw that he was covered from three directions. He dropped both rifles to the ground.

“Now get the hell down from there!” was my next swiftly obeyed command. I watched closely to see if he had any hidden weapons as he dropped a knotted bull rope over the side. That dude was an easy 400, pounds but he climbed down like it was a piece of cake. That took an incredible amount of strength.

As he neared the ground, the rangers backed up, keeping him in their crossfire. That man lay face down without even being told. He knew that he had been caught by some seriously dangerous people. I gladly climbed down to join my friends and the mystery of the cabin. Barry and Travis still had their eyes and the machine gun trained on the only door. Johnny put his M-14 to the big man’s head and told him not to twitch. Donald took a nylon rope from a side pocket and bound our captor’s hands like he did it on a regular basis.

The big man was about three feet wide and Don could get his hands no closer than ten inches apart. He dug out some more rope and hobbled the man’s feet about eighteen inches apart. “Now roll over!” he growled.

“Stand up!” was the sergeant’s next command. Donald was in his normal role as a policeman and took command of the situation. “What’s in the cabin? Your life depends on the truth!”

Tiny looked up and didn’t see any pity, “They’re all dead, there’s nothing to fear.”

Barry took a chance and pulled the door open. It was a thick, heavy affair that dragged open slowly. The big man didn’t lie. The cabin was a meat locker full of bodies. They were all sizes and both sexes. They appeared to be smoked or preserved in some way. Some near the door weren’t even whole as if he had been cutting his meals from them.

Most of us had children and there was talk of saving the taxpayers some money. Barry pushed the door shut. We were all tired of looking at that. I felt sorry for the county coroner.

I climbed up the knotted bull rope to search Tiny's bedroom. I found a machete and two other wicked looking knives. There was some meat up there too. God, I hoped that this man got the death penalty.

The helicopters followed the stream up and were able to land in two small clearings. This would be my first chopper ride in over twenty years. This would be a good one.

. . .

With the securing of the prisoner, and having heard Sergeant Donald read him his rights, we should have had a sense of relief. I, for one, had an uneasy feeling instead. The cabin had way too much meat for one man. The stream here was large enough for a sizable boat.

While the FBI Agents that came in with the choppers were looking around and taking pictures, I corralled Edwin and suggested that we do some looking of our own. I told him my thoughts about the giant selling meat to Satanists or other cannibals.

Satanists come in all colors and from all walks of life. When I was a teenager, I read about a group of cannibals in Upstate New York. Before I left Wisconsin, there was a serial killer arrested in Milwaukee who was also a cannibal. There were devil worshippers in every state in the union and all over the world.

I told Ed that we were looking for some sign of watercraft or activity of that nature. We were less than five hundred feet below the island when we found what I expected to find. There were two large stakes driven into the sand about fifteen feet apart. They were about three feet out into the water and parallel to the shore. There were tracks of all sizes aplenty here. Evidently, Big Foot had friends. Wading out to the stakes, we could see the obvious marks in the sand from a flat-bottomed boat. Now, to report our findings to the people at Camp Cannibal.

My theory, my find, and hence my decision, on who to report it to. I figured that Don had taken the responsibility to head up this mission, so he should have the pleasure of informing the FBI that they overlooked something. I didn't want too much attention until I could clear my warrants. The ten thousand-dollar reward money would clear up my child support, pay off David, and leave me a few bucks to buy a junk car to get around in.

Edwin stayed in the brush near the stream in case a boat came at the wrong time. I sent Johnny back to boost Ed's firepower. Talking to the Sergeant brought the expected reaction. The FBI agents were excited at the implications. All kinds of questions arose. The mission had outgrown its original squad.

We were to be re-supplied, reinforced, and brought out some extra clothes. The cabin had to be emptied quickly and all the re-supply and reinforcement done ASAP. Body bags as well as extra radios and batteries would be needed. We were in imminent danger of being compromised by the air traffic.

Our squad, minus the Sergeant, was to setup river watch approximately one mile downstream from what everyone called "Camp Cannibal". We called my house and released the decoys. Then we put the PRC-77 on the same frequency as the helicopter's radios and began our hike downstream. Ed took over point since he saw as well as I in the daytime and his height may enable him to see farther.

The sun came out and cheered us up. This was our first chance to dry out since we started. We walked roughly a mile and set up far enough in the brush to allow us to see without being seen. Just like in combat, we took off only one boot at a time. The warm sun was like medicine for the soul. Barry had the volume low on the radio. Johnny was set up another twenty yards into the brush as a listening post.

When I told my three friends about the ten grand, they were ecstatic. The financial affairs of Vietnam veterans with PTSD are usually in a state of woe. They knew that there was another mission ahead, but expressed concern over losing jobs and not seeing their wives. I assured them that the FBI was picking up the whole tab. In addition to drawing deputy salary, their lost pay would be made up. The authorities would notify their families as well as their bosses to alleviate any stress there.

Now they were really happy. All of us missed the action. Now our forty something year old bodies and brains could get the adrenaline flowing again. We were buzzing so much that Barry almost missed the call to reunite. When we got back, the camp was as we had first found it. There were some rough looking youngsters at the river to greet us. They turned out to be the first watch. As we entered the clearing, Sergeant Donald greeted us. He appeared to be still in charge.

We were briefed in the cabin, which served as the command center.

All vestiges of the former occupants were gone. The place even smelled fresh as if it had been sprayed with disinfectant. Don assured us that we were surrounded by a perimeter of specially selected police akin to SWAT, to the tune of thirty-six men. It was a whole platoon. He said that they were well armed, experienced men, most with combat experience. Some were even Vietnam Veterans.

We were given dry clothes, waterproof ponchos, anti-fungal powder for our feet, extra socks, and heat tabs. There would be no more cold food. There was to be noise discipline around the clock, no fires, and cooking was to be done only in the daylight hours using the compressed Trioxane heat tabs. We were given camouflaged thermoses for hot coffee at night. The dog would come with us since our position was back downstream where we had just left. Johnny would come with us as well as one of his SWAT friends.

The radio procedure was the same as the trip out, only we'd be reporting to the cabin as the new base. Barry exchanged his PRC-77 radio for a smaller PRC-25. The big radio would be needed at the cabin so Don could communicate with the FBI who was now set up at my house. Johnny's SWAT friend had a night vision scope on his fully automatic M-14 rifle.

Our orders were; All traffic, boat or pedestrian was suspect. Don't shoot unless fired upon. Report all traffic to base with attention to detail. Now we should get outfitted and to our station ASAP. I shook the Sergeant's hand and wished him safe hunting.

...

We waited to change clothes until we bathed. With security downstream another one hundred yards. We took turns in pairs. The cold water made this a speedy affair. Soon we were snug as bugs in rugs or something like it. Two men watched the river all the time while we took turns building dry sleeping positions with the camouflage ponchos. We made three low-profile hutches in a triangle with five yards in between. Just a little brush over their tops made them virtually invisible, unless you knew that they were there. The center was our cooking area. The miniature camp was thirty meters into the brush so river watch was always in sight. We'd have to rig a rope signal for guard at night.

There were chores enough to go around. Thermoses to be filled for night- time, trash to be buried daily, river watch and guard in the brush, plus radio duty twenty-four hours per day. The general consensus was that we'd be the first to sight intruders. My motto was, " Expect the unexpected."

I assumed command of the group without argument. All of the major discoveries and positive suggestions had originated with me. Sergeant Donald would have serious competition when I became a regular member of the force. SWAT would have appealed to me more, but I don't like big cities and Conroe didn't have a SWAT team yet.

Ed and I shared a poncho tent, Barry and Travis paired up, Johnny and the new man, Rick, filled the last tent. We were settled in well before dark so we could heat supper with no danger of compromising light discipline.

There was about a half of an hour of daylight left. I wanted to explore our immediate area, something that we hadn't had time to do yet. I went out alone which may have been a mistake, but I felt comfortable since I had the dog with me. I started at the river watch and went downstream fifty meters with the intention of making an arc that would end up fifty meters upstream of river watch. I made my plan clear to everyone for obvious reasons. Our mission wasn't to make fools of our selves by shooting each other.

The dog walked slowly, three yards ahead, strictly business as he was trained. Spike alerted just before I was about to swing inland. I crawled forward slowly with the dog close behind. This was a good dog. Twenty meters ahead, I could see a man at the bank. He appeared to be fishing. I smelled a rat. This guy didn't appear to be your garden variety of fisherman. Everyone carried a gun in the woods, but his was an AK-47 worn on a sling in a front to back, horizontal position, classic mode for quick firing. It was almost dark and he was literally in the middle of nowhere. I suspected that he wasn't alone but I couldn't see anyone, which meant nothing. I sent the dog back to summon help while I kept an eye on my well-armed fisherman.

Moments later, Barry and Travis crawled up with the machine gun, help in spades. That was a very good dog. The fisherman's boat was a V-hull. This meant that if he were parallel to the shore, only the stern would leave a mark. Who knows how many customers the headhunter had? Just then, two men with similar armament left the brush and greeted the first man while dragging a dead alligator between them. It appeared as if they were just poachers, but everyone was suspect.

They put the six foot 'gator in the boat and made their way quietly downstream with an electric trolling motor.

We used Santa Claus as a password. That kept us alive as we rejoined our curious friends. Spike was worth his weight in gold. We called in our report and I requested an extra radio and six more men. The radio and men would be flown out tomorrow and rappelled in one mile upstream from our base. That way they would be less likely to compromise that position. I told the Sergeant about the boat traffic and poaching problem. He said that the FBI had a camera on the bridge that our river passed beneath. It was a live camera with the monitor at my house. They also had a houseboat with a speedboat tied to it in the bay where the river emptied. All of this was only seven miles farther downstream.

It sounded like our sting couldn't fail, but Murphy's Law never sleeps.

I still wanted to finish the sweep of our area even though it was dark now. Travis volunteered to come and we brought the dog. We went back to the river and walked downstream to where the poachers had been. We couldn't see much in the dark and started our swing into the sparse woods. Now we were glad for the dog's company.

Of course the bigger arc took us deeper into the woods. We found the water hole where the alligator's hibernation and life were cut short. We found several more water holes on our moonlit jaunt through the creepy forest. We heard the scream of a bobcat sounding like a dying woman. The dog alerted once for a small black bear. The bear didn't even challenge us, choosing to shuffle off quickly. We came upon some stone ruins that would need daytime exploration. The ruins might be a major find. We couldn't be sure in the dark, but it looked to be a busy place. Was it animal traffic or from people? It was too dark to tell.

There were no more major discoveries on the way in. "Santa Claus" was our salvation once again. That same password would gain entry to our main camp as well as my house. Time for river watch and the comfort of other human beings. I radioed in our finding of the ruins and told them that I would wait for the extra men before further exploration.

The night passed uneventfully. The dog never alerted. This was good, since we all needed the rest. The whole operation was wearing on our nerves. Only the new man, Rick didn't seem drained. For me, this living nightmare started in the cemetery when I literally stumbled onto the first hunter. I was in this nightmare for the duration. I could never sleep in my house until all the demons were exorcised. I wouldn't feel like a man until the end and right now, the end just wasn't in sight.

It was sickening to think of Satanists and cannibals in my own country. It was like civilization was on a downward spiral. According to history, we had made little or no progress on moral or spiritual issues. The evil outweighed the good and seemed to multiply faster. I refused to accept that I was on a losing side no matter what the odds. The few dozen men out in this swamp were waging a war that not many men had the stomach for. Each one was a hero in my book.

The new men arrived by nine AM. I moved them off the river's edge and introduced them to the rest of the troop. River watch had already frozen them until the password was uttered. I let them get settled before I picked some men to check the ruins. If I'd asked for volunteers, the camp would be empty. I picked Ed, Travis, Johnny, and Rick. Barry stayed to man the machine gun should it be needed.

The new men looked solid with mile deep eyes. They carried themselves with the confidence of men who had passed the test. They were just younger versions of what Vietnam did to us. I had no doubt that they'd fit in and would be a compliment to SWAT.

We took Spike, only this time we didn't walk down the river. We paralleled it inside the brush to avoid being seen from the river or from across the river. We moved in a "V" formation with the dog setting the pace. When we came upon last night's trail, Spike hung a left like he could read my mind. We wound our way through the alligator ponds and followed the dog to the ruins. The other four men set up a loose perimeter with their backs to the ruins. Spike roamed wherever his nose led him. The ruins were full of people tracks, all different sizes including those of the giant. That must be why his tracks kept going the night before we found him.

This meant that he roamed around in the dark a lot. These ruins were well over a mile from the cabin and his tree fort. What was the attraction of this particular place, especially at night? There was an unsolved mystery here that I couldn't quite bring to focus.

I called in the security to put them behind the cover of the walls and get their thoughts on this puzzle. The very first thing that Ed said was, "Good God, look at all this blood!" everyone saw it but me. I'm colorblind. The rain had mixed it into the mud to the point that it was invisible to my eyes. The dark spots on the walls were made from blood too.

The horror was in everyone's eyes. Rituals or feeds were conducted here. None of the blood was fresh. This was our second day of sunshine. I had two thoughts that I hoped weren't true. One was that our poachers were involved. That alligator which they'd put in the boat came from one of the holes in plain sight of these ruins but they carried it back whole. It was not butchered here. Surely they were aware of this place and all the blood, yet they seemed totally calm. My second thought that the big dude we arrested at the camp was the wrong guy.

God help the world if the real monster was still out in the dark and all that we had was just a brother or just some big guard for the smoke house. Those knives and the machete could have just been butcher's tools instead of murder weapons. There were too many unanswered questions.

We would have missed these ruins if the dog hadn't seen the poachers. One thing was obvious, we would have to watch this place. I radioed our little camp and told them the situation we had. I had them take the chance of hitting two rocks together to get a compass fix on the river camp. It was loud and clear since it was less than one hundred yards away. Using the back azimuth, either team could reinforce the other, even at night.

Next, I called Sergeant Donald. He had been monitoring our conversation. He said that they would modify their perimeter and send us six more riflemen. I told him to have them put their backs to the river and take eighty-five paces, then make a right face and follow that azimuth for about a mile and a quarter. When they spotted the ruins, they should come ahead. I told Donald to curtail night patrols except in force and to be ready for anything. I reminded him of the three men with their AK-47's.

His response was that he, too, expected the unexpected. I thanked him for the extra men and signed off.

We would have to wait for the reinforcements to come before we could break for chow since our rucksacks were at the river. Any patrol from here on out would have to have six men and the dog. We would make three camps forty yards apart along our azimuth. The machine gun would be in the center camp. This meant that the ruins wouldn't split us up too badly. We would have a radio at the river and at the ruins. Runners from the outer camps could keep the gun position informed. We would use the password "Santa Claus" answered by "Happy Easter".

Spike alerted in the direction of the base and we took cover. We spotted them first thanks to the dog. They moved up cautiously and the lead man said "Santa Claus".

I stood up and said "Don't shoot!" There were six sober looking troops armed with M-16's. I'd have to be sure that there was a night vision scope at the two outer positions. Spike would stay at the camp nearest the ruins.

I briefed the reinforcements including the Happy Easter response. I gave them the azimuth and told them to make a low profile, three-poncho tent camps twenty yards along the azimuth in the direction of the river and to camouflage the tents. I reminded them to be constantly vigilant and to watch the dog for an alert. I gave them the fire and cooking discipline and told them that I would be back with the starlight scope after I'd chowed down. We left them with the PRC-25 radio and the knowledge that this camp might be the most dangerous spot.

Finally we could eat. We compassed our way straight to the river camp and "Santa Claus'd" our way in. I counted the paces in between. It looked as if we would have only thirty yards in between camps, which was more to my liking.

. . .

After lunch, I called a strategy meeting. First I filled Barry and company in on all the implications of our find. Not just the blood at the ruins, but the possibility of the headhunter's still being out there. We could assume nothing. Those poachers may have been just that, only poachers. If they saw the blood at the ruins and didn't have all the facts that we did, they would attribute the footprints and gore to competition for the game in the area. Poachers were in abundance from Brownsville to the Keys, nationwide, as far as that goes.

Of course, they could be connected too. With human meat being one of the selections along with catfish and alligator tail. They looked like desperadoes, but they had made no attempt to approach the smokehouse. They may have even become victims themselves. The headhunter may be an independent entity with no friends at all. His role might be as a hunter and provider of meat. Since the smokehouse was full, it made no sense for him to carry either of the dead hunters back with him.

I decided to call base to see if the FBI had a fingerprint match with Tiny and the prints on the cross found in the elderly lady's neck back in the Seventies. Sergeant Donald said to wait one and he'd call my house for confirmation. It took ten agonizing minutes for the chilling reply. There was no match on the prints. Tiny was being held without bond on suspicion of murder, cannibalism, and dealing in human flesh. The public defender was cooperating with the FBI since the circumstantial evidence was overwhelming. The boat carrying the poachers never showed up on the monitor of the bridge camera. That was a lot to digest. None of this information was good news.

Cell phone service was sketchy at best in this low piece of ground. I requested a third radio, a PRC-77 if one was available since we would have to patrol as far downstream as the highway and the bridge. Don said that the PRC-77 was a good idea and one would be flown to the drop off, two miles west of us. He said that he'd send six more of his men since we were spread so thin. I asked if we could keep the new men. He replied, "Most affirmative."

That would mean that I could keep my three camps and still have a roving patrol. Once again I shared hunches with Sergeant Donald. He said that with the astounding news about the fingerprints, that anything was possible, especially that we may have several adversaries. He said that if the FBI would send someone to run camp cannibal, that he'd like to join us. He said that he'd request another platoon and enough PRC-25's to have a radio for every sixth man.

"Excellent ideas, Don. I was afraid to ask for so much. The radios are as important as the chow that we'll be needing soon." Before I signed off, he said that the cabin was stacked with LRRPS, pronounced "lurps", which was slang for dehydrated food named after the elite troops that conducted the **L**ong **R**ange **R**econnaissance **P**atrols. There would also be C-rations for the hard core.

Don showed up at 1:30 with eleven more men, three of the small radios, a big radio, and another dog. This one was a black German Shepherd named Otto. The new dog was a little bigger than Spike and looked to be about the same age. He sniffed everyone at the river watch to acquaint himself. Since we now had thirty men, Otto would need a good memory.

I took Donald on the 25-cent tour while Otto was saying howdy to all. When we got to the Ruins camp, he bristled at Spike. Soon their tails dropped and wagged happily. Don seemed appalled at the blood. "This could be the blood of women and children," he said vehemently. This thought was already on everyone's mind.

Don took me aside and said that he wasn't out here to take command from me, only to share the adventure. I told him that two heads are better than one and his input was always welcome.

I asked him if any of the new men were qualified with the machine gun. He said that we'd have to poll all of them since Johnny and Rick were the only ones that he knew personally.

I laid out my plan as follows; We would have four permanent positions along our azimuth, fifteen meters apart. The machine gun, Spike, and a starlight scope would be at the camp nearest the ruins. There would be six men to a camp with six men patrolling with the new dog. At night, Otto and two men would join river watch where the other starlight scope would be. The other four men, when not patrolling, would beef up the camp by the ruins.

We had to find new gunners because I wanted the patrol to consist of the original six of us. Rick would stay at the river and Johnny and Don would join him at night. That would put a leader at both ends of this on-line defensive position.

Now that we had enough men to hold the fort, we would be able to send six men in empty packs to fill up on LRRPS. I asked Don to take over while I got five more volunteers to hike to Camp Cannibal. Naturally, Edwin, Travis, Barry, Johnny, and Rick were asked first. All were willing to stretch their legs. Ed walked point and I carried the radio. Barry was rear security. Travis said that he felt naked without his gun so I offered to let him carry the radio and he flipped me off. Gotta love him.

We left without either dog, but Ed had walked point more than a time or two and he managed to pick out the tents in the brush before we were heard or spotted. Once Christmas and Easter greetings were exchanged, we walked towards the smokehouse where Ed was surprised by another checkpoint. They were expecting us since radios were in vogue. We climbed the low hill and went up to the cabin's open door.

There were three men at desks all facing the door. They were in camouflage like everyone else but they looked like FBI. Introductions were exchanged. "So, you're the famous Derrick who started this mess? We cleared up your problems in Illinois and Wisconsin. Margaret calls your place often to check up on her hero. Just please, avoid future messes," said the man at the center desk. There was a hint of a smile in his eyes.

"No problem, and thank you for your assistance with my 'problems'," I replied. I didn't like speaking with seated men while I stood. I felt that my friends and I were equal to any man.

"By the way, the reward has been doubled on the head hunter. There's also an extra grand apiece on all convictions for trafficking in human flesh, murder, or kidnapping. Don't try to wrap this up single-handedly and be alert on your patrols. Now you can grab your chow and safe hunting to you all," spoke the man at the center desk.

The LRRPS were light. We stuffed our rucksacks. I put a small box of Halizone water purification tablets into a side pocket. As we left, I looked around the camp and couldn't see a man anywhere. This was a well-run camp. I looked into the sleeping tree and some huge, dark haired man waved back at me. I nearly jumped out of my skin until he showed a badge and flashed a peace sign. These guys seemed to have thought of everything. Their end of the mission was being handled very well.

The hike back was uneventful. I radioed our approach to avoid wearing St. Nick's name out. Don had been busy too. All four camps were set up with camouflaged tents for our element as well as the rest of our men. Our tents were at the Ruins camp. He was anxious to use the daylight for a patrol. I told him that the chow run wanted to chow down prior to the patrol, so would he please pass out the chow where necessary. We walked to the ruins to check out the new gun team and repack our rucksacks. After we ate, we picked up Don at the river and commenced our tiptoe through the tulips.

Barry and Otto the dog got along like they knew each other in a former life. I took point and Ed walked slack. Travis was next with the PRC-77 radio, followed by Johnny and Don. Barry was our eyes and ears at rear security. We kept well into the brush parallel with the river.

The farther that we walked, the more that it looked like a river. When the brush thinned out, Johnny and Don took left flank twenty yards out. We were about three miles along when I spotted the boat. It was a flat-bottomed sixteen-footer with two nasty looking creatures in it. A pale, skinny, white dude was in the center and a big black man was steering the electric motor. No way could you hear the boat until it was along side. We ducked down and radioed our river watch to let it pass. Then I called base and told them to be expecting buyers.

We continued the patrol along the river. After a while, we heard river watch radio base that the boat had passed. We decided to go one more mile before turning back. Shortly, base called us. They said that the customers tied up at the stakes like it was a routine for them. They walked up to the tree fort and called to Tiny, which was even the name that they used. They said that they wanted meat. The skinnier white dude said, "Make two of them kids and one a woman." Those were the magic words that earned them the right to remain silent since everything they said could and would be held against them in a court of law.

Base said that this boat didn't show up on camera either, another mystery. Otto alerted and we all sunk down. A man was running at us. It was the fisherman from the group of poachers. He had no weapon that I could see. He collapsed in a heap when I stood up and said, "Freeze!" Our flank men moved up and we set up security. The terrified fisherman seemed glad to see us.

The story that we got out of him confirmed our fears. He said that he and two of his buddies were out to do some fishing the other day when this giant of a man stood up in the river and turned the boat over with one hand. The giant had a big, curved knife and cut off his friend's heads while our man was backing towards shore. When he got in shallow water, he turned and ran into the woods, running at every sound and not sleeping since it happened. He just found the river again and thought that he heard something and started to run again when we caught him.

I asked him if he could show us where he was attacked. He said that he'd rather die first. I believed him too. We had to head back to beat sundown. I didn't want any casualties among my friends. The fisherman was glad to be surrounded by armed men, even after Don arrested him for poaching. We didn't need handcuffs, our friend wouldn't think of leaving his newfound safety. We radioed base and asked for a patrol to pick him up in the morning. I told both river teams to have two men awake and to pay attention to their dogs. Then I asked base for clearance for the river teams to shoot any giants in the water.

"That's negative. He must be given the chance to surrender," answered base.

"Escape is more like it," I thought. I kept it to myself.

We reached our camp before full dark. I pulled a man from each of the center positions and sent them to the river. They heard our report and were glad for the extra men. Now, hopefully, we'd get a good night's sleep. Somehow, I doubted it.

...

We were shown to our hutches and introduced to all the men. The man who seemed to run things was older than me and had 'the look', so I asked. He had been Army, infantry, 1st Cavalry in '68 and '69. He said that he'd asked to be sent out here and asked to be stationed at the ruins. His name was Jimmy and he had been a squad leader in Vietnam where he made sergeant in the field. I picked up the hint and said that he'd be running the camp anytime that Sergeant Donald and I were away. I told him that his ideas were important and to share them freely.

We had an ex-Marine with service in Beirut and Desert Storm at the river with Donald and two more ex-Marines that had served in Tripoli when there was a mess at the embassy. It seemed that this hastily put together bunch of volunteers were from the lunatic fringe of the police and military, just what we needed. I hoped that they saved some barnstormers for Camp Cannibal.

As always, situation reports were called in hourly. The river checked in first, then down the line to us at the Ruins camp. At our camp, we had two men on guard at ten and two O'clock using the ruins themselves to designate twelve O'clock using the standard aviator's method of direction.

At 11:30 PM, the dog at the river alerted. That camp was at full alert now. They reported voices downstream. I told them to sit tight and report any changes. They said that the voices were moving inland.

In a very few minutes, Spike alerted. We could hear voices too. By now, every one of my men was wide awake. The approaching group wasn't even trying to be quiet. Some were even laughing. None of the men at the Ruins camp moved a muscle.

The intruders went straight to the ruins like they were going to a bar. They had a few shotguns in sight. There were six of them. We inched our way forward to see and hear better. Closer inspection revealed that some of the strangers wore handguns. The group looked as sturdy as a bunch of construction workers. Their general conversation kept referring to the show at midnight.

River watch reported more voices headed our way. I sent Travis, Barry, and Don around the eastside of the ruins to form an "L" shaped ambush. Then I called the five men from the nearest center position to move up by us. I knew that the strangers at the ruins would have the protection of the walls if shooting broke out too soon. Our best chance for success was to wait for the rest of their men to join them, then move right up to the walls. We could force a surrender or fire point blank if necessary.

The second group consisted of two large men with assault rifles. They had what looked like a family between the two of them, tied at the neck and strung together. There was no father among the captives, just a woman, two small boys, and two young girls. All were naked and shivering. All were bruised like the abuse had begun earlier.

I called the other two center camps and sent them east along the river to look for boats and to cut off escape. These bastards were coming with us dead or alive to the last man of them. Now we crept up to the walls.

The conversation from inside the ruins went to this effect; When they were done with the fun here, they would exchange the new bodies for cash and some meat at Tiny's place.

Now all fifteen of us were at the walls on two sides. We would have to be careful not to hurt the family who was huddled on the ground in a tight, pitiful group. I tossed a trip flare across to the entrance of the ruins. "Sheriff's Police!" I hollered. All of my men stood up at once. The two big men jumped the flare thinking to escape. The first six froze in the face of all those automatic weapons.

We could hear gunshots from the river. The fifteen men there could easily handle those two. We disarmed the creeps in our care and tied them together at their necks. Blankets were brought from our camp for the traumatized family. "God, how do you heal a mind?"

We heard gunfire. The report from the river came over the radio. They had found the boats unguarded with a dead, white male, early thirties. The two men from the woods came out shooting and were both killed. We had no casualties on our side.

I called base with the news. He said that their river team had heard the shots and called the smokehouse. I said that there would probably be more customers and the giant was still out there. I said that we would conceal the boats at our position tonight and send the family and the prisoners up in the morning.

With the camps back in position, we made a special tent for the family. We couldn't build a fire, but everyone at the ruins gave up their blankets. Nothing could replace their father, but they were safe now. One of our guys gave up a set of clean fatigues to the mother. The mom had no smiles left in her. All of them were totally traumatized.

None of us got a wink of sleep that night. We were filled with resolve to wipe out this plague of demons. It was an act of God that we had our camp set up where it was. Once again, the dogs had proved priceless. We'd have to send for a third dog so the river watch would always have one when we went patrolling. The Giant liked the river and he was still our most unpredictable foe.

All of the possibilities were wearing me out. My PTSD was beginning to sap my energy as well. There was so much that I'd forgotten trying to surface. Some hot coffee would help. I remembered the old military saying, "Take two salt tablets and drive on!"

. . .

We roused the family at dawn and fed them. Then we loaded them into the first boat so they wouldn't have to look at their captors. We'd left the string of rats face down in the ruins. Since there were no extra blankets, they did a little shivering of their own. Their guards were happy to get them on the second boat. Some of them might talk, that was their only value, period. We dumped their dead friends on top of them.

There was a cop steering each boat, as closely to shore as the loads would allow. There would also be six men on shore keeping pace. I reminded the steersmen about Big Foot in the water. I also said that live prisoners gave information and dead ones had to be accounted for. Our string of rats was none too popular. The 1st Cavalry man, Jimmy, took charge and walked point on the bank.

With the expedition on its way, I radioed base of their coming and requested another dog and more ammo. Now we needed a thorough cleaning of the area to avoid scaring off any other rats that may come our way. With the house cleaning in order, we could split the guard and get some sleep. My patrol squad had to sack out undisturbed since I wanted to hike to the bridge and back. We still had to find out why the boats didn't show up on the FBI monitor.

I slept like a rock. We awoke to a cold drizzle. The boat patrol had returned with the blankets. The base was developing a small armada. I got the news from the patrol that a 'V' hulled boat had floated past the camera. It was capsized with the motor still attached. The speedboat had retrieved it, but no sign of bodies yet. It was almost certainly that of the poachers.

I called the houseboat and asked them to stay on the far side of the bridge until we could determine where all of the invisible boats were coming from. The six of us ate and filled our canteens with coffee. We put a LRRP and some heat tabs in our side pockets. First, we would have to meet the new dog. He'd already met everyone else. It was another big, male shepherd with a steady disposition. We couldn't afford any barking dogs out here. We were getting well-trained animals. I'm sure that we were borrowing them from other police departments.

With Otto moving cautiously up front, I took point with Travis at slack, or second in line. Sergeant Donald had the radio, followed by Johnny, Edwin, and Barry. Like yesterday, when the brush thinned out, we moved farther inland with Barry and Edwin taking up the left flank. We had just passed the place where the poacher had collapsed at our feet when I saw the first unmistakable boot print. It was too deep to be washed away by the light drizzle. So the poacher really had heard something. I wondered if the big man had watched us steal his prey. The dog hadn't alerted a second time, but it was still possible. Dogs got shot in Vietnam occasionally. If the wind was wrong, and a well-camouflaged enemy remained motionless, the dogs were no better than a man would be. A man might do better just by listening to the jungle, or in this case, the forest.

Over on flank, Ed said that he'd found tracks too and they were headed deeper into the woods.

We joined Ed and Barry and formed up on line with Ed and me in the middle as trackers. Otto took up his place while the other men were the eyes and ears in all directions except the ground where all of Ed's and my attention were riveted. Again I reminded them how this guy loved to double back. The tracks were so big that Ed could put his size twelve's in them with room for all four knuckles in front and three fingers at the side. I'll bet that the black bears around here were afraid of this guy.

Travis grabbed my arm. Otto had alerted. We sunk to the ground and crept forward. I looked in the trees, remembering Tiny's sleeping quarters. That's when I saw the man hung upside down in the tree. His head was gone. At first I thought that this was why the dog had alerted, but his stare was straight ahead. Something must have moved. We kept advancing and we struck gold. There was old Big Foot with his back to us. He appeared to be eating and I wish I didn't know what. We got as close as we dared before shouting, "Sheriff's Police!"

He spun like a cat with his big knife raised. Then he did the unexpected, he charged. Ed and I were right in his path but we did the expected, we fired on full auto. His charge knocked us both to the ground, but he was already in his death throes.

"Are you guys gonna share, or should we leave him on you?" that was Travis asking.

I for one couldn't breathe, but Ed said, "Sure!" for both of us. It took the four of them to roll him off even with Ed and I helping from below.

We were covered with blood, but at least it wasn't ours. "Now how do we get this big freaking elephant back, not to mention the two dead poachers?" I said.

Both of the heads were there, but the brains were gone like the first pair from the hunters had been. We couldn't compromise the mission with a boat sent so far downstream, and a helicopter was out for the same reason.

"I know," I said, "Let's drag him down the hill to the river and float him back. We can float the poachers too." Don and Johnny were appalled but the rest of us just laughed. "I'm serious, it's the only way."

Dragging the dead giant was as tough as it sounded. When we cut the one poacher from the tree, Travis picked him up in a fireman's carry.

Ed and I were already a gory mess, so Ed gathered up the heads and I picked up the other body and we took off after Travis. I heard Johnny ask Barry what it was like in Vietnam. Barry laughed in his face and said, "Don't ask!"

...

Floating our grisly raft against the current is something that I never want to do again. The current isn't as strong along the shore, but it still required all six of us pulling and pushing to get the job done. Otto was the lucky one. He trotted along on the bank. Travis took the radio from Donald since he was the strongest.

We had no plan 'B'. If a boat came up the river, we'd just have to deal with it. I'd like to *think* that the sound of the automatic weapon's fire would discourage brave explorers. The problem was, the traffic on this river is anything but good Mousketeers.

Dragging our tired butts out of the river at our little camp was one of those happy moments that I shall always cherish. We hadn't radioed in our little surprise so surprise it was. The camp was buzzing about the crazy squad and their ghoulish raft. Now I decided to call base to risk a boat. When I gave my report, they agreed to the boat. It would be a night mission, but with the headhunter dead, the night lost much of its terror. Hell, originally, only six of us came out at night looking for the giant and busted Tiny more or less at home.

When the boats showed up, they realized that they couldn't get the giant into one. The oversized Neanderthal would still have to be towed. Once again, Travis and I loaded the bodies and Ed loaded the heads. All three of us stripped and threw our clothes on the bodies. We washed as well as possible and walked back naked but proud. When we got to the ruins, we were the ones given blankets. Base wanted to interview the entire squad. I told base to deliver dry clothes for all at first light, and we would return with the delivery patrol.

Once again, sleep would come hard. I was ecstatic with the progress, yet I knew that the mission might be only half done with more demons to overcome. The devil on Earth perpetuated this cannibalism and murder and we may have to pursue him to Louisiana. If our dearly departed headhunter operated so far away recently, anything was possible.

Sure, we had slain this beast, but the devil told Jesus, "I am Legion." This was not a comforting thought to try to sleep on. My thoughts were spinning in circles. Someday soon, an accounting would have to be made for all the missing men and the cash that they carried. I felt like we had struck close to the top when we killed those two who had kidnapped the family. I had a feeling that they were kingpins and the giant was a pet of some evil master.

The headhunter never bothered the customers or the kidnappers or the spectators at the ruins. All of his victims were non-players. I expected his fingerprints to match those on the cross. He's also likely to be tied to the slayings in Louisiana.

I must have passed out during these thoughts. Mercifully, no one woke us for guard. My first glimmer of consciousness was when we were awakened and told that the re-supply was here. We dressed hastily and loaded all of the soiled fatigues from our camp into empty rucksacks. Plain coffee for breakfast and we had to hit the trail.

The hike to Camp Cannibal was like a romp in the park. I felt like I was leaving the front lines and heading to some safe rear area. I knew that this false sense of security could get a man killed, so I brought my faculties back to earth. For all that I knew the biggest battle could still be waged at the smokehouse. It was certainly a logical place. Whoever ran the show might simply bypass the ruins as his workers playroom. Human meat was his business and something was wrong at his warehouse. Those sobering thoughts restored my respect for the men at the base.

The man in charge was named Schultz. He was the one that I spoke to when he said that my problems had been cleared up. Schultz greeted us warmly. He got down to business right away. "First, where does the reward go?"

I told him that it was a six way even split on the giant. Each of us could instruct him on where to send the funds. The two kidnappers-presumed-killers were terminated by the river watch. I gave him their names. If the six rats that we sent in bound at the neck were worth anything, that money would be split among the men at the Ruins camp. I told him that I would radio specifics when I returned to my men.

Then I told Schultz that barring interruption, our next patrol would be to the bridge. I asked to be given extra clothing in waterproof bags since I wanted to cross the river. I told him that the far shore had been ignored too long. We may be under surveillance from within the more dense brush a little farther inland on the lower bank. I'd like to have breakfast here and grab some more LRRPS and heat tabs. Then we have to move out. It's eight miles one-way from here and then seven miles back to my camp.

We were outfitted as I requested and he offered to take us across here by boat. I thanked him and told him that he might want to order some anti-tank weapons in case they were attacked by boat. He liked that idea. When we were done eating, we hopped into one of the flat-bottomed boats with Otto and one of their river crew who would take the boat back.

Once ashore, Otto took the lead happily with Edwin at point and me second. Donald carried the big radio followed by Johnny, Travis and Barry at his favorite spot of rear security. We went inland twenty-five yards and headed east. We couldn't see the river, but there were plenty to watch it for us. If there was any boat traffic, the radio would keep us informed. The brush was sparse along shore, since it was the low side and flooded often. Barry and Travis moved out to right flank. The sun was out and I prayed that snakes wouldn't be about. We'd been fortunate so far and I didn't want to lose a dog.

Travis waved us over. They'd found the remains of an old camp. What looked like muddy rocks turned out to be three more heads. These were old and nearly filled with mud. We carried them to shore and radioed across. We couldn't see them in their cover, but they had a visual on us and would pick them up soon. With new DNA testing, a lot of missing persons would be accounted for. That smokehouse was full when we opened the door the first time.

We resumed formation and continued to march. I figured that we'd hit the bridge shortly before 11AM. Donald called our river watch to advise them that our guys would be across the river in zero five minutes. They were told to call us when their dog alerted. We would then come closer to shore for a visual. From then on, we'd have to watch for river traffic from closer to shore.

We got the call that the dog had us. We moved towards the river and they informed us that we could be seen. Once again, we couldn't make them out. It was a good job of camouflage. Seven miles to go. It grew steadily warmer. Again I thought of snakes. I told Ed to make Otto heel and I would let him know if the dog alerted.

We found the bridge and the answer to the mystery at the same time. We were a quarter mile west of the bridge and straight across from us was a dirt road. Of course! Over the years, every bridge winds up with one of these dirt roads. They start out as two tire ruts in the mud. As more and more fishermen used them, they became hard packed roads. The boats were all launched and removed from here.

I reported to base and suggested that the camera be moved to this location. Base gave me frequency of the houseboat again to expedite this procedure. We were told to wait for the crew to provide security. This gave us a chance to chow down as we looked up the dirt road from inside the brush.

The speedboat showed up in about a half of an hour. It dropped off two men dressed like tourists who hooked up a new camera. They wanted to leave the one on the bridge. They said that a second monitor was being hooked up at my house as we spoke. They used a hand held radio to call their boat back. The river was quite deep here, so we bummed a ride to 'our' side of the river to look for clues on the dirt road.

There was plenty of evidence of boat and vehicle traffic here. The giant had been here too. I wanted to follow the road out to its source. I had a hunch that I wanted to check out. I left the radio and four men hidden at the river while Travis and I hurried up the road. We were in enemy territory and knew it. As I suspected, there was a chain across the road with a No Tresspassing sign on it. There was enough slack in the chain for a car and boat if someone held the chain up. That explained how the poachers gained access. The lure of easy money cost two of them their lives.

Basically, this was a private party for the property owners and his select, human flesh-eating pals. We went down the hill and joined our friends. Our first move was to get away from the road and then to radio my house. I told them about the locked chain and asked them to find out who owned all of this land. I was under the impression that it was part of the Sam Houston State Forest. Maybe the land north of the river was private. This could provide a major clue.

We switched back to my camp's frequency and told them to expect us at two PM. Now, to walk back seven miles. We waved at the camera and someone broke squelch twice.

. . .

Seven more miles, it don't mean nothin'. Actually I wished Mr. or Mrs. Big would just surrender so we could all leave this swamp. I didn't really think that a woman would surface at the top of this organization, but every possibility had to be considered. That giant that we killed could have been some rich woman's stud. Old Big Foot wasn't pretty, but he must have gotten lonesome once in a while.

A sudden thought struck me. Not much, but better than lightning. I called a halt, no complaints there. While we were still close to the road, I had to find some answers that could only be found there. We had to double back, not a very popular idea, but the logic was hard to argue with. We still had two LRRPS apiece, heat tabs, Halizone, and plenty of daylight. Clues found by the road could be invaluable, and might not be there for long. We wouldn't have to hurry back. Jimmy from the 1st Cavalry could run the camp. Our radio battery was still fresh. We really didn't have any reason to hurry.

With the thought of a leisurely walk back, my idea went up in the popularity poll. I informed all parties of the new plan and off we went to play Dick Tracy.

We got a call on the horn that the giant that we shot was a match for the fingerprints on the cross. That bit of information was no surprise. The FBI had plenty to work with now. Boat registry, a new camera, property ownership, and six rats to wrestle information from, not to mention testimony of the mother whose family we had rescued. Maybe the G-men would be able to wrap this without another shot being fired. Maybe the tooth fairy would put a zillion dollars under my pillow tonight too.

I wanted to start my search at the highway past the chain where cars would have to stop to raise the chain, or unlock it for trucks. We set up in the woods at the top of the hill. I stripped to the waist so as not to look too military. I went out alone when no cars were coming. There were overlapping tire tracks and the prints of many feet. I found the giant's tracks here too. They went to the locked side of the chain, across, and back again. So Big Foot had gotten out of the passenger side and let someone through. I stepped over the chain and read his tracks getting back into the car. Now I knew why his tracks weren't on the road going down, he had ridden. So Big Foot had a social life after all. Why not? He was such a pleasant fellow.

Next question, why was there no sign of a return trip? My guess meant more getting wet. The squad had flanked me all the way down. I waved at the camera again and we got back on command frequency. I told the powers that be that there was probably a car in the deep water by the bridge. They said that they had divers on the houseboat to check it out. If there were bodies, they would be recovered. The plates and VIN numbers would have to be written down. They said that a salvage effort on the vehicle would compromise the operation. It was difficult for me, but I refrained from saying, "No shit, Sherlock!"

Since we didn't find Big Foot's trail near the river, he must have walked in the water again, or swam. Where we had found him was much further upstream. Knowing the giant's habit of backtracking, I had another theory to explore. I figured that if we walked uphill, that we might cross a manmade trail. The rest of the squad agreed and we set out with this intention.

We did find a trail about three hundred yards up the hill. It appeared to run parallel to the river. This was farther North than our previous explorations. This newly discovered trail could cause serious trouble for both camps. I radioed this discovery to Camp Cannibal. I said that we would follow it east to its source, then turn around and follow it west. We would report any further developments immediately.

We started off with Otto in front and Ed and I walking abreast on this wide trail. We were studying the ground, trying to read its story. Barry had the big PRC 77 radio on left flank with Travis. Don and Johnny were on right flank. The flanks walked slightly forward of Ed and I. Ed spotted them first. There were tire tracks like from a trailer or golf cart. The tread marks had been rained on several times, but were still readable. Sometimes they would disappear altogether. The ground was harder this high up.

The wide trail led to the back yard of a rather fancy estate with an impressive house. The place didn't have a very homey look to it. The grass needed mowing and there were no flower gardens or pretty shrubs. I got the distinct feeling that most of this house's functions were held behind closed doors. We could tell that someone was home because there were glasses on the patio table as if a meeting had just ended. Some of the glasses still had liquid in them. There was also an electric golf cart with a small trailer attached parked in plain sight.

The news of this find would open some eyes. We were all convinced that there was no place like this place, anywhere near this place, so this was definitely the place. We regrouped and moved back down the trail several yards and went into the brush so I could call Schultz. I told him to alert the houseboat as well as my house that we had a highly suspect house that required surveillance. It would be easy to find from the description of its architecture and I asked Ed what color it was. "Oh, yeah, it's blue-gray."

I told Schultz that we would resume our westward march. I asked him if his men had done much patrolling. When he said, "No.", I held my anger and suggested that his men might look for the other end of this trail at his location. I couldn't believe that he hadn't sent out any feelers. I would be willing bet that his men had wondered the same thing.

We hadn't gone more than a hundred meters when the horn crackled. It was Schultz. They had wheeled tracks from a small vehicle on a wide trail parallel to the river that seemed to pass through their camp. He asked if he should send a force to meet me. I told him not to. The last thing that I wanted was friendly troops firing at each other from adjacent parallel trails. I said that we would come to him. If our present trail led straight to the smokehouse, that should be enough to get a search warrant on the house at the eastern end. We'd have the head of the serpent, but had we cut off all sources of supply by killing the kidnappers and the headhunter? If we couldn't get the rats to spill some secrets, we might have to stay in the woods awhile longer.

I called Schultz again and asked to move my entire camp to the dirt road with the chain. That way they could intercept all traffic, yet be near enough to the estate to reinforce operations there.

Schultz came back, "Excellent idea, expedite the move. There was a car found in the water by the bridge without any occupants. We're still running the plates and VIN number."

"Roger that. Expect us at your location in zero three hours," I told him.

We moved out in the same flank forward formation with the dog in his favorite position. Sergeant Donald radioed the planned move to our camp and told Jimmy to stay in the brush with the river in sight. Same rules, boats without obvious captives are to be allowed to pass. When they reach the dirt road, they are to arrest and detain any and all newcomers for suspicion of poaching, tresspassing, or whatever seemed appropriate.

Jimmy from the 1st Cavalry seemed to like this. "Roger and WILCO, out."

I told him to shoot the motor of any vessel that they needed to stop.

We'd gone about four miles without anything new on the trail. Don and Johnny halted abruptly and waved us over. There were two bodies hanging upside down in a tree, both headless. The bodies were those of a young male and a young female. It looked like their clothing had been used to cook the heads.

Where would these kids have met Big Foot? And what would make them trust him? We'll never know, but I was sure that it was their car under water at the bridge. We had another delay as we cut the bodies down. Travis picked up the man, I carried the female, and Barry put the heads in a waterproof bag after giving his extra clothes to Ed. Sergeant Donald radioed Jimmy and the camp on the move to watch for us at the river.

We reached the river early and set our burdens down. We hadn't been there five minutes when Otto alerted. The horn crackled and Jimmy said that their dog had alerted. I told him to move up slowly and keep his eyes open. I moved past Otto and eventually made eye contact with Jimmy like we'd seen each other at the same time.

We linked elements inside the brush line, under the trees. I had them wrap the bodies in ponchos. We told them that the heads in the waterproof bag should be the last with Big Foot deceased. I asked them to haul the bodies to the dirt road for extraction by the speedboat. The camera would let the houseboat know when they were there. Next I got on frequency with the houseboat and filled them in.

Back up the hill and on the trail once again, I wondered aloud if Big Foot took the bodies to the smokehouse or if someone picked them up on the trail that the cart used. Both times, they were hung near the trail on the downhill side. Ed had found hack-marks on a tree near where the bodies were hung. We'd have to watch for more of the same. This time we would go down the trail combat patrol style with the slack man watching the trees.

Once again we moved out with flanks forward. Johnny gave Sergeant Donald a break on carrying the radio. We used to call the PRC-77 "The Monster", because it was so heavy.

After another mile or so, Sergeant Donald halted us again. He came over to tell us that we were at the camp where we had killed the headhunter. Sure enough, the hack-marks were on the tree on the south side of the trail. Someone would have to come along soon to retrieve the bodies. We would have to go back to where we found the young couple and set up an ambush.

I called Schultz and told him of the change of plans and why. He could send his party up to us. I told him to have his men watch for a green T-shirt on the trail. Our ambush would be set up twenty-five yards beyond. If their dog alerted or if they found the shirt, stop and call our patrol.

Now we could move back to the first set of hack-marks and set up our ambush. God, I hoped that Big Foot wasn't expected to report any time soon. It was their move. All that we had to do was wait.

...

On the way to the first set of hack-marks, it hit me. I had to have those bodies for bait. We'd have to wait until the people in the cart actually cut them down and loaded them before we could make an arrest. I got on the radio and requested that the speedboat should intercept the platoon and deliver the bodies to the party of two who would be waiting at the river's edge. Haste was a must. We needed the bait to make the bust airtight. They got my drift and said that they'd comply in about eight or ten minutes. Now we'd need some luck or we could wreck what looked like a wrap on our operation.

Travis, Barry, and I headed the three hundred meters down to the river. No one was eager for the walk back, uphill, all the way, with our stiff burdens. Whoever carried the waterproof bag would be security. Here is where I might have an edge. As a roofer, I was used to carrying loads up ladders. That's why I grabbed the bigger package when the boat showed up.

My big, muscular friend Travis said, "When it gets too heavy, son, just put it on my other shoulder."

Well, here's where his cigarettes were going to kick his butt. I'd quit in 1970. He still had the habit. I had another ace in the hole. I'd shingled entire roofs where I'd carried two bundles every trip and had occasionally carried three bundles, as recently as last summer. That is one of the reasons that my body is so dense that it doesn't float. Barry was only too happy to watch his idiot pals in their macho competition.

With my M-16 in my left hand and the body on my right shoulder, I started off first. I was determined to make it to the ambush ahead of Mr. Prize fighter. Let me tell you, I had never climbed a three-hundred-yard ladder before, and I had to stop twice, but I still reached the ambush first. Travis had more respect when he reached the top. He had been looking at me as the 125 pound soldier that he knew over twenty years ago. He finally saw the additional 65 pounds of muscle that a lifetime in construction had glued to me. Edwin said that he wouldn't have shot the giant if he had known that I could kick his ass. That made us all laugh.

Travis and I let the other three unwrap the bodies and wrestle them in the tree while we crept up to pull guard. Ed came up to get us and he showed us how he had the ambush set up. Sergeant Donald had never had to do that and Ed had sat in hundreds during his 32 months in the jungle.

This vegetation wasn't as dense as we would have liked, but he had us in three groups of two behind some clumps of palmettos. This is where our camouflage clothing would serve us well.

"Where's Otto?" I asked. Ed took me to the clump of palmettos where Barry and Travis were and there he was, lying down.

"I just told him to stay, and he hasn't moved yet," laughed Ed. It was a good thing too, because his black fur made him stand out. Our positions formed a 'V'. We would have the men from the cart in an inescapable position. I pointed the weakness out to Ed if someone waited by the cart. He volunteered to conceal himself nearer to the trail to cover this possibility. I warned him to locate out of the line of fire.

I told Ed to keep the radio with him by the trail and keep an ear out for the group from Camp Cannibal. "When they arrive, keep half with you along with their dog. Hold their PRC-25 and send the PRC-77 back to me with the other half of the men."

Otto sat up and I got on the horn. "Base patrol, if that's you, say the password." Santa Claus came over the air and Ed went out to greet them. Nightfall was coming. The people from the house would have to make a move soon or wait for sunup, unless! Unless they had night vision glasses. I sent Johnny up to swap his M-14 with the starlight scope for Ed's M-16 and told him to warn Ed of that possibility. We got five more men at our position.

Were we ready? I couldn't think of anything. I turned to the rest of the squad for input. Travis, who also had a year in Panama in Jungle School that I didn't, said we should move a six-man team from the dirt road to the river directly downhill from us.

"That way, they could pick off anyone who slipped through the dirt road ambush or back us up if we needed it," he said.

I implemented that very good idea with a call on the radio.

Barry said, "Call the houseboat for FBI activity. They may have a way to warn us of goings on at the estate." That was going to be my next call, but I thanked him anyway. We all stood a chance of being killed. Everyone should feel a part of the plan.

As if on cue, we received a call from the houseboat. They had urgent news pertinent to our operation. The horseshoe driveway in front of the blue-gray house was full of Bronco and Blazer type vehicles along with a stretch limousine registered to the homeowner. The other vehicles were registered to mercenaries and felon parolees.

The home across the highway had been evacuated and staffed with fifteen U.S. Marshals. Also, many of the mercenaries had federal warrants on suspicion of white slavery traffic on an international scheme including traffic in children smuggled to and from Brazil. They were also suspect in kidnappings of teenage girls who were turning up in Japan and Belgium. Some of them had been found dead. The home and the limousine belonged to the pastor of a church of questionable reputation. His church was affiliated with others in Houston, Beaumont, Shreveport, and Baton Rouge.

The final transmission from the FBI at the houseboat went like this; "Gentlemen, tonight's operation should net enough evidence to enable us to shut down this blight on humanity and get the death sentence for the bulk of the players, if not all of them. Once you make your arrest at the bait tree, notify us ASAP. We have a federal judge on the boat ready to sign a host of warrants. If a single shot is fired at one of your men, you are cleared to terminate all hostiles with extreme prejudice. When your position is secured, stand by to reinforce operations at the estate. Your men will be the blocking force to prevent escape into the woods. Be careful, and you can return to your families after tomorrow's reports are filed. Thank you all for your brave sacrifice and may God be with you."

After that transmission, you could have heard the proverbial pin drop. That was a lot of food for thought. We knew first hand how ruthless and despicable our foes were, but the scope of the operation was overwhelming. We were on the brink of a great victory against evil.

It was full dark now. I was convinced that if the golf cart came now, it would certainly have night vision devices of some sort. Every minute of waiting was an eternity. Three or four eternity's later, Ed said, "Get ready. My dog alerted."

Nothing any more sophisticated than a hand held spotlight was used for the enemy to scan the trees. They stopped at the hack-marks and three men came down our trail waving flashlights. When the bodies were spotted in the tree, two of them laid down their rifles and commenced to cut them down. That's when I threw out a trip flare and hollered, "Freeze!" My command was echoed on the trail by Edwin. We got no resistance when eleven armed men in uniform seemed to materialize out of the darkness. We tied the prisoners to the bait tree and Ed came down, leading another rat at gunpoint. We tied him with his friends and I left four ferocious men and the new dog to guard them. As my group climbed to the trail, I heard one of my men say, "Please try something."

I called the report to the houseboat. "The rats took the cheese. I'll have thirteen men in their back yard in zero five minutes. I grabbed the spotlight from the cart and we turned it and the trailer over as a precaution. When we reached the estate, we spread out in the back yard in the prone position. I called the FBI with our new situation report. They said that a helicopter would flood the back yard with illumination as the Marshals went through the front door. The order to terminate was repeated.

This was it. The chopper appeared overhead as we heard the front door crash. The shout, "US Marshals!" carried out to us.

Shooting in the house started immediately. "Semi-automatic firing,"

I ordered. "Choose your targets from your twelve O'clock." The back door burst open, the chopper lit up the yard and the rats came out in a panic.

"Sheriff's Police, freeze!" I yelled. To a man, the rats began firing wildly on full automatic. They couldn't see us and all the lead was passing harmlessly over our heads. We picked off several of the child-molesting, child-murdering, kidnapping sons of bitches before weapons were dropped and hands were raised. "Cease fire!" I yelled over the din. That wasn't an easy order to give. I'm sure that those of us who had seen the inside of the freshly opened smokehouse or witnessed the captives at the ruins had a hard time complying with that command. We weren't cowardly murderers. The survivors could die of old age in Huntsville Prison or face execution. Hell was the bottom line for all of them.

When the smoke cleared, the dead outnumbered the captives. That was including the four live ones at the bait tree. Not one of my men had so much as a scratch. Two of the US Marshals had been shot. Neither one was seriously wounded. Thank God for vests. I radioed the FBI to watch for us shortly to show up with the cart. Then I called the guard at the bait tree and warned them of our approach. We turned the cart and trailer upright and went to get our last four prisoners.

We loaded the rope-bound rats in the trailer and put the headless corpses along with the heads on top of them. Sergeant Donald got behind the wheel while the rest of us escorted it to the estate. I called our backup squad at the river and told them to walk up the hill to the cart trail then join us at the house. Then I called the camp at the dirt road and told them to walk up to the highway and go north to the first driveway on the left. "We have some body bags to fill. See you in fifteen minutes."

...

We drove the prisoners around to the front door. The Marshals had really done a job. The double doors were designed to swing out, not any more. Now they looked like four hours labor for two men.

I found the headman and asked if it was really over. He said that some buyers and suppliers were probably still out. It might be as simple as checking the Pastor's church records and arresting people at their homes.

I said that the suppliers that we killed didn't look like churchgoers.

Then he told me of their mole at the local parish and the conduct that their man had witnessed. Everyone at the church had partaken of human flesh.

"He had a difficult time faking his end and had to leave when he became suspect. His testimony will put a lot of people away. The pastor had been killed during the raid, but some of those who had surrendered in the back yard were facing death penalties. One or more of them are bound to roll over and save us some time hunting down suppliers," he said.

The cameras were to remain in place. The estate and house would be cleaned and repaired. The Limousine would be left out front, and anyone who knocked had better be selling Avon or Girl Scout cookies or they would be arrested. Schultz and crew would vacation at the smokehouse for another two weeks. He would ask for six volunteers from my group to ambush the ruins.

I got his permission to collect the volunteers and he agreed. The entire operation had taken place in less than one week. I was hoping that my original patrol would stay out the extra two weeks. When I confronted each one separately, Johnny was my only holdout. He had two small children and a wife to go home to. My next and obvious choice was Jimmy from the 1st Cavalry. He jumped on it.

I went back inside with my personnel roster and requested Otto for our dog. I told him that I had the utmost confidence in my squad. He said that we had filled the airwaves for the last several days and he wanted to meet my hero squad. I brought the original squad and Jimmy inside for introductions. He shook everyone's hand like he was truly honored. He was the local bureau chief and it was *him* that was honored to meet *us*. That made us feel appreciated.

He said, "I did background checks on all of you. It's no wonder that you never took any casualties, I'm surprised that you took any prisoners."

I told him, "We're deputy Sheriffs, not murderers." I thought that he was implying that Vietnam veterans were ruthless killers and I called him on it.

"Take it easy, I was a platoon leader in the Marine Corps. It's just that the war along the coast was very confusing," he said.

Before the atmosphere grew any more uncomfortable, I changed the subject. "Is it alright if the platoon chows down in the back yard? Most of us missed supper." He agreed to that. The plan was to move the remainder of the platoon to camp cannibal for extraction tomorrow. Tonight, we would all set up at the ruins. Johnny could bum a ride to Houston with one of the Marshals who weren't needed at the sting operation at the estate. Temporary repairs were performed to the doors while we all chowed down out back.

It was decided to split into two groups. One would walk the cart trail and one would parallel the river. I took my group the river route so we wouldn't miss the Ruins camp. We could radio the trail team and either link-up with them, or set up for the night, rejoining in the morning. We would decide when the situation arose.

The houseboat could tell us if anyone appeared on camera. I assumed that Schultz had kept track of the day's adventure over his PRC-77, but I wanted to apprise him of tomorrow's extraction. With that conversation out of the way, my group walked the three hundred yards to the river and turned right to tackle our seven-mile hike. Travis had recovered his machine gun and was happy again. When we reached the ruins, we were too tired to make tents, so we wrapped in our ponchos and crashed where ever there was room.

Jimmy said that his guys had gotten some sleep so they would pull guard. I thanked him for the break and reminded him to report to the smokehouse on the hour. Sleep came in minutes. I was so tired that I had vertigo before passing out.

...

Sun-up came too soon once again. It had rained during the night and I hadn't even noticed. I wish that we'd have showered at the house last night, but the FBI was right to restore normalcy as soon as possible. Guests could arrive anytime.

We linked the entire platoon at the ruins. After we ate, I had them pool their ammo, chow, dog food, clean clothes, trip flares, and fresh radio batteries. We let them keep one full magazine apiece. We kept the PRC-77 and one PRC-25. We also robbed them of heat tabs and water purification tablets.

Our supply at this point would carry the six of us easily for a while. We said goodbye to the departing men as they sent half along the river and half along the cart trail, which was much closer here. We were back to six men again. Now we would have men at the river and men at the ruins. Personally, that was spread too thin. Hopefully all of the bad guys were dead or in jail, but I wasn't naïve enough to believe this.

Expecting the unexpected had kept us all alive through these and other more harrowing experiences. Edwin, for one, couldn't even remember most of his first tour in the Big Red One. He only remembered parts of the rest of his time in Vietnam with us in the 101st Airborne. Hell, at first he didn't even recognize Barry or me. We all had PTSD and traumatic amnesia.

Sergeant Donald talked about all the bodies from the Persian Gulf war. "I'll never get the smell of death out of my nostrils." He said that it was like driving through hell with occasional groups of lost souls surrendering to the Allies. He was as shaken with his nightmares as the rest of us.

We could remain in a group at the ruins until the camera picked up players. The two men would have to go to the river. The machine gun had to stay at the ruins. The camera could tell us how large of a party was approaching and if they had hostages.

We set about making and camouflaging our poncho tents. We decided that between the cameras and Otto, that we'd only need one man on radio watch. The dog would sleep at the guard post all the time so the guard could see if he alerted. It sure would be nice to catch up on some sleep. The four of us from the 101st still hadn't really had time to visit and catch up on where our lives were now.

The first four days were spent doing nothing except to call the smokehouse with negative situation reports every hour. We all scrubbed in the chilly river and did our own laundry. Lots of coffee and bull sessions. Camp Cannibal had been shrunken to thirty-six men again plus the Tiny look alike in the tree, and Schultz and his two friends in the smokehouse. They kept Spike at the river watch and another dog at the place where the cart trail met their camp. The tranquillity was disarming. On the fifth day, Schultz complained of boredom. He wanted to come out by us.

"Just bring more coffee for us and two backup men for yourself. Follow the river down and listen for Santa. Bring full rucksacks if you plan on staying," I told him. I was looking forward to getting to know our commander better.

When Otto alerted, I waited until I saw the whites of Schultz' eyes before I froze him. He said, "Santa Claus," but I could tell that he still couldn't make us out. He jumped when I rose up only ten feet away.

I said, "I hoped that you just learned something. This is no picnic out here and a nasty surprise could come at any time." He seemed to appreciate my little demonstration. It had driven a point home.

"Now that you've opened my eyes, show me the rest of your operation," said the Lieutenant. I thought that he might bring his two friends from the cabin, but he had chosen two rather large men who looked as if they might have been FBI also. They must have been hidden among his perimeter whenever we entered his camp. He introduced them to me as agents Smith and Jones. Now I had them figured as CIA. They all had full rucksacks, so they must have planned on staying.

I showed him the invisible camp at the ruins and explained the plan. The three of them nodded approval and offered no changes. Now Schultz wanted details of the last action at the ruins. He said that he wanted to hear it from the horse's mouth. Once again, they were impressed at how well it was carried out.

"If you hadn't have moved right up to the walls as you did, it would have changed the outcome of the bigger picture, not to mention the casualties that your men would have taken," said Lieutenant Schultz. Then he elaborated on current events of that 'bigger picture.' Congregation members were being arrested in five cities and their suburbs spanning two states. Many of them were talking. The doors at the blue gray house had been repaired and the bullet holes plugged and painted over. Several people had rung that particular doorbell. The garage at the estate had been converted to a walk-in cooler with more bodies. The refrigerator in the house had the liquid form of the date-rape drug along with PCP and meth-amphetamine. The master bedroom had a regular library of snuff videos, most involving women and children. The perpetrators made no effort to hide their faces and some of those faces had yet to be accounted for. Two had been among the dead in the back yard, one had been the pastor, and Big Foot was also a common player.

As disgusting as this news was, I was past the point of being shocked. This news only strengthened my resolve to see this through. "You said that some of the faces in the video weren't accounted for. How many is 'some'?" I asked Schultz.

Then Agent Smith took over the briefing, "Some, Mr. Johnson, is twelve. That's twelve mercenaries who have killed just about everything that walks, crawls, or flies, with a penchant for human prey."

Now Agent Jones spoke up, "Mr. Smith and I sat through the screening of those videos. There are no rules of engagement when dealing with these men. Our orders come from the president of the United States. Make no effort to detain these men, they are to be exterminated on sight."

Then he produced a large manila envelope from his shirt and showed us the 8x10 blow-ups of the filthy dozen. I was surprised at how clean cut they looked. Except for their eyes, they looked like typical businessmen.

While my squad scrutinized the photos, Mr. Jones continued the briefing. "We'll leave the photos with you. The videos of these men were taped at these very ruins. They were all filmed on sunny days. We have every reason to believe that these men are local. We can only guess that they have been out rounding up new victims for their videos. They have probably been out of state. We're not certain if they will stop at the estate first, or come directly here. This should be a daytime operation that could very well go down on the next sunny day. The new password is "Vengeance". The challenge is "Divine". Now if you'll excuse us, we'll be escorting the Lieutenant back. You seem to have this end under control. If that dog of yours alerts uphill in about a half-hour, it will be Smith and myself on the high- speed trail on our way to the estate. Break squelch twice and we'll come back with Smith and Jones. They may need us at the house." With that said, the three of them left.

We sat studying the photos a little longer. All of the men were Caucasians with blond hair and blue eyes. Their eyes looked bad as if they were staring out of hell. Creepy looking, but nothing that we couldn't handle. Hell, it was only two to one odds, I know that at least four of us had lived through worse. They'd most likely come down the river in flat-bottomed boats. Our biggest problem would be killing the Ariens without hurting any hostages. Killing these devils would give us pleasure. Now, to plan our daylight ambush and a backup plan. The sun was already coming out. We had two aces in the hole, Otto, and the cameras.

. . .

The time to hit them, ideally, was before they left the boats. They would have no cover, and the only escape would be the cold water. The motors could be put out of commission with a burst from any of the automatic rifles. In the event of any trying to escape under water, Ed, Sergeant Donald, and the dog could serve as the hunter/ killer team. The captives were at the root of our problems. This could turn into a running battle down the shore or in the woods.

A lot rode on the report from the camera monitor. If the mercenaries had captives, we would simply have to hit them before they reached the cover of the ruins. Now was the time to consult the rest of my think tank.

First, I laid out my plan about the only two possible ambush sites. When I asked for suggestions, none came. Everyone came to the same dead end in planning, how to protect the inevitable captives. Jimmy said that we should pray to protect the innocents involved. He offered to lead.

"Dear Lord, give us strength to overcome these evil men. Please don't let any innocent blood be spilled. In Jesus name we pray, Amen."

We all said "Amen".

Now to prepare both ambush sites and hope that our prayers were answered. My thoughts were that the Ariens would bypass the house until the filming was done. Then they would take the bodies to Tiny for processing before going to the estate for payment and socializing. My guess was that we would be movers, shakers, and risk takers once again.

The ambush site by the river was fairly simple and probably the better of the two. This being the higher bank, there was a natural depression approximately fifteen feet from the stream. We could lie prone, peeking through the foliage and firing from point blank range.

The inland site would consist of two groups of three men about five meters apart along the trail leading to the ruins. These would be harder to conceal because the brush thinned out under the trees. The machine gun would be in the position closest to the river since I expected the bulk of the mercenaries at the rear, and some were bound to try escaping. Once we were satisfied with our handiwork, I held another meeting.

"Friends," I said, "I believe that the enemy will arrive at night. I know that they film on sunny days, but they will want the cover of darkness to mask their arrival. They can't afford to be spotted by a semi from the bridge. They'll have to be in at least three vehicles. Probably vans or panel trucks with tinted windows. If all twelve show at once as I believe they will, they will need three flat-bottomed vessels to move everything to our location. I tend to believe that they will arrive just prior to daybreak. I've not seen any sign of overnight camp around here. Another possibility is that they'll show around dark to play with their victims until the sun is high like the first bunch of rats had planned. These men are sadists who would perform their work even without pay for no other reason than that they enjoy what they're doing. When you have them in your sights, remember, each one that you kill means saving countless innocents."

There was a unanimous acceptance to my theory and a total agreement to necessity of annihilating these demons on Earth. We all expressed an eagerness for this to be over soon. Everyone moved to the depression to await news from the camera watch.

I called base to find out if Smith and Jones had left. Schultz said that they were just leaving. He also said that the big man from the tree fort that we had arrested was indeed the brother of the headhunter and had some manslaughter charges pending on him. He had been sought for bail jumping until we found him. There was an undisclosed reward for him too. He'd let us know how much as he got further information. "By the way, the twelve Goldilocks were worth twenty-five grand apiece, dead or alive," said Schultz.

No wonder Smith and Jones or whatever their names were headed to the estate. They expected the Ariens to show there and they wanted a share of the three hundred grand. That kind of money was hard to obtain legally for one day's work. Many people would risk their lives at a chance like that. Many, but not all. I suspected that our friends at the agency were keeping secrets. The CIA men would have stayed by us if they thought the mercenaries were coming to the ruins first.

I stood by my hunches. We'd greet our incognito CIA men by the trail and play as dumb as they thought we were. Then we could have lunch and wait for our wealth to arrive. Travis and I took Otto just north of the trail along with the PRC-25. The agents would be looking for us on the south side. If I had to guess, I'd say that they meant to pass without saying hello. My hopes were to surprise them for the second time in one day. I wanted to keep them off balance and instill a little respect for Vietnam Veterans.

We didn't have long to wait. Their shit was pretty much together. They were both on the uphill side of the trail on a collision course with us. They were moving quickly and almost soundlessly. When they were ten feet away, I gave the challenge, "Divine!"

When the lead man said, "Vengeance," I could hear the disappointment in his voice. He tried to cover his disappointment by saying, "Too bad you won't be at the house for the real fun."

I told him that we had enough killing for several lifetimes. "You younger, less experienced men have to get your feet wet too."

This conversation ended on that note and the agents moved along, keeping their secrets to themselves, as did we. I hoped that these two killers didn't try to ambush the dirt road alone. Who knows what harm might come to innocent captives in an undermanned, wild shoot out. Those two looked crazy enough to try something like that.

I called the rest of the squad at the water to warn them of our return. I said that we'd send Otto in first. When we were linked up at the depression facing the river, I told them about the agent's jibe about missing the fun. Then I suggested that Smith and Jones might be mavericks after the money with no regard for safety of innocents.

Barry suggested that I call the estate with an estimated time of arrival for the two, and call the houseboat to keep an eye out for pedestrian traffic on the camera. I implemented those ideas sans any personal suspicions. I figured that the Chief could read between the lines. I'm sure he felt the intrusion of the pair of rogues too.

We didn't get any news from the camera for the remainder of that sunny day. That night at about eleven PM, the radio finally crackled. We had actors on stage at the dirt road. Three maxi-vans in camouflage paint all towing similarly colored flat-bottomed boats. The priceless camera watch gave us all the details. The first van backed to the water unloading its craft. Six blonde men entered the first boat and waited while the second boat was put in. Boat number two was tied to the first. The first two vehicles were driven into the brush and camouflage nets were spread over them. Four men were tending these duties as the third van backed to the river. The four men helped launch the third craft, which was tied to the center boat by one of the men. Then this man threw a rope to shore and all the boats were pulled into line, parallel to shore.

The prisoners were unloaded through the side door of van number three. All were small children or teenagers. All seemed to be Caucasians, and all appeared to be female. They were tied together at the neck and roughly jammed into the center boat. There were a total of nine hostages without an adult among them. Two men held the boats steady while the last van was parked and covered. Now the six men in the shore party climbed into the rear boat and they headed upstream, presumably to the ruins.

The camera watch reported two assault rifles in the lead boat and only side arms for the rest. Our prayers hadn't been in vain. The captives were safely separated. I put Travis, Barry, and Sergeant Donald on the east-end of the ambush to insure that the machine gun with its greater fire power and range would make escape impossible. Also, it put a Starlight scope on the approaching end. Edwin, Jimmy, and I were on the western side with Otto.

I would initiate the ambush by simply opening fire when the lead boat was on line with my position. There would be no calls for surrender. The safety of the children was our main priority. We had only a few quiet moments left. No one spoke. Travis was bathing the gun barrel with LSA gun oil. Ed took Otto a few yards west of our group and told him to stay. This was finale time on the set of our personal horror show.

We made our last report and killed the volume on the radios. I swear that our beating hearts provided the only sound for awhile. Sergeant Donald signaled their approach. There was a bright, full moon. I wondered if the bad guys planned it this way. At any rate, it would work to our advantage.

They were coming excruciatingly slow. I guessed that they were looking for the trail that led to the ruins. An eternity later, the lead boat was abreast of my position. After my first shot, pandemonium broke out. The noise was deafening. The slightly slower firing M-14's and the machine gun could barely be distinguished from the din. Hell, if we were firing blanks, we might have scared them to death.

We never received a single round of incoming. The first and third boats were sinking fast. Ed and I ran into the water to the lead boat with drawn pistols. Barry and Travis were charging the last boat with guns in hand. Sergeant Donald and Jimmy ran to the center boat to reassure the children and to keep it from drifting. Ed and I fired into the lead boat where two men were still moving. There were no more shots fired. The machine gun had done its grisly job well. The center boat was dragged as close to shore as possible. We were all wet now. Jimmy and the Sergeant cut the center boat free and dragged it as far ashore as they could with all the weight, then they helped the children ashore before they helped us retrieve the bodies so the current wouldn't carry them away.

Twenty strenuous minutes later, we had three hundred thousand dollars lined up on shore.

The children were in a non-responsive, shocked condition. I got Schultz on the horn and requested an immediate extraction for the children. I told him that the blonde rats could wait for morning. The kids wouldn't get in the boat again, so we convinced them to walk with Ed, Sergeant Donald, and I to the camp at the smokehouse. We requested a patrol to meet us and finish the escort duty.

After we released the children to the patrol, we headed back to our friends by the bodies. It was only twelve thirty AM. All of this seemed to take hours, but only an hour had passed since the first shot was fired. I volunteered for radio watch with Otto sleeping next to me. I couldn't sleep anyway. It appeared as if bad guys in our neck of the woods would be as scarce as hen's teeth, for awhile at least.

By one AM, all six of us were sitting up, wide-awake. I called the estate for permission to build a fire. They said, "Sure. If the camera spots anything, we'll let you know."

We'd damn near wiped out bad guys as a species. I really didn't think that any players in our show were left. There would be a festive mood around the fire. Five of us had seventy thousand dollars coming and Jimmy had over fifty thousand coming. Even Otto was awake and happy.

Jimmy and Sergeant Donald pulled the two holy boats up as far as they could while the rest of us looked for firewood. That was a rare commodity this close to shore so we went inland under the trees. We searched in pairs, still not quite believing that the woods were safe. Upon our return to the river, we all pitched in dragging the boats out of the water. We dumped them over to get rid of the water. Sergeant Donald and I tallied all the equipment from the boats while the others built the fire. We turned up a lot more than the two rifles spotted by the camera. There were ten AK-47's and two RPD light machine guns. There was video gear galore.

Next we turned our attention to searching the bodies. There were a total of twenty-four pistols. Every man had a backup piece concealed. Me too, of course. I still had the bottom line in my pocket. There were twelve wicked looking knives of all descriptions along with numerous throwing stars and steel balls. We left the wallets sans money with the bodies to make for easier identification. Many had been shot in the face and head. Travis walked over and said, "I'd like to see some smart-ass lawyer get these guys off on a technicality."

That was the first time that I had laughed in days and it felt terrific. It was time to wash off the blood and join the party.

At six AM, the radio crackled. It was the smokehouse wanting to know how many boats would be needed. "Send two with one pilot each. We'll walk in when the boats arrive," I replied.

We didn't have long to wait for the pickup. The boats came with two good motors, that would be one more than we had. We tied the flat-bottomed boat that still floated between the two from base. Then we put in the equipment and the bodies were spread out between the three.

We took off on foot for base as soon as the grisly armada was on its way. I carried the PRC-77 and Edwin carried the PRC-25. Thank God that it was only a mile or so. We should have piled our rucksacks on the boats, but I didn't think of it. It turned out to be a short, pleasant stroll. The camp was being dismantled when we arrived. The bodies and equipment had just started to pile up in the clearing nearest the river.

We walked up to the open door of the cabin to be met by Lieutenant Schultz' beaming face. "It looks like I had the right men in the right place," he said, extending a welcoming hand to all. "Smith and Jones scared me. I was afraid that if I left them at the ruins, they might have caused casualties among the innocent. I told them that the twelve mercenaries would stop at the house first. They work for the CIA and were sent by the president to insure that none of the twelve survived. I never underestimated you six for a moment.

I said, "It took the collective brains and courage of the whole team, not to forget the dogs, and a lot of praying."

Schultz spoke up again, "Whatever it took, you're all heroes now and the media are waiting to get their hands on you. Just remember to stress the safety of the children when they ask why there were no survivors among the twelve demons. We don't want any liberals screaming "Murder!" on us. This was a well run and well executed mission. We'll never know how many innocent lives were saved by the events of the last two weeks. The predators killed on this operation weren't worth one single innocent life. Now you can take a break and wait for the helicopters. The first bird is yours. My men will clean up here and retrieve the two junk boats from your camp. Thank you, you're on your own time now"

...

The chopper dropped us on the road in front of my home next to the quiet neighbors. The agents were already packing their van. The press and local TV crews were there. I felt like hiding with the Jones'.

The media really put us through a grilling, exhausting and redundant, and everything in between. I'd guess that all of our faces would be plastered across front pages nation wide. We'd probably appear on several TV shows as well. There we would be, in all of our unshaven, unwashed glory looking more like criminals than the clean-shaven anti-Christ's that we'd just killed. At least a picture of Big Foot and that curved machete might redeem our image.

So, now we were national heroes. We had large rewards coming and our stories would be worth something too. With all that said, I still only had a bicycle for transportation, and it wasn't even mine. The FBI had better have left the phone hooked up or I'd be pedaling to the darn 7-11 pay phone to call Margaret. I'd like to call my children too. The FBI had promised that my mess had been cleaned up. My ex's would be impressed. What I'd like to do is get custody of all three children. They would like the Houston climate better than they would like the frozen north.

Sergeant Donald took me aside and said that I was a shoe in for the Montgomery County Sheriff's Police. If I went through training, I'd be a sergeant within a year. That would look very good on my appeal for custody.

When the FBI and the media were gone, we went inside to see what they'd left me. Furniture, nice stuff too. Beds in every one of the four bedrooms. There was linen in the linen closet, drapes, two reclining chairs, a futon, and food in the refrigerator, but no beer.

The phone was still working, Hallelujah! I let Sergeant Donald call his wife first. She'd be picking him up sooner than soon. She'd also bring lots of beer. I called Margaret next. She was so excited that I was embarrassed. She insisted on picking me up before I got drunk. I told her to give me time to shower and wait for me to call her. (I can't let her run my life, even though she'd probably do a better job than I.) I also wanted to call the bank to see if I had liquid assets yet. I wanted a car and the freedom that goes with owning one.

What about clean civilian clothes for my friends? Jimmy might fit in mine, but the other three were too tall, period. Then Jimmy said that he had a wife waiting for a call too. So, as Sergeant Donald's wife was pulling in, Jimmy called his wife. She was about forty minutes away in Spring, Texas. Now I called the bank. There was twenty grand ready with the other fifty available by tomorrow.

Next, I scrubbed up while my three friends ran up my phone bill and drank beer. When I came out looking and feeling like a new man, I was greeted by wolf whistles with an "Oh baby!" thrown in. Sergeant Donald was gone. He left the message that the beer was on him and that he would call me tomorrow about my job. I was hoping to catch a ride to the bank with Jimmy and his wife. And for my next wish, I could buy a cheap car.

The Bureau was sending a car in the morning for my friends to take them to the airport. We still hadn't been able to visit properly. We exchanged phone numbers and addresses before we forgot. My friend Barry had lived six hours away from my last home in Wisconsin and I never knew. Travis and Edwin lived an hour apart in the Tampa area and they never knew. It looked like the Conroe area was my home once again. It sure felt like home. I hadn't realized how much I missed it.

Jimmy agreed to drop me at the bank when his wife pulled up. "How could you live next to a cemetery?" she asked.

I told her that I liked it quiet and my neighbors kept their mouths shut. She laughed, but I could tell that it wasn't her cup of tea.

I wrote down sizes for clothes my larger friends so I could get jeans and T-shirts while I was out. I looked back as I drove away and remembered that I wanted a rake and lawnmower soon.

I said goodbye to Jimmy and his wife at the bank after getting his phone number. He was a Harris county cop. I was sure to see him again. At the bank, I withdrew twenty five hundred dollars with the thought of a decent used car or van in mind. The bank manager greeted me like a celebrity. He gave me his brother's business card at the Chevrolet dealership at the north end of town. I walked the ¾ mile with horns honking and people waving the entire way. The dealer said that my money was no good there. He would give me a new car or van of my choice if I would agree to do some commercials for him.

"No problem, just draw up the papers and show me where to sign!" was my natural response. It was hard to believe that I was a hobo less than a month ago. I drove out of there with a white window van and an agreement to do six commercials in camouflage fatigues and six in street clothes. I drove to the Wal-Mart and picked up clothes for the three men at the house.

There was a strange car in the drive that looked like an unmarked squad. Upon entering, I was greeted by Conroe's police chief. He had an interesting offer that I just couldn't refuse. He wanted me to organize and head up their town's first SWAT unit. He said that I could choose my men from his force or bring in outsiders as I wished. I was told to limit it to six men to stay within the town's budget. My rank and pay grade would start at Sergeant. If I did well on tests, I could study for the Lieutenant's test and take it the next time they were scheduled. "There is a book on the table that will help," he said.

I said that I would be honored to lead the SWAT team and thanked him for the opportunity.

When he shook my hand, he leaned closer and said in a loud whisper, "Try to keep these boys here in town."

After he left, I took my friends outside to show them the van and tell them how I came by it. That opened their eyes to their individual commercial value. Regretfully, they all had to leave in the morning, so I carried in the clean clothes and let them fight over the shower.

It was a damn sight easier to breathe in there when the last man toweled off. I was now down to one razor and all out of after shave. It don't mean nothin'.

I called Margaret to tell her that I'd be wasting tonight with my killer friends who had to leave in the morning. She claimed to understand, but who knows with women?

. . .

We took our beer over to the cemetery so my friends could meet the neighbors. “Boys, these are the Jones’s. Jones’s these are the boys. We’re sorry that you can’t have a drink with us, but we’ll have a few for you.” I felt naked without my M-16, but I still had the bottom line in my pocket.

Barry said, “I wish they would have let me keep Otto, he sure was a good dog. I’m going to try to buy him. They can’t want more than a couple of grand for him, maybe a little more with all his training. He could get killed. They make him do a lot of dangerous stuff.”

I reminded them of my cottonmouth problem and said, “I can’t get a dog until I have my balance of nature back.

Travis said, “You Point Men are all unbalanced and nature is a poor excuse.”

Edwin jumped right in, “I have no excuses. I’m just plain crazy and I liked walking point.”

I said, “Let’s go inside before we wake the neighbors, and watch out for Big Foot’s other brothers.” Even I didn’t think that was funny. Hell, he and Tiny could have a big clan. Just the two of them was already a big clan. I laughed my way all the way to the house.

Ed said, “See, he’s as nuts as me. Ya gotta be to walk point.” Then Travis defended his service carrying the machine gun. He used to walk right behind me with it. Meanwhile, I told Barry my joke about the ‘big’ clan and we were both laughing.

“What’s so funny,” said Travis. “A machine gun is as important as a radio!” Then I told him and Ed what we were laughing at and pretty soon we were all laughing. Every time the word big entered the conversation, we’d crack up all over again. I didn’t say it then, but I made up my mind to check into Big Foot and Tiny’s sibling situation. I was the one who lived next to a cemetery at the end of three miles of unlit dirt road. I was scaring myself just remembering. I would have to get a dog soon. Maybe a short hair that knew his snakes by smell. That was it, I’d get a black male short hair and build him a house by the front door.

Ed and Travis were passed out in the recliners and Barry was curled up on the futon. I turned up the space heater and passed out in the master bedroom with the door open.

...

We were all awake and done with our three 'S's before the airport car came. We said our "good-bye's" and made sincere promises to keep in touch. One last round of handshakes and hugs, and I was alone. I had gotten used to being alone and even preferred it, but I was going to miss those guys. Once again, our lives had been in each other's hands, and they were still good hands.

I called Margaret's to see if she wanted company. She said OK, trying not to sound too eager. This was Sunday and she didn't have to work, so why not? I could see that I'd have to smooth some ruffled feathers. That was OK too, she had some nice feathers. She was amazed when I told her about the van and the job as SWAT team leader with a shot at Lieutenant. Sure I could come right over and yes, she wanted to come shopping and to lunch. Now the eagerness was back in her voice. I'd get flowers and candy on the way.

She smelled real good when I got to her place. Then she kissed me like it was the natural thing to do. King Kong was talking in my ear. I told her that I needed to use her bathroom, but what I wanted was to get inside with the door closed. That chick was a mind reader, because when I came out of the ladies room, she was seated on the couch and patted the seat next to her.

It was after two PM when we finally left, starving. The shopping could wait until after lunch. Every where we went, I attracted attention. My face was in the papers and on TV. I could tell that Margaret got a kick out of being with a celebrity. This would raise her status from unwed mother to Derrick Johnson's girlfriend. That was fine by me. She liked me when I was on a bicycle before I got into dragon slaying. I had slain some in 1970 that she hadn't forgotten either.

Shopping wasn't any less fussed over than lunch. I had a hard time getting people to take my money. They'd been living in fear for a long time. They could breathe a collective sigh of relief now that Dodge had been cleaned up. Almost everyone's life had been effected in some way. Their quality of living had improved a thousand-fold.

Where was all this gratitude when we returned from Vietnam? Texas treated their veterans better than a lot of states. I would make it a point to join the VFW and spread the news that the entire squad had been veteran's and five of the six that freed the last group of children had been Vietnam Veterans.

I think that a few items on my shopping list intrigued Margaret, but she kept a lid on her curiosity well. She would have to get used to a quiet man. I normally spoke only when a question was asked. Even then, half the time my response would be, "Who wants to know?" My children were the only ones that I felt comfortable opening up to. Their questions were always given careful consideration. My answers were designed to suit their best interests. I never lied to my children. Sometimes, when they were little, I'd tell them that a fuller explanation than the one I'm giving would come when they were old enough to understand.

Margaret loved the van. She said that it made her high enough to look down on other people. I guessed from that last remark that she felt looked down upon. Getting to know each other was not going to be easy, neither one of us was good at opening up.

My final stop was the animal shelter. They didn't have what I wanted but they had what I needed. He was a one hundred-pound Rhodesian Ridge Back with enough 'puppy' in him to bond to a stranger. They only charge sixty-five dollars for their animals to cover shots and food. Here I had a pedigreed lion dog for nickels and dimes. They said that he was picked up as a stray, so he had no name. I named him Sinbad after a big tomcat that I used to own. That cat would rather fight than eat. The only thing that he liked more than fighting, he had to fight to get. I'm glad that people aren't like cats in that respect. A simple, "yes" or "no" was fine with me.

Margaret and Sinbad got along well. That was important since she and I might become an item. I'd have to find a way to get Sinbad used to children. If Margaret and I were still together when the baby came, I didn't want any sibling rivalry. I presented this problem to her.

She said that her nieces and nephews could visit to see if my dog would tolerate children. Their ages ranged from six months to eleven years old. We decided that next weekend would be a good time to start. Her nieces and nephews slept over often and their families each had large dogs. This might be easier than I thought.

I drove back to my place. I'd have to make phone calls to my children and to David. I was hoping to buy this house that had been so hard to rent. By now, my children would be famous at their schools. Their father was the key player in the elimination of several 'bogeymen'.

David said that I could have the house and the two acres on both sides of the road nearest the cemetery for twenty-eight thousand dollars. He wanted the rest for development. I asked him how much land on that road was his.

He said, "Two hundred feet wide on both sides of the road clean out to highway 105."

Then I asked, "How much per acre after that?" He told me that I could buy acres for twenty-five hundred per acre since I had increased the value of the land just by living at the end of the road. I told him that I wanted four more acres, two on each side of the road and adjacent to the land that we'd already agreed upon. That put his sale at thirty-eight thousand dollars, which still left me comfortable considering my new job as well as the remainder of the reward money. My nearest neighbor would be over seven hundred feet away. I could live with that. I could put a gate across the road with a streetlight above it and another light by the house. The gate would never be locked. I had to let people visit and tend the cemetery. It was such an old graveyard that most of the kin had probably died or moved away. I really didn't expect too much traffic there. In a pinch, I'd take my own lawnmower to those weeds.

David liked my proposal and we agreed to meet Monday evening to complete our business. The taxes must have been eating his lunch ever since he made the original purchase.

Calling my children was pure joy. They were all full of news and love. The two oldest ones, Travis, (named after my friend and slack man) and Rebecca, were excited at the prospect of coming down for the summer. Annie, the little one from my second marriage, wanted to come too. My plan was to get them to fall in love with Texas so they would want to stay with me.

Margaret wanted to be out of here before dark and the sun was going down. I opened Margaret's door and let Sinbad into the back. We picked up some Chinese food on the way. I wanted her to have a little time for 'us' and not leave her a pile of dishes.

...

Monday morning, I chained Sinbad to the front porch and gave him an old carpet to lie on. I had to meet with Conroe's police chief to sign in and pick up my gear. The gear included a belt radio and a radio for my van. The idea being that I was on call twenty-four hours per day. The rest of the gear was my kind of toys. I got an M-16, a .357 Combat Magnum revolver, body armor, several sets of black and camouflage fatigues, some mace, a black leather belt, a folding lock blade knife and a black wallet with a Sergeant's star. Other than studying for my detective's exam, my time was my own. The test was given on the first business day of each month.

So, now I wasn't just a rookie, I was an instant Sergeant. I wondered, but I didn't worry, if the other officers would be upset at my instant promotion. Before I left, I asked for a list of his men with military experience and their phone numbers. Then I asked him to post a notice, requesting volunteers, putting my radio call sign, 'Swat One,' along with my home phone number at the bottom. Once again, I thanked him for everything.

He said, "I'm sure that neither I, nor this city will be disappointed. I wish that your very efficient friends could have stayed."

"Likewise, captain. In a pinch, I'll be your one-man army. I also have a good dog which I would like to have trained after a month or so when we've had time to bond."

He made the list of men from memory. There were only four men on the force with a military background. I was curious to see if any or all volunteered.

When I got home and turned Sinbad loose, he made a fuss over me. I guess that he was still a little insecure. We went inside and I left a phone message for Margaret to call me after work. I left Sinbad in the house so I could check out the cellar. I took a lamp and extension cord with me. There weren't any on the stairs. The ones that I electrocuted had all been cleaned up. The light showed that a few little ones had straggled in. The big ones den up first because it takes longer for them to warm up. They are very slow and more vulnerable to coyotes when they are cold. That's why their instincts send them underground first. The little ones have to eat as much as they can to keep from malnutrition over the winter. The adults can go as long as a year without eating and still remain healthy.

The snakes were dispatched and I picked up the bodies on a shovel for safety to bury at the edge of the swamp. Now it would be safe to let Sinbad out again. We went back to the cellar so I could examine the tools and junk hanging on the walls. I wanted to build a curb under the cellar door so the Cottonmouths couldn't get in any more. The foundation was brick, so the crack under the door was their only means of access.

Sinbad started growling. I turned to see another little snake coming down the stairs. The dog charged the snake before I could grab his collar. He rushed at it, but made no attempt to bite it. The snake stayed on the stair with it's head tipped back and his mouth open 180 degrees in the classic 'trap-jaw' position. The dog knew that it was a bad snake just by its musk. That took a load off my mind. As long as the dog stayed near the house, I could let him run loose. I killed the snake and buried him near his buddies.

The wooden curb only took a few minutes to make. Now the dog and I could explore together. I checked the belt radio to see if the range was sufficient. The dispatcher said that they had me loud and clear. I went inside and picked up the M-16 and some full magazines. Then I locked the house and took the dog on his rounds. I paced off my new property lines and kept Sinbad close. If I did this at least once per day, my dog would learn his territory.

I wanted to buy and post signs against tresspassers and hunters. I decided to see if David was home so we could conduct our business. He was, so I asked him to meet me for coffee. The M-16 could be stored in the van, but I wore the revolver and the star. Soon, I hoped to have a detective's shield for that little wallet that the captain gave me.

The first thing that I did at the coffee shop was to give David his five hundred dollars back. When I asked him about the rent owed, he said that the FBI had covered it.

By coincidence, we used the same bank. The paperwork was over in a flash since David had called ahead to set the wheels in motion. We both left the bank as happy men. He told me that after he sold another five acres, the rest was profit. The property taxes that he'd been paying all those years would help offset the capital gains tax. We parted company smiling. I'm sure that he and his wife Pauline would be celebrating that evening.

Sinbad was waiting in the van. He picked up on my happy mood and seemed to be happier too. I changed my mind about sending him for training. He was a house pet, even more, a friend. I would just work with police or National Guard dogs if the need arose again. Now, off to Wal-Mart for signs, wood, and nails. I wanted those posted before Margaret called. I might even have time to do a little studying for the detective's exam. First, I wanted to see if anyone had signed my volunteer list.

I swung by the station and introduced myself to everyone that I hadn't already met. My notice had only three names, but I hoped for improvement every time a shift changed. I checked the names against the list in my pocket. One of them matched. I wondered how the captain was going to make up for the five-man hole in his work force. Surely, a town this size would produce plenty of applicants. There might even be a waiting list.

Next, off to the house to post my new property. Sinbad could join me to note the boundaries once more. That dog was good company. Neither of us talked much. Words aren't always necessary among friends.

...

Having posted the signs, I went inside to shower. I could study afterward while I was waiting for Margaret to call. When I got done with my shower, Sinbad was lying right outside the bathroom door. He got to his feet immediately to greet me. This would make up for some of the loneliness without having my children around. He followed me into the bedroom as I dressed and he sat by my chair as I studied. Neither of us would be lonely again.

The phone rang a little after four O'clock. The man on the line said that he and his partners wanted to apply for SWAT. I asked them to stop over if they had a few minutes. He said that they knew where I lived and would be over in five minutes.

Five minutes later, a car with four men pulled up. They got out of the car still in uniform. Sinbad slipped past me and ran out to do battle. I hollered his name and he retreated to my side. "Good boy," I told him. "It's OK, they're good boys too." I had the dog stay on the leash until I greeted the officers.

The one who spoke up said that they all wanted to volunteer. They were Bob, James, Al, and Steve. They were all about thirty and looked sturdy and fit. These turned out to be the ex-military that the captain had mentioned.

Now it was time for Sinbad to apologize to my new friends. I told the men to stand still and let the dog sniff them first. I walked him over on the leash. None of them showed any fear. Soon, Sinbad was wagging his tail, so I let him off the leash. I invited them all inside to discuss the details.

All of the men had been Army Airborne. They signed up as a group for Desert Storm. They all went to the 101st who parachuted inside Iraq. Bob said that the Elite Guard of Saddam Hussein didn't even stay long enough to introduce themselves. All of these men were rappel qualified too. They were perfect. I told them that I'd been in the 101st also.

Steve quoted my unit and the years of my Nam service. Al said that I was already a legend at the station. James was more quiet. He did say that Desert Storm was no picnic. I could feel that he expected to be rejected like the WWII vets did to us. I told him that no war is a picnic. I said, "I heard that the Highway of Death looked like Hell on Earth." That seemed to disarm the situation and put us all at ease.

Back to current business, I asked them how they felt with just the five of us. I told them that I was authorized for six, I just would rather work with former military than work with a sixth man who not only would have to be trained, but may prove to be a liability at some crucial moment. "All of us know that training is no substitute for experience which is what we already have," I stated factually.

They agreed to a man that the possibility of a weak link wasn't worth the risk just to fill out the team. With that aside, I asked who would best be qualified to be our sniper if we should need one. The other three all pointed at James, the quiet one. James said that he'd been a sniper in Iraq and that he'd had to take lives before. He said it like that and not "to kill" as many people would have. I thanked him if he was volunteering and he said that he would do it.

"Now I will have to consult the captain. I think that he'll approve of our five-man team for the reasons that we have already discussed. It's been a pleasure meeting all of you. I have every reason to think that we shall work well together. Thank you for volunteering. I was hoping that you would. I'll meet you at the station in the morning. Goodnight gentlemen," I said.

Pretty soon, Margaret Ann would be calling. I'd have to ask her how her day was. Dinner out should cheer her up. I let Sinbad out and commenced to study once again. I was having trouble concentrating. Those four men were obviously as close as I was to my three friends who had just left for Michigan and Florida. They had said that I was a legend.

This might make them more willing to follow my orders and to impress upon me that they, too, were capable of becoming legends. I decided that this situation was best for Conroe and the success of each and every mission.

I closed the book and went outside to check on Sinbad. When I called, he came from the north side of the house. He was excited and obviously wanted me to see something in back. When we got around the corner, he had another snake curled up by the cellar door. This was one I was looking for. It was a speckled king snake about three feet long. It looked like a female by it's short tail. She was cold when I picked her up. She made no move to bite, but seemed happy to be held in my warm hands. I heard the phone ringing and unlocked the back door to answer. I had the snake in one hand and the phone in the other. All that I heard was heavy breathing. Margaret laughed and said that it was more fun as a duet. That remark didn't go over my head, "Could we dine out before our asthmatic duet?"

Now she was really laughing. Dinner sounded fine to her. I told her what Sinbad just found. She asked, "Is that good or bad?" When I explained, she said to name it Eve and put it in the cellar.

"I was hoping that you'd understand, I'll be over in fifteen minutes," I said. So I put the beginning of my Cottonmouth solution in the cellar and went in to wash my hands. I locked the back door and turned on my new yard lights. I put Sinbad inside and locked up before heading to Margaret's.

She had just gotten out of the shower. She looked and smelled great. I was tempted to call for a pizza delivery, but I didn't want her to think that I only wanted her for one thing. She was dressed so nicely that I assumed she wanted to go out.

When we got to the restaurant and were through ordering, she told me that she was going to order a pizza, but she didn't want me to think that she only wanted me for my body. I laughed and told her of my exact thoughts. Yes sir, she and I would get along great.

...

Tuesday morning at the station, the five members of the city's new SWAT team were sitting in the break room waiting for the captain. He joined us with a sincere smile. After "Hello's", he got down to business.

"I assume that you've had time to get acquainted with Sergeant Johnson. I hope that you all know that Derrick is studying to take the detective's exam. This job will have its privileges and its drawbacks. Effective immediately, you are all removed from street patrols. Most of your time will be your own. You will be on call twenty-four hours per day. This means that no one can leave a twenty-five mile radius of city hall except for emergencies. In order to get state funding, you will be acting as the SWAT team for the entire county." At this point of the captain's speech, Sergeant Donald of the county police walked in.

"I hope that I'm not late, Captain," he said. Of course I jumped up and shook his hand. He continued, "The county team is short one man, I'd like to be that man."

I looked at the captain and he nodded. "Welcome aboard," I said. "How did you know about this, or were you in on the whole plan?"

Sergeant Donald said, "The captain and I have been playing with this idea since before you came into town. We got to know each other at the gym. Our children study Karate together and we go to the same church. Your performance over the last two weeks told us that we had the man to head up the team. You were a born leader with a complicated and intelligent yet open mind. The trials in the swamp appeared to be just routine for you."

I thanked them for their flattery and especially their confidence.

The captain spoke up, "This meeting is over. You new men report to the arms room to pick up your gear. Keep your radios with you at all times. Take them with you when you shower and leave them on your nightstand next to your bed. Derrick, come up to my office for a briefing."

In his office, he took on a very serious tone. He said that aside from the occasional call for hostage situations, our primary assignment was to wipe out any vestiges of Satanic cults. "We're not after wannabees and we're not going to run rough shod over anyone's civil rights. We do have a sinister core of devil worshippers of indeterminate size. They managed to avoid that other group of high profile monsters that we dealt with recently. We have the Klan, the Skinheads, and the Black Power groups covered. Those kinds of trash are in a distinct minority here. We still have an unusual amount of missing persons that the DNA lab boys couldn't account for in that wealth of bodies that you and the FBI turned up. Most of those bodies were gathered from people who were tourists or transient families hoping to find greener pastures. The more secretive group that we are seeking now is a complete mystery. Any speculation that I might share with you may point you in the wrong direction. That is why I've decided to let you fly by the seat of your pants. I will supply you with the current file. It is one that I was hoping would be wiped out with that massive joint effort in the Sam Houston National Forest which you were just a part of. A few bodies have turned up, most of the missing are still that, 'missing'. Everything that I have is in the file that I'm giving you now. These people may be every bit as dangerous as those damn cannibals. They certainly know how to hide." He rose and shook my hand and wished me "luck".

...

He said that they were very good at hiding. That meant that no one was exempt from suspicion. Unfortunately, that meant that even my team might be members. I would hate to think that, but I would consider it anyway. Expect the unexpected. That is why I decided to keep the file and my knowledge of this separate cult a secret. The captain only invited me to that meeting. Maybe the captain was as paranoid as I was. I was chosen to investigate the case on the merits of past performance and maybe, too, because I was an outsider. I decided that I would have to talk to the captain again and soon, right after I met the other team members in the parking lot. I'd just tell them to take the rest of the day off and remind them to keep their radios turned on.

Once I'd dismissed the team, I went back inside. The captain raised his eyebrows when I told him that I was going to keep the file for my eyes only. He agreed with my reason why. He admitted that he never would have been that cautious. He said that once again he was reassured that I was the best man for the job.

As I left the building, I was wondering if Sinbad would be comfortable around Sergeant Donald. He had accepted the other four members readily enough. Country folks say that a dog can sense the devil, something that I'd always instinctively believed. His introduction to Sinbad was something that I would be paying close attention to.

...

As I drove up the road to my house, I saw David's truck on the side. He was parked behind another vehicle with a surveyor's logo on the door. They were way off in the trees, so I just honked and waved. I had to get home to let Sinbad out. Then we could try to catch David before he left. The dog was happy to see me and happy to be out. While he was sniffing the bushes, I put the bicycle in the van. Next, Sinbad hopped in. He loved to go for rides. I'd held David's bike hostage long enough. It would be a good excuse to visit.

They were just walking up to the road as I pulled up. "Hi there stranger!" I said. "I was going to sell the bike at a yard sale but no one would come down the road."

David laughed as I loaded the bike into his truck. Sinbad hopped out and was busily sniffing the two new people. They passed his inspection and he wagged out his happy acceptance. David said good-by to the surveyor who seemed happy to be leaving the big dog.

David was truly impressed with my canine friend. "How much did you pay for the lion dog?" he asked. "Those are an uncommon breed. They are all heart in a fight."

"David, you'd just be mad if I told you," I said. "Let's just say I got a deal."

He said that surveyors would be out all day tomorrow. They'd have to mark my boundaries last since they had to start at highway 105. They'd be done that same afternoon. No building would start until the lots started selling. He and Sinbad got along real well. David was a good Christian man. The dog that didn't like him should be put to sleep, or at least its master should. I promised to bring Margaret over for supper soon. He said that Pauline still wouldn't come down here. He had an appointment with a Realtor, so he took off. Sinbad and I went back home. We walked around the house to check on Eve in the cellar. I turned on the lamp. After awhile, I spotted her up in the tools. I would have to buy a big male for her. They shouldn't cost much since they were local animals. It was a surprise finding such a big one out of the ground this time of year. Something must have disturbed her.

I was past due for cutting my grass. Sinbad would have to get used to the noise. This was a monumental undertaking of staggering proportions. It hadn't been mowed since before David knew the history of the house. I would pick up all the sticks in an area, mow, rake, then, mow again. As

I worked my way along the West side, I picked up some rib bones. They looked too small to be human, maybe from a small dog. As I worked my way towards the northwest corner, Sinbad brought a surprise to me. It was a tiny skull, unmistakably human. God, when will it end! I dropped the rake and started a serious search. Eventually I discovered several sets of tiny remains. Something told me that these weren't related to that last operation. That bunch would not have left the bodies. Whoever dumped these tiny angels here had no use for their victims once they were dead.

This was more like the classic Satanic sacrifices that I'd heard of since I was a kid. The groups would start by killing cats until the congregation took that step over the line from which there is no return. Satan has always wanted his minions to kill babies. They were the most innocent, therefore the most desirable. The devil is capable of rewarding too. He can't give eternal life even though he promises to. He can, however, provide material wealth. For some men, this is enough. Since they don't believe in God or Satan, they play their evil games with no thought for the consequences to their immortal souls. They call themselves Atheists or Agnostics, but they comprise the 'legion' that Satan claims to be.

I felt suddenly exhausted looking at these tiny remains. Instead of giving in to the helplessness that I felt, I prayed for strength and wisdom. The inspiration that I had was that now would be a good time to call Sergeant Donald. Then Sinbad could help me in my analysis. I would instruct him to come alone and I would keep my discovery to myself. If there were anything to be learned from him, it would only be in his eyes for only a fleeting moment.

I thought it best to put Sinbad in the house. I hoped that Sergeant Donald would be as shocked and disgusted as I was. He had been a brave ally in those last dangerous weeks. I would want a witness on my behalf in case I had to kill him. David would make a very credible witness. I prayed that he would be done with his appointment. I was able to reach him on his car phone and gave him a few necessary details. He thought that I was being paranoid, but he agreed to be here in twenty minutes. I'd call the sergeant after David hid his truck. Hopefully, Donald would be at home and I wouldn't have to expose my call on the radio.

David showed up on the button. I drove his truck around to the far side of the cemetery. Sinbad let him walk right in while I hid his truck. My dog's behavior was a tribute to David's character. I outlined my theory and emphasized the importance of him keeping his eyes glued to the sun sheers covering the window on the western side of the north west bedroom. He could see out, but no one could see in. Then I had to tell him what I had found while raking the yard. He sat down and the color drained from his face. He said, "Derrick, I thought it was over." I told him what the captain had told me. Again I told him that I may have to kill a man and I'd need a witness.

Evidently he had absorbed the implications. He asked if he should call 911 if Donald wasn't alone.

"Only if they split up," I told him. "Keep Sinbad with you. If he growls or barks, let him, just keep your presence a secret."

Now to call Sergeant Donald and try to pick up on his voice inflections. After three rings, his call was forwarded. I expected voice mail, but he came on, "Howdy Derrick. (caller ID no less) What can I do for you?"

"I found something that I wanted you to see before I called the other guys. I need you now. Come alone. How soon can you make it?"

He said, "I'll need about a half hour."

I told him to make it sooner if possible, I'd be waiting. I was getting bad vibrations from the time he picked the phone up. It was worse after I said that I'd found something. He sounded cocky, like he knew something that I didn't. He probably did, but he might take his secret to the grave.

"David, leave all the lights off. Let the dog roam at will and don't stop him from doing anything. I still don't know who my friends are around here other than you. Hold off on 911 unless they split up. If they stay in a group, I can handle them. He may show up alone, that's still a possibility."

I left him with the M-16. I knew that David couldn't bring himself to shoot anyone, but he might be able to bluff them. I wore my .357 and had my .38 special in my pocket. I also had a hundred-pound lion dog that would come through the window if I called him. He might just do it on his own.

I went out and sat on the steps facing the road. He wasn't due for fifteen minutes, but I didn't want to be caught napping. I had just sat down when I heard gravel crunching up the road. I hoped that it wasn't some unexpected guest. That would wreck everything. The car didn't look like the sergeants, but he was driving. He wasn't alone. Unless someone was hiding on the floor, there was only one passenger and he was in the back seat. The car was a four-door Mercedes, all black and brand new. The fancily dressed man in back was the owner or I'll never make lieutenant.

He pulled right up to the steps in an obvious move to intimidate me. I didn't let him have the upper hand. I waited until he and his extremely tall and skinny friend exited the Mercedes, then I yelled in his face, "Mister, I'll kill you and slim if either one of you even look funny!"

Sinbad was jumping against the door like he wanted out. His savage barking was making the windows rattle.

I said, "You were supposed to come alone. Who is this jerk?"

Still confident, he said, "You'll find out very soon. Now I hope that you have something important to have disturbed me."

"Of course, wise guy, just step around the corner. When they saw the pile of tiny bones, they both started laughing.

Sergeant Donald said, "I thought that it would come to this. Now I'll introduce you to my friend." He and his friend turned around. Slim already had one of those sissy foreign pistols in his hand so he was the first to die. Donald went for his pistol and Sinbad burst through the window before I could shoot. The sergeant lost his pistol when the dog hit him. All that he was doing now was screaming and trying to protect his face. I took the time to yell, "What's so funny?" before I called the dog off. His face and both of his hands were a gruesome wreck.

I shouted, "David, call an ambulance!" Then I knelt down by my blind friend and said, "You'd be dead too if I wasn't afraid that I'd kill my dog. You'd better tell all you know or the dog and me will visit you in the intensive care unit. Give me the dead man's address or I'll let the dog play some more." I wrote down the address and picked up the two pistols. Then I frisked my former friend and took his belt knife and ankle gun. He didn't move. He couldn't see, but he could feel Sinbad's hot breath as the dog growled in his face.

I got on the radio and asked Chief Walker to come along with the coroner and a police photographer. By the time the ambulance arrived, I'd already stopped the bleeding. I told them to treat him but to wait until the chief came before they took him away. David came out and handed me the M-16. I asked him to put Sinbad on his leash and to please wait out here by me.

When the chief showed up, I took him over to the pile of bones. He started crying. “One of those could be my baby.”

When he regained his composure, he told me that his infant son had been kidnapped while in the care of a sitter. The sitter was hysterical. Neighbors saw the car fleeing the scene, but the crime was never solved.

David and I filled him in on everything. Sergeant Donald had passed out, so we waved the driver off. I told the captain that we should probably post guards at the sergeant’s hospital bed. I said, “He knows too much for them to let him live.”

The chief called to place the guard order. He ran the registration for the Mercedes. It matched the ID on the dead man. The address didn’t match the address that Sergeant Donald had given me. I pointed this out to Chief Walker.

He asked, “How well do you trust the other four members of your team?”

“Sir, at this point, I trust you, David, and my dog. You know those men better than I do, how do you feel?” I asked.

He admitted that he didn’t know them as well as he thought he knew Sergeant Donald. “I’m still trying to digest the fact that the Sergeant was a bad guy.

I replied, “How do you think I feel? My life had been in his hands only a little while back.”

“Evidently Sergeant Donald was fighting for different reasons than I was. I was out to eliminate the bad guys while he was only eliminating competition. He had such convincing cover. Today, he underestimated my paranoid mind as well as my ability. That dog saved his life purely by accident. By the way, I’d like you to meet my friend, Sinbad.”

As we approached the porch, Sinbad got to his feet, but he wasn’t growling, as he had been when my volunteers showed up. I let him off his leash while still holding his collar. Chief Walker came up with his palm up and Sinbad just sniffed it. When I let go of his collar, he just sat by me. That was a good sign. It was also a red flag for my volunteers and I pointed that out to Walker.

“That dog was charging them until I called him back. One or all of them are no good. We can’t take a chance on using them on this case. If we get too close to the heart of this beast, one or all of them could turn on us. Let me see if I can appeal to my army friends again. Until then, how about you, me, and Sinbad delivering that Mercedes tonight?" I asked.

Evidently this suicidal idea appealed to him. He was tall enough to pass for Slim and the sergeant and I looked and dressed alike. Sinbad could lie on the floor in the front. I'd leave his window down. We decided to try the address that I got from Sergeant Donald first. My instincts told me that someone was waiting for this car.

David was allowed to go home. His statement could wait for morning. He was to report directly to the captain. The fewer people who knew about this, the better it would be for the success of the operation.

I had never driven a Mercedes before. I just had to call Margaret and we'd be off on our adventure.

Sinbad didn't like this car. On a whim, I popped the trunk open to make sure it was empty of living or dead. There was nothing more exciting than a spare tire. Chief walker sat in back and Sinbad lay down on the floor in the front seat. With everyone in place, we set off into the rapidly approaching night.

The chief had to direct me to this unfamiliar part of the city. Naturally, it was in a fancy neighborhood. We found the address easily enough. When we pulled in, another tall, skinny dude came out. The headlights were in his eyes as he hurried to the car. "Did you kill him?" he asked.

Captain Walker got out with his gun drawn. "Freeze, stupid!" he ordered.

Then I got out and told him that he had the right to remain silent and the chief would tell him the rest of his limited rights. We cuffed him and moved him to the back of the car so the lights would still work to our advantage.

Another man came out and asked, "Hey, Sergeant Donald, did you guys get him?"

I stepped in front of the headlights with my pistol out and said, "No, they didn't get me. Now, walk towards me slowly and quietly." I backed up into the shadow again as he carefully followed instructions. Once he was in the shadow with me, he was read his limited rights and we used the cuffs to link them together on the steering wheel with a growling dog in their faces. Now Walker and I were supposed to search that huge house, no way.

"Chief, why don't you watch these jerks and we'll let Sinbad flush the quail?" He liked that idea. I'd have to memorize the Miranda Law or the captain could wind up with a sore throat. I walked up to the front door and opened it, then I told my hairy friend, "Go get 'em!" I hurried around to cover the back door.

I could hear Sinbad inside. He had at least one more. Two men came out the back door with more of those sissy guns. They didn't feel like freezing so I used some lead to show them how. I dug out the bottom line and stuck it in my belt as I reloaded the .357. Shots were fired out front. I went into the house with a gun in each hand and exited through the front door with the headlights in my eyes. I could hear my dog happily chewing on someone while the chief tried getting him to stop. I called him off immediately.

The chief had a stiff one on the ground and it looked like Sinbad's was dead too. All this before we even checked the address where the car was registered. I took the dog back inside while the chief called the State Police. That was an excellent idea. We needed help and we couldn't ask any of the locals.

The house was empty. Walker wanted to ID all of the bad guys, so I watched the ones with the matching bracelets as he started fishing for wallets. The one he shot and the one that Sinbad wasted were both County Cops. The ones in back were just residents of the house. The two survivors lived there too.

The State boys had surrounded the other address already. They sent some men to take over for us here after we explained the situation. I drove the Mercedes again. This time, Walker sat in front and the dog got in back.

The State Troopers at the other house informed us that they had sent their dogs in first and hadn't found anyone. We left the Mercedes with the State Patrol who could wrap up for us. Then we caught a ride back to my place. The chief said that we could count on help from the State until this was over. I said goodnight and entered my house a very tired and lonely man.

...

Sleep didn't come easily Tuesday night. The empty house that the State Troopers had searched didn't make sense. Walker and I had surprised those jokers at the first house. They couldn't have had time to call anywhere. By the time the dog entered, it was every man for himself. There was no time to reach out and touch someone. Either the house was truly abandoned or the State Patrol had missed something. In the morning, I would ask Chief Walker to come out there with me. I wondered if he was safe anymore. He and I had removed eight key players in the first skirmish. Hopefully, we'd already cut off the serpent's head, but I doubted if that was the case. This operation had gone on for an unknown number of years, like a hidden cancer. That kind of organization and secrecy took more intelligence than those arrogant fools that had tried to kill me possessed. We may have hurt the serpent badly, but I was pretty sure that its head was still intact.

My first call Wednesday morning was to the captain's house. I caught him at breakfast. He said that forensics were going to turn my yard into an archeological site. "Tell them to cut the grass too," I joked. "The reason that I called is your first guess."

He said, "My first guess is that the empty house bothers you as much as it bothers me."

"There were cars in sight, someone had to be there. I have some thoughts that I'd rather share in person. Can we meet somewhere, like where all those State Troopers meet for coffee?" I was speaking in code. I was counting on him understanding.

He said, "I know the place. I'll see you in fifteen minutes." Now contrary to the myth, cops don't live at donut shops. The State Cops were staked out at both houses. Any coffee they'd be drinking would be on the job. I'm sure that the captain would go to the second house, that's where the mystery was.

I loaded Sinbad, my M-16, and a five-cell flashlight. I put my body armor on too. Then off I went to the designated coffee shop. As I was pulling in, Walker was right behind me. We flashed our badges to the stake out and parked as close as we dared. This would totally blow the stake out, but I was convinced that the answers would be inside the house.

"Here is my not so far fetched theory," I told the chief. "There has to be another way out of the house. It must be undetectable from the outside. That makes it a tunnel. You build on concrete slabs in this part of the country. This home is almost certainly built the same way. It would be easy to cut a hole in the concrete and dig a room or a tunnel. The entrance might be in a walk-in closet, or under a large piece of furniture. When the State Police searched last night, they would have noticed any hollow sounding places in the floor. That makes our entrance underneath something large."

"You already have a detective's mind. Your test depends mainly on knowing the law and arrest procedures. Let's take the wonder dog inside and have him show us where to start," said the chief.

He put on his armor too, then we got our flashlights and M-16's before entering. Sinbad was eager to enter and went ahead of us as soon as the door was open. After running in and out of every room but the closets, he came to a halt by the door to the foyer closet near where we waited. Walker covered the door as I opened it. Sergeant Donald was in there, dead. His face was a mass of bandages as well as his hands. He had a chest wound that wasn't there before and his throat was cut.

Walker said, "I asked for a guard to be posted when we were still at your place last night, but I don't know who was assigned. I had better call the dispatcher right now." I listened to the conversation. The dispatcher told the chief that Bob and James had showed up just as she was getting the order. They had volunteered for the task, saying that the injured officer was a friend. She asked if she should change the guard. Walker told her that Sergeant Donald was being guarded as a criminal suspect and we had found his body miles from the hospital.

Walker called the hospital next. They said that Sergeant Donald's wounds weren't life threatening, so he was treated and released. He left with the two officers sent to guard him.

We couldn't raise Bob and James on the radio. They either weren't answering, or had fled the area. Walker put out an all points bulletin to arrest officers Bob Ingram and James Putnam on suspicion of murder. We did reach Al and Steve. We told them to suit up and join us at the house. I whispered, "Don't tell them where it is."

Steve came back on the horn immediately to ask for an address. Either he passed the test, or he was a quick thinker. I told Captain Walker that Sinbad would be the litmus test on their character. He admitted that the dog had been a big help so far.

"Where is Sinbad now?" asked the chief. "He was in here a moment ago."

We found him sniffing under the couch in the family room. My money was on this being our door to the unknown. We tried to lift it and found it to be attached. After a bit of maneuvering, we discovered that the floor underneath was hinged. By pushing on the back of the couch, we opened the floor to expose a set of wooden stairs descending to God knows where. Sinbad started into the hole, but I called him back. We closed up to wait for Al and Steve.

They showed up minutes later a few moments apart. I studied their faces as each pulled up. No emotions could be read there. Sinbad greeted them as if he'd known them since a pup. There was none of the original hostility as had been displayed when the four of them had come together. Thank God, we needed all the friends we could get. They said that they had been monitoring the radio last night and this morning.

Al asked, "Why are we suited up for action at an empty house?"

"A picture is worth a thousand words," I said. "Follow me to the mystery of the empty house." They were genuinely astonished at the fancy door.

"Walker said, "This was Derrick's discovery. If anything ever happens to me, I want you two to push for him to be Police Chief. Now tell us what you know about James and Bob."

They told of how James seemed to enjoy his power of taking lives from a distance. How Bob, at times, had gunned down men with their hands in the air. He claimed that it would make the other prisoners talk.

"Gentlemen, you may be called upon to kill your friends. If you hesitate, your children will grow up without their fathers." Then I showed them Sergeant Donald's body in the front closet. "We believe that this is the work of the missing team members. They volunteered to guard him at the hospital and drove away with him when he was released," I told them. "Now," I said, "Sinbad is dying to find out what's behind curtain number one. Let's go."

. . .

Before we entered the stairway, we radioed the State Patrol of the body in the closet and of our foray beneath the couch. When the trap door was reopened, Sinbad went down cautiously like he was hunting. I followed my dog and Walker brought up the rear. My flashlight revealed a light switch at the bottom of the stairs. The switch illuminated a twenty by thirty-foot room with ornate columns supporting the slab above. The room had twelve chairs facing a throne at the far end. So there were thirteen people involved, eight of whom we'd already accounted for.

There was a dais that contained both the throne and an altar. The altar contained the body of an infant whose throat had been cut. A note was left on the seat of the throne which read, "Parents of Texas, do you know where your children are?"

We could hear traffic upstairs. Walker went up to report our findings. "Spread out and don't touch anything," I said. "We're looking for one or more exits from this theater." The chief joined us while Sinbad did what he was good at, nosing around. Naturally, the dog found the passage and naturally, it was behind the drapes in back of the throne. Further search proved Sinbad's exit to be the only one.

A forensics team came down the stairs. Walker spoke up, "The password is 'Salvation', memorize it! Post a guard at the tunnel entrance and shoot anyone who doesn't know the password, even if they are in uniform, no exceptions."

Once again, Sinbad led, followed by me with Walker bringing up the rear again. There was no light except for the Chief's and my flashlights. The tunnel slanted downward for several yards before leveling off. I assumed that this was done to avoid tree roots. There were no side passages. This tunnel was straight as an arrow and built for speed. Sinbad was moving slowly which was unusual for him. He was hunting something that worried him.

My flashlight beam picked up something on the floor in the distance. The tunnel appeared to be partially blocked at that point. Sinbad continued moving slowly, and I followed his lead. The blockage on the tunnel floor turned out to be the bodies of four people. James and Bob were among the dead. The other two were women. I was wondering when sex would rear its ugly head. They looked to be victims to a burst from an automatic rifle, quick and messy. Evidently the man who sat in the throne felt like I did, a partner is a witness.

That left us with only one clever and very ruthless man to find. I hoped that our prisoners from the night before would tell us their leader's name. Without their help or some kind of miracle, Mr. Big might get away.

Our radios weren't working down here, so we left the bodies where they laid and walked over them. There hadn't been any M-16's by the bodies. That meant that if we cornered our prey, there would be no quarter, which suited me just fine. Anyone who killed babies didn't deserve to live.

Sinbad started to move more quickly now. I could see a tiny dot of light ahead. That had to be the exit. We had to jog to keep up with the dog. Soon, we were all squinting in the bright sunlight. We had arrived at a steel grill high in the side of a man made drainage canal. The grill was easily opened on its hinges. The grade was steep but negotiable by all members of our party. First we went up the rise to look for tracks along the top of the ditch. There were no signs at all. The grass wasn't trampled and there were no prints in the bare patches. Back at the grill, I could make out a faint, recent trail going diagonally to the bottom in a direction away from the road.

I asked Walker if he would bow to my experience and let me take over the track down. When he agreed, I told him all that I'd already figured out. I told him that the man was very light, one hundred twenty pounds or less. He was carrying his shoes, but was wearing his socks to avoid making easily read tracks. He knows about me from Sergeant Donald, so he knows that my tracking abilities are better than average. He must also know that doubling back is something that I'm hip to. I asked the chief if he would take Al and Steve to the ditch along the path that our light friend used. I had to point him in the right direction since none of them could see the marks that were plain to me.

"Just wait for me at the water's edge," I said. "I have to check something before we continue."

I went straight down the steep embankment to look for any sign that he'd doubled back. There were no signs in the sandy bottom of the shallow canal or in the mud on either bank. I joined my friends and picked up the trail. The man had jumped to the water to avoid making tracks in the mud at the water's edge. Then he proceeded south for fifty meters or so and took off his socks. His bare footprints were easier to spot than the stocking covered tracks. I'd have to remember to thank him if we got him alive.

The radios were working again since we were out of the tunnel. I asked the chief to scramble a helicopter to follow the canal. "They will be looking for a short man of about one hundred and twenty pounds. He will probably have two rifles slung and one cradled in his arms. Tell the chopper to fly high and not to linger over the suspect so as not to arouse suspicion. Have the pilot bring rappelling equipment for two men in case the trees are too close for an insertion.

Walker did all that I asked and gave a description of our group and location. When the chopper finally landed in the canal bottom, I asked Al and Steve to go with the bird. "When you spot our quarry, fly past about a mile so he won't see you come down. Then send the bird and equipment back for us. We will set down on this side of him, close enough to be heard, that should drive him right into your arms."

The radio on the chopper came on our frequency. I planned to send the bird back up to keep us informed of our fugitive's whereabouts. The bird came for Steve and Al and left Walker and I to continue tracking on foot.

We found the place where our prey put his socks and shoes on. The trail was easier to follow. He had quite a long head start. This made the chopper reconnaissance vital. All that our efforts were accomplishing was to make sure that he had indeed stuck to the canal. My only real concern was that he might double back to ambush his pursuers. I was so worried about this possibility that I had Walker climb the east bank and parallel me as I tracked from as high up the western bank that I could and still see the tracks. The bird radioed us that they had a visual six miles south. He would drop his passengers and pick us up in ten minutes.

The noose was tightening on our baby killer. He had wanted me dead, well not as badly as I wanted to send him to hell to meet his maker. Walker and I rejoined at the canal bottom. We were looking for a break in the trees so the bird could set down. We had a visual on the bird. He had found his own landing zone and we ran to the chopper and boarded.

The pilot said that they were so high that the target never even looked up. He felt sure that they hadn't been compromised. As we approached the drop zone, Walker said, "If the little murdering bastard starts shooting, let me take him out."

"He's all yours captain," I replied. I could understand his desire to kill the man who almost certainly had killed his infant son. I certainly had no mercy for such a creature. As far as I was concerned, the killer could join the beast that he had served for so long. As soon as we had a visual on our diminutive demon, the chopper dropped like a rock. He was still a quarter of a mile ahead. The chopper was able to land. We asked him to wait and monitor our frequency. Walker jumped out and started running up the canal.

"Go up on the high ground I told him." Now we were on opposite sides of the ditch running along the edge of the tree line. The captain wanted to catch up with him before he ran into Steve and Al. We had him in sight. He was running too, but the three rifles that he was carrying were working against him. We were gaining rapidly. Satan Junior gave up running and started firing my way. After all, it was my face on television that he associated with the demise of his evil games. I almost fired out of instinct for self-preservation, but I remembered my promise. I dropped to the ground to make a smaller target and the captain took him out with a single shot to the head from one hundred and fifty yards. As we descended into the canal, Al and Steve came running from the south.

The man was older than he looked from a distance. He was the kind of person that you wouldn't even give a second glance to on the street. He could move invisibly through a busy mall. Well, the devil could see him now and forever.

. . .

There was no way that I could get Sinbad back on the helicopter. There was nothing to do but start walking. I asked the Captain to radio the house with the tunnel and have them remove the bodies and to remind them of the password. I'd been shot at once today, that was already over the quota that I scheduled for myself. Actually, I was aiming for zero tolerance in the 'shooting at Derrick' thing, thank you very much.

Sinbad and I reached the tunnel at about two-thirty in the afternoon. We were both very hungry as our growling stomachs attested to. 'Salvation' was our salvation when we hit the throne room. We made our way upstairs and found the captain conferring with the forensic team. When he saw me, he offered to buy me lunch. That being the best offer that I'd had in two days, I took it. I poured a packet of dry dog food on the floor of the van and Sinbad wolfed it as we drove.

We went to a 'sit down' restaurant rather than a fast food joint. We both needed to sit down and there was much to discuss. There were still some unanswered questions that the Crime Scene Investigators were seeking answers for. Waiting was not one of my favorite things to do. The Chief was patiently waiting to find out whether or not his son's remains were found in my yard. I was waiting to find out if this morning's finale was truly the finale. Texas was in the 'Bible Belt'. I always remembered my earlier stay here fondly. If such goings on could take place under the noses of these fine people, what must the rest of the nation harbor?

Since all that we could do was wait, we decided to do it at our homes. Sinbad was happy to see me. I always gave him a hamburger patty when he had to wait. If he kept working with me, someday he would be killed. The same was possible for me, but at least we would have given our lives for a good cause.

When I got home, my yard was full of people. There was a considerably larger display, sadly, of the tiny remains. Sinbad had gotten used to meeting strangers. Evidently no one here gave him bad vibrations. He went straight to the door, probably still hungry and maybe even tired.

After I fed Sinbad, I went out to speak with the forensics team. They had a crummy and difficult job. I didn't want to give them the impression that I thought that I was better than they were. They had one of those jobs that no one wanted, yet someone had to step up and do it.

The good news was that they hadn't seen any snakes. The bad news was spread out in the front yard in little piles. It was hard not to cry. I found the Coroner and asked if he'd like to see the cellar. He said that he'd like to very much. I told him that the long, skinny snake was a pet and shouldn't be harmed. He said that when they were done with my yard, they had planned on checking the cemetery too. That grass is thick enough to hide more of the same.

I told him, "There is a lamp and extension cord in the cellar. I'll make coffee for you and your bunch." They already had a port-a-potty delivered, so that problem was covered.

I carried my table and dining room chairs outside, then brought out the coffee. I left a message for Margaret, then took the dog for a ride to the 7-11 for more coffee, cream, and sugar. I also got some rolls, bottled water, and soda pop. Not everyone likes coffee, and I didn't want anyone to feel neglected.

I dropped the goodies off on the table and instructed the yard crew to make themselves at home. I had a message on the answering machine when I got inside. The Chief called to give me the week off. He said that it would be at least that long before this puzzle was put together. All that I had to do was stay within the twenty-five mile radius and monitor my radio.

That was good news, I hadn't had time to mentally recover from the first mission. Things happened so quickly on the second operation that I was still trying to accept the fact that it was over so rapidly. God, I hoped that it was truly over. I felt like it was over. I had no haunting feelings of stones left unturned or loose ends not tied. My instincts are usually right. Still, Sgt. Donald had fooled me.

I decided to visit the boys in the cellar. They were probing in a pattern to a depth of two feet. I would be surprised if they found anything, but they had to check. Eve was in her favorite hiding place among the tools. I reminded them to keep the door closed and to watch their step on the way out.

Next, I went by the Jones' to check on the crew there. They hadn't made any new discoveries. I put forth the theory that 'some of the remains may have been carried off by animals'. I volunteered the services of my dog and myself to search the surrounding area. I still had an hour to waste until Margaret called.

We walked fifteen feet inside the property line for the two acres nearest the house. Then we walked fifteen feet outside the line, still no find. We were already very familiar with the property line itself and had never seen anything suspicious. It occurred to me that nearly all of the remains were found on the western side of my home. That was either where they were dumped, or it was where animals had brought them from their original dumping site. I decided to approach my search as if there were a primary dumping ground nearby. The sense in this theory was that people so secretive as the Satanists wouldn't be likely to dispose of the evidence where it could be found so easily. Had they known about the remains on the western side, they surely would have done something about it. This meant that the dump was elsewhere.

That bit of logic required serious consideration. Now I had to try to think like the scumbags responsible for this horror. They would want an easy, yet remote place to hide their handy work. Slim and Sergeant Donald had anticipated my findings, Donald had practically said as much. That meant that the dump was very close.

We had bloodhounds here once, but they had been searching

specifically for Big Foot. We never had them nose around except at the cemetery and then into the swamp on the trail of the headhunter. Before I called for bloodhounds, I'd give Sinbad's nose a chance. I never saw where he had found that first skull. Sinbad was at my side as usual. Putting myself in the place of a man hiding something so grisly, my first thought would be to put it in the thickest set of woods in the most remote area imaginable. That happened to be on the north side of the house along the edge of the swamp. Next question, why dig with a whole swamp to throw bodies in? Since Sinbad's feet hadn't been wet when he brought the skull, he didn't go in the swamp. He could have just found it like I had found the ribs, or he might know where more are.

I took a chance on a modified game of fetch. As sick as my idea sounded, no stone could be left unturned. I walked the dog over to one of the neatly arranged piles of bones and he naturally started sniffing them. Then I pointed to the area of suspicion and said, "Go get it." Sinbad took off for the northwest corner of the yard far beyond where the forensics team had been looking. He scratched at the ground for a moment and dug up another skull as I watched. So, there were two cemeteries at the end of the road, one of them unmarked.

I went to the cellar to share this new find with the coroner. They were running out of floor anyway with only a few large rocks to show for their efforts. I led them to where Sinbad had resumed digging. I called the dog to me and let them take over. Now I could take a shower and begin my week off.

When Margaret called, I asked her if she could handle Sinbad and me overnight. She said that we were both welcome. I threw some clean clothes and dog food in a bag, grabbed my shaving kit, and went out the door.

...

I called the Chief from Margaret's to fill him in on the latest at my house. I also warned him that the number of victims would probably total the number of full moons times the number of years that this had been going on. He could also figure that the man chased out of the tunnel was probably an obstetrician or gynecologist, and that many of his victims could have begun as abortions. The steady number of sacrifices required would have brought too much attention. Therefore, if my theory is correct, the doctor's records would show an unusual amount of still born or aborted births. The frightening implications of this theory, I'm sure the Captain grasped.

The chief was very quiet during this presentation. I guessed that he was struggling with his emotions. "Chief, my radio is on twenty-four hours per day if you need me for anything." He thanked me and hung up.

I imagine that he'll never lose the picture of the infant with its throat cut on the altar. He had held up well at that point. His rage must have driven him on right up to that single shot that almost certainly killed the murderer of his son.

We only had two live suspects from that mess. They would almost certainly cooperate when they hear that all the rest are dead. They will have nothing to fear but the death penalty, which they might avoid by talking.

Margaret finally came out of the shower. The pounding noise you heard was King Kong beating on my chest. "That's a nice teddy, but you can't wear it to dinner," I told her while my eyes feasted.

"Dinner can wait," she said as she walked right up close to me.

Dinner did wait until it was more like a midnight snack. That was my favorite excuse for being late for a meal. Just think, we had the rest of the night ahead, how would she ever wake up tomorrow? (I have an idea)

The poor girl made it to work on time. She looked tired, but she was smiling. This weekend, we were going to introduce Sinbad to her nieces and nephews. He and I went to my friend the Chevy dealer to talk about the commercials. I told him that I had a week off so this was a perfect time to complete his project. He said that he'd make the arrangements today and we could start shooting tomorrow. He assured me that it would only take two days.

So now, I could go bumming with my dog. I figured that it would be a good time to go husband hunting for Eve, the queen of the cellar. Before I bought one at a pet store, I wanted to try my luck at catching one. I gassed up the van, then Sinbad and I went on a safari. It was a warm, overcast day. Rain looked imminent, but there were no storms in the forecast.

I wanted to look on the south side of the San Jacinto River to insure that a different gene pool would provide the mate. First, I had to buy a pair of welder's gloves. Safety is a must in an area with three kinds of rattlesnakes, coral snakes, copperheads, cottonmouths, and fire ants. I've also on occasion had to swat bumblebees and wasps, rather frantically too I might add. Did I leave out scorpions and black widows and fiddle back spiders? I didn't mean to.

When I finally found a suitable place to hunt, I parked on a piece of hard ground with no vegetation. The place was perfect for my purposes. It was an illegal dump with empty beer cans in abundance. In leaner times, I'd gathered aluminum cans for the meager income they brought. I slung my M-16 across my back. I already had my .357 on my waist and my .38 special in my pocket. My badge was pinned on too from pride as much as force of habit.

Sinbad picked up on my good mood and he ran around like a pup. This time of year, most reptiles were under cover to stay warm. I hoped to find some adult rat snakes too. I brought three sacks to separate the species.

I was busily digging through piles of debris when I heard the sound of motorcycles. I moved out of sight, being suspicious by nature. I watched from hiding as they drove past the van, all the way to the dead end of this out of the way dirt road.

There were six bikes. The riders were wearing colors. They were obviously not your AMA group on a Sunday excursion. Two of the bikes had young girls on the back. The girls looked like minors. I crept the two blocks to where the group was parked with Sinbad at my heel. Still out of sight, I got to within thirty feet of them. The girls were as young as they had looked when they went by. They were in their early teens. The bikers already had the beer out and were passing joints. I radioed for backup and waited. As far as I was concerned, this was a crime in progress. I could only hope the backup arrived before I was forced to make a move.

All of the men wore pistols and two of the bikes had shotguns in scabbards. I hadn't yelled "Sheriff's Police" for a while, but I was clearing my throat for that moment. If I had to go it alone, someone was bound to die. Most of the hard-core bikers I knew were veterans. They weren't likely to take me seriously, they were more likely to try to kill me, then kill the girls as witnesses.

I hoped that Sinbad wouldn't give me away, he was already growling low in his throat. I didn't think that the noisy bunch would hear him thirty feet away. The scene hadn't gotten out of hand yet. They were just drinking and smoking so far. They didn't stray too far from the bikes. I had hoped to get in among the bikes for cover. They were less likely to shoot at their machines. That idea looked out of the question now. I hated waiting. I couldn't make my move without endangering the girls. So far, all that I had witnessed were misdemeanors. I wanted to avoid shooting. With enough back up, we were likely to keep this calm. The fly in the ointment would be if there were felony warrants on any member of this hard looking bunch. They could turn this into a hostage situation. I wished that I had been wearing my body armor.

Finally, the sound of approaching vehicles reached my ears. I had asked for a silent alarm. A few moments later, the partyers reacted to the sound of the cars. They headed for their bikes at a run. The girls were running into the woods. This was my chance, "Freeze! Sheriff's Police!" I shouted as I stepped out with the M-16 in the ready position. One man pulled his gun and died with a three-round burst center mass. "Who's next?" I asked. There were no volunteers, but the hatred in the air could be cut with a knife. (I suppose they hated me too.) Sinbad was barking frightfully as well.

When the three squads pulled in, I let them take over so I could round up the girls. Sinbad made that easy. The girls didn't appreciate the rescue very much. They probably didn't even know that they had indeed been rescued. They had to be arrested on drug and dram shop violations. They might know something about their boyfriends that the police would like to find out.

All six had federal warrants. The dead one was being sought for murder and armed robbery. When the girls heard all these priors and warrants, they were more likely to appreciate their rescue and cooperate.

I felt it necessary to deliver a message to the five before they were hauled out of there. I made it face to face and very sincerely. I told them that if either of the girls were harmed for their part in the arrest, I would assume that it was the work of all five, in which case, I would reward the guards at Huntsville handsomely to make their lives painful and miserable on a daily basis. They knew my face and reputation from TV. That coupled with the swift death of their brother convinced me that my message would be heeded. I stripped the bikes of any weaponry, being sure to tag it to the license plate of the bike it came from. Then it was locked in the trunk of a squad. I told the deputies that I'd wait until a truck with a cherry picker came for the bikes.

I still wanted to look for snakes, which I resumed after the squads pulled out. The body was taken away by a silent ambulance just before the truck for the bikes showed up.

My first day off hadn't been very restful. Finally I could continue my quest. Sinbad just watched me as I tore up pile after pile of debris. After two hours and several copperheads, I finally turned up a very large female rat snake. The next hour produced two young males of a similar species.

Sinbad and I had worked our way halfway back to the van by this time. I was hungry, but I had the fever of the hunt. I cut the heads off two of the copperheads and peeled their skins off to look for parasites before letting Sinbad eat them. I liked my snake meat well done, so my appetite would have to wait. There was a long spell of not finding anything, then I got very lucky. I found a four-foot male king and another three-foot female king. I freed the rest of the copperheads. Something had to keep the rodents in control. However late it might be, I wanted a shower before I ate, so we went straight home.

...

The digging crew at the house looked exhausted. I think that this was their first mass grave. Their stress was on their faces. According to the Coroner, they had nearly eighty sets of small remains. The piece of property that they were digging in looked like it had been hit by an artillery barrage. Now they were excavating the ground between the holes so as not to miss anything. I could see the pattern they used. It looked like the cemetery was about fifteen feet square. He said that all the bodies were found within a foot of the surface.

The area was full of ants to add to their misery. The coroner felt sure that when the holes were connected, they would have found all that there was to find. He said that coyotes were probably responsible for the unearthed ones. The fire ants compelled the animals to remove the bodies from the gravesite.

The whole scenario was like a scary movie, only we didn't have the option to walk out of this theater. They were expecting to be done before dark and glad for that time to come.

After my shower and a salad, I called David to see what night was good to cash in on that dinner invitation. He conferred with Pauline and said that tonight would be a good night. "Pauline wants to meet Margaret so she can warn the poor girl about you," said David.

"Tell Pauline that I'll come alone unless she promises not to spill the beans." I could hear his wife laughing when my message was repeated.

We made tentative arrangements for six O'clock since I still hadn't cleared it with Margaret.

I had a minor problem with my new snake population. I could put the two king snakes in the cellar with Eve. The female rat snake would be safe down there since she was too big for them to eat. The two younger rat snakes would have to stay in the bag overnight until I could buy an aquarium for them. In March, I could release all the males and keep the females until they laid their eggs. Then the females could be released while I incubated the eggs to insure maximum survival rate. Ants and raccoons have a way of finding most snake eggs.

Margaret called just after five. She was looking forward to meeting Pauline and comparing notes with her. I wasn't worried. Pauline always spoke well of me. (I figured that she only did that because she didn't know me that well.)

I fed Sinbad and walked him around my six acres again. Then I locked him in until my return. I remembered to board up the broken window, which required a trip to the basement. My king snakes seemed content. They had all gathered at Eve's favorite spot. It looked like they were 'denning' together.

The dig was completed and the men had leveled the yard. The coroner was bagging the remains individually. I would have to plant some forest floor flowers there soon. Right now, the soil was soaked with insecticide and disinfectant. It would take several rains before the soil was palatable for vegetation.

I put the yard lights on and said goodnight to the coroner and his men. As I drove down the dirt road, I said a prayer for the nightmare to be truly over. News from the FBI had been encouraging on the former case. That dragon had many heads and it appeared as if we'd cut them all off. The rest of the body was falling, one man at a time. People who were afraid to come forward before were giving the FBI an earful now.

The Satanic group that we had just eliminated was much smaller. We may not need the testimony of the only two survivors, in which case, they could be eligible for the death penalty. I say, "Who cares?" and "Good riddance." The two houses should provide an overwhelming volume of evidence. It was an act of God that I moved into David's house when I did. The whole thing was wearing me out. Just when I get some time off, I ran across the bikers. Breaking up the 1%'ers (the outlaw element) would probably be my next assignment. My team was down to three. We would need reinforcements and a new sniper. I was a pretty fair shot, but when it came right down to it, I preferred to do my killing face to face if killing was necessary.

I was still lost in thought when I pulled into Margaret's. She looked scrumptious as usual. I asked her to drive because I was distracted by my thoughts. I had to join the VFW and try to find some volunteers there. I needed combat tested personnel to fill out my team.

I told Margaret about the taping of the commercials tomorrow. I directed her to David's house. River Plantation can be a maze, even to the folks who live there. We threaded our way through the winding streets and rang the doorbell. Pauline expressed gratitude at my leaving the dog home. David must have told her about his leap through the closed window and his attack on Sergeant Donald. I wasn't about to tell her that Sinbad had killed a man less than an hour later. David and I offered to do the dinner dishes, but the girls said that it gave them a chance to be alone. Doing the dishes isn't "Girl's' work, it's just plain work. We were both extremely grateful that they had volunteered. That left us free to discuss things of a less delicate nature. The TV and newspapers could never replace first hand knowledge any more than reading a dirty magazine can replace being with a woman.

The state police provided the press release on the tunnel house as well as the first house that the chief and I busted. Hell, they didn't even have the details unless they interviewed Walker. Lately, I'd been too distracted to watch the news. David said that Chief Walker and I had been given proper credit. That meant that someone was bound to be after us for a story. Cracking into and ending that cult had been almost as big as Big Foot and the cannibals. (That would be a great name for a rock group.)

Those Satanists had turned out to be better at murdering babies than facing armed men. The three cops involved had turned out to be poor security. Their leader did us a real favor when he killed James. There would have been a different ending if a sniper had been watching the grill at the end of the tunnel. Again, it was an act of God.

When the girls joined us, all four of us were talked out. It was time to go home. This time I drove. I suggested that we do a dinner at Walker's house soon. Margaret was excited at that prospect. Tonight I just kissed her goodnight at the door. If I wanted to pass the Lieutenant's test on the first try, I had to study every chance I got. The first business day of the new month was coming up soon.

When I got home, the forensics team was gone. Sinbad was glad to see me as always. I strapped my M-16 across my back and we walked the property line again. I wasn't looking forward to the commercials, but I sure liked that van. I lugged the table and chairs in before sitting down to study.

...

I was just starting to get the Miranda law memorized when Sinbad got up and went to the door. Then I heard the sound of motorcycles. There was a bunch. I put all the lights on and dialed 911. Then I put Sinbad in the old- fashioned cast iron bathtub and told him to lie down and stay. I grabbed the M-16 and went out the back door. I had just enough time to climb the TV antenna tower to the roof, when the bikes started pulling in the front yard. I was familiar with the drill. The group madness that goads the outlaw bikers on is their mistaken belief that the whole world is terrified of them. The idea here was that they all ride around the house and shoot out the windows. This practice is supposed to deliver a message, one of intimidation. Tonight, I think they hoped to kill me.

There were eight bikes in all, single riders. The expression in the infantry is, "When you are in the kill zone, charge!" The wisdom in any battle is to gain the high ground. I already had that part covered. My M-16 should even this skirmish out. I didn't do anything foolish like hollering "Freeze!" I just waited until the house was surrounded and the firing started. There were only eight fish in this barrel. I tried not to kill any, just knock them off their bikes.

With all of them down now, I felt it safe to tell them to freeze. The hip roof allowed me to stand on the ridge and watch all my fish by turning my head either way. The squads were pulling in now.

The first cop out laughed and said to the bikers, “Which one of you all called 911?” I loved it!

There was an ambulance coming up the drive. It was going to be crowded. I climbed down to survey the injuries. “Who’s going to pay for the damages to my home?” I asked.

“We’ll have our fallen heroes take up a collection,” said Walker who was one of the late arrivals. “Just send the bill to the station. Their confiscated bikes should bring a few bucks at auction. They won’t need them for a minimum of five years, probably a lot longer once we check for warrants and parole violations.”

“I’ll come downtown and file charges for attempted murder on every one of them. I just have to check on my dog first.” Sinbad turned out to be fine. The bathroom was an interior room and he stayed in the tub. I took this attack on my home very personal. I desperately wanted to find the headquarters of this bunch of domestic terrorists and crash their party. I realized that I couldn’t do it alone. I had been lucky twice, that couldn’t go on forever. The Chief and I could work out a plan involving a large enough force to overwhelm the opposition.

So, we were off to file charges and hope that bail would be denied or set impossibly high. The charge was attempted murder of a Police Officer. That would make them high risks to flee. I begged the press to go nuts on both stories about the bikers. The 1% bikers need to get the message that intimidation wouldn’t work. Conroe and the rest of Montgomery County were not safe havens for criminals.

The trip downtown had to be done tonight because of tomorrow’s taping of the commercials. Locking the house was a joke with all the broken windows. With all the lights on and Sinbad to watch the place, it should be safe enough now. I ought to be running out of enemies pretty soon. I only had eight papers to sign. The clerk could fill in the blanks at his own pace.

When I got home, I swept up the glass and fixed a place for the dog and me to sleep in the bathroom. Those jerks hadn’t missed a window. It was going to be a tad chilly this evening. There was no sense turning on the space heaters. It was time to walk the property line for the last time tonight. David probably knew some reliable people to fix the place up. Me, I was still waiting to start my week off.

. . .

Morning already, I didn't even know what day of the week it was. I just hoped to get two day's taping done in one. I also hoped that the first five bikers were still in the county jail when their eight bandaged buddies showed up. Then they could mourn the loss of their brother in a group session.

My house didn't look any better in the morning light. Damn those jerks! At least they lost their precious motorcycles. This place looked better before I got here when it was abandoned.

I was driving down David's property values. Half of the yard was dug up, the grass looked terrible. There were tire tracks everywhere. All the windows were broken and only one had been boarded up. If I didn't own the joint, it would be funny.

I called David for help. I could pay the crew at the end of the day, or reimburse David if they were done early. "Please get someone to mow the grass in both my yard and in the cemetery. Your lots will never sell if prospective buyers come to the dead end to turn around." He promised to take care of everything.

At the Chevy dealer's, everyone was excited. Some at meeting me, others because they would play some part in the commercials. They filmed me in black SWAT fatigues, camouflage fatigues, and civilian clothes. It wasn't my first commercial. The last one was over twenty years ago and I wasn't the star. I felt a little foolish but I guess it made me look humble, which everyone loved.

I had lost track of how many people that I'd killed since my return to Texas. All of them had been bad guys of the worst sort. I was a celebrity of no small stature in this part of the state. My commercial value was akin to sports heroes. This was good for the image of cops in general who get overlooked most of the time.

Miraculously, we wrapped the shoot by 4:30 PM. God, I needed quiet time. My PTSD was starting to eat my lunch. Margaret and Sinbad and I had to drive 24 ½ miles out and rent a room. First, I had to go home to see if my dog had eaten anyone in my absence. The cleanup and repair crews were still painting inside the house. Sinbad was chained to a tree near the cemetery where David was still cutting grass.

I said hello to my dog and went to talk to David. He said that the glass and Glazier were the most expensive items. I wrote him a check for the amount that he quoted. I knew that he was giving me a break, I also knew that he'd be offended if I made the check out for a penny more. I was ecstatic at having it taken care of so quickly. The place looked livable, like I pictured it in my dreams.

The handymen were packing up when I went back to the house. Sinbad would have to stay outside, away from all the wet paint. I chained him to the porch before showering. When I dressed and went outside, David was driving his mower up a ramp into his pickup. What a relief! Now, I had the nicest house on the street. The freshly mown lawn would be harder to conceal anyone or anything in.

I thanked David profusely before going in to call Margaret. She had just gotten out of the shower herself. I asked her over to see the place. She said that all the bogeymen were dead or in jail, not to mention that half the bikers were locked up. Therefore, she felt safe enough to drive out alone. I was trying to get her to like the place. She might live here some day. Maybe after there were other houses on the road, it wouldn't seem so lonely.

Margaret was her usual cheerful self. She greeted Sinbad happily and complimented the improvements to my home and yard. I told her about my desire to plant flowers where the children had been buried. She said that she knew just the right kind to bloom in the shade. Then finally, I got a hug and a kiss. "So first you say hello to the dog, then I get some token affection. Can you spare it?" I asked.

"Oh Derrick, don't start. You know that you mean as much as to me as that dog. Just don't ever ask me to choose," joked my comedienne. She said that she had a three-day weekend, just some vacation time that was owed to her.

"Well, dear, I finished my commercials today and I too have the weekend off. Shall we grab your favorite nieces and nephews and camp out here? We'll have a picnic every day. They can see the snakes and play hide and seek in the six wooded acres that I pay taxes on. I'll build the gate and Sinbad can be the mobile burglar alarm.

Margaret asked if she could see the inside before we picked up the kids. There was one room in particular that I wanted to show her. The dress code was extremely casual in that room.

It was past dark when we called her sister about her children spending the weekend. She agreed and said that they got out of school at 3:30 and would be ready by 4:30. We had both forgotten about school. That gave us another day to ourselves.

I called Chief Walker to invite him and his wife out for dinner and drinks. He said that they had already eaten, but they would be happy to stare at us over drinks while we ate. We met at a fancy restaurant with a liquor license. No pool tables and strictly enforced dress codes. I guess that Walker wanted to help me spend some of that reward.

We did our best not to talk shop, but the girls were busy getting to know each other and forgot we were there. We were in no danger of boring them as long as they were ignoring us in the first place. I laid out my idea on getting rid of the rest of the bikers. He said that they were probably our last dragon to slay. He said that he would work out a plan tomorrow, and we would implement it when my vacation was over. He also told me that he and his wife were planning a new baby. They both agreed that the town was becoming a nicer place once again.

We said our good-byes and left for our respective homes.

...

The weekend was over too soon. The kids loved Sinbad and vice versa. It helped that Sinbad was still a kid himself. Basically, he was an overgrown pup. He wouldn't settle down for another year. We were already planning on borrowing her brother's baby and toddler next weekend. Maybe Sinbad would let them ride on his back.

Margaret was back at work and I still had time off left. Tuesday was supposed to be a warm day for late February. The swamp and its waking animal life were calling me. The little green Anole lizards were everywhere today. Expect the unexpected. I took both of my pistols and the M-16, plus ammo for all three.

I had eaten an early lunch and put some dry dog food in a plastic bag. I decided against body armor and just tied my shirt around my waist. Sinbad was happy to go exploring. I had a place in mind that I'd never visited yet. It was the big island where the river split upstream. That was where Big Foot had backtracked the first time.

The trail to the stream was still visible and easily followed. I knew that it wasn't the shortest way, but it was the easiest way. The trail was more or less the only fairly dry path through the swamp. There was no sign of recent travel, which pleased me greatly. No news is good news. When I reached the stream, I turned west towards the island. There were myriad tracks from either Coyotes or Red Wolves. It amazed me how so many predators could share one environment. The last time I was out here, I heard a Bobcat and saw a Black Bear. The poachers already knew about the Alligator holes and you could almost guarantee a Puma or two.

We, the human race, are by far the most dangerous creatures on the planet. We alone are capable of destroying the planet, and may very well already be doing it. I'm certain that the Lord never intended it to be that way. The Native Americans may not have built railroads and skyscrapers, but they had clean air and water and a harmony with nature that this country shall never see again.

Just the dog and me this trip, no giant bogeyman looking to cut off my head and no other humans to break the silence. This hike was like therapy for my PTSD. I planned to sit on the island with Sinbad and just wait for whatever wildlife came along, not to kill except in an extreme emergency. I was the intruder in their shrinking sanctuary. It was enough to be allowed to share their home for awhile.

Sooner than I remembered, I came to the fork. The swamp must look smaller in the light of day. The stream seemed more shallow than when I first crossed it only weeks ago. Was it really only weeks ago? Here in the sunshine with a full belly, it seemed like ages ago. It was probably from less rain lately. It might be the work of Beavers too. No matter, it was theirs to do with as they pleased. Who would know better? I had so many bad memories of bulldozers wrecking habitats that it further alienated me from people, especially government. My house at the dead end was nice, but I'd rather live out here, especially if David developed the rest of the street.

It was about time that I radioed my location to anyone who might care. The dispatcher expressed her jealousy at my freedom on this gorgeous day. I asked her to remember how I'd earned my little vacation. She said that she didn't begrudge me one minute, she was just envious. I told her that I wanted to return to the smokehouse tomorrow, but today, the island was my goal. We did the over and out routine and I continued my peaceful explorations.

This was no island. It was a small hill. The two streams had separate sources originating who knows how far west. This hill may go all the way to Frazier Street, the business route through town. I paused long enough for Sinbad to wolf his food. I decided to explore the hill further and look for signs of human disturbance. I let Sinbad take the lead knowing that his nose would find things more quickly.

We roamed around randomly without seeing so much as a beer can or cigarette filter. The only tracks were from animals. We went down the south side to follow the stream back. Still, nothing but animal tracks were visible. We crossed here before the stream got deeper. Once again, only animal prints. The trees were sparse here, so the sun seemed warmer. Walking back went much faster. The dog hung a right on the trail. He knew where home was.

I missed the wilderness, but being wet and muddy is for pigs, not me. I hosed off the dog and my boots. Then I put them both on the southwest side of the porch to dry in the sun. I brought out Sinbad's food and water dishes. I even got a chair for myself to sit awhile. Margaret would be home soon, so I'd be showering before long. She was starting to show. It wouldn't be long before we'd be going to Lamaze childbirth classes. She'd already had an ultra-sound and we knew that a boy was on the way. She had picked Nikolas Ryan to be his name. I suggested Eli, but she turned that down flat.

I showered and left a romantic message on her answering machine. Then I went back on the porch in the sun. I could hear the phone ring out here. I would leave Sinbad inside when I left. The belt radio went off. It was Walker. He said that it was his turn to pay for dinner. I was glad that it wasn't bad news. He did say that we had to talk over some things. I told him that I'd call back when I heard from Margaret.

The phone rang as soon as Walker signed off. She told me how sweet my message was. I told her about Dinner with the Chief and his wife again. She said that she had enjoyed their company. I told her to pick a place since it was his turn to buy. "The place we went to last time was fine," she said.

We met at the restaurant at 6 PM. The mood was light and happy. After dinner, we ordered drinks. The ladies were in their own world, oblivious to us.

Walker shared the latest news with me. That outlaw motorcycle gang was either enlisting new men at a feverish rate, or assembling members from affiliated chapters. The Captain figured that they had to kill me to send a message to Conroe that the bikers were here to stay. The man I had killed turned out to be a major player. He was the master of ceremonies for the Montgomery County chapter. All of the men arrested had been the hard-core nucleus of this chapter. The word was that they were in the process of electing a new local president. All of the heavies from the Houston and Galveston areas were throwing their hats in the ring.

These new faces each came with a history. Most had done time for manslaughter. The one most likely to succeed had beaten his rap. He was guilty as sin, but several witnesses claimed that the victim had pulled a gun first. Then, somehow, our Teflon hero managed to beat him to death. The gun was totally generic, registered to none of the players. It had been reported stolen more than a year prior to the incident. It even had the victim's fingerprints on it. The victim was a working man with a family and no prior arrests.

The biker gang, now totaling in excess of thirty, was under surveillance at their local clubhouse. Walker said that he scrapped the idea of a mole as being too dangerous. I agreed with him heartily. Any stranger trying to infiltrate this bunch would stick out like a sore thumb. They'd just turn up dead or missing.

"So, that's what we're up against. My only hope is to use you as bait and overwhelm them with numbers. Hopefully they will make it a shooting war so we can rid the planet of the whole bunch. Mercy will be granted for anyone who drops his weapon and lies down. That any of them will do just that is doubtful when considering the caliber of these hombres." His last statement pretty much ended Walker's speech.

I reminded him that I was still waiting to collect for the last time my home was trashed. "If they come out in numbers like we're expecting, I may need a new home."

The Chief said that a check was ready and waiting at the station. He also said that the chapter had funds, which could be seized to cover a new home if necessary. "The FBI will be in on this because of the organized crime aspect. That beefed up our budget to hire the manpower necessary. Besides county and local police volunteers, the FBI is providing a dozen men. We are authorized to bring in your friends from Michigan and Florida if you can convince them that it will be a worthwhile cause. With your three friends, our force would total almost forty men."

"Chief, I'll be your bait if you'll allow me to mastermind the operation at my home," I stated.

"The FBI warned me that you'd want it that way. Their same team that helped us with the mercenaries and that headhunter with the big feet are the twelve who will show up again. They said that since it was your life on the line, and in light of your past performance, that you could set up the operation. All they asked for was to know the plan ahead of time," said the chief.

"It sounds as if time is short. Let's use the pay phone in the foyer to start the ball rolling right now," was my advice.

We started by calling the FBI and telling them to arrange for my friends to be flown in. They assured us that all three could be flown in by 10 AM tomorrow if they were willing. I informed them that my friends wouldn't leave me hung out to dry when they heard the news of the personal attack on my home. We would hold the meeting at the airport to expedite matters.

We went back to our table. I don't think the girls knew that we were gone. They barely acknowledged our return. I ran a plan by Walker that we both agreed was the best option. It was a night- time operation. We felt sure that the bikers would attack at night. He wanted to know how long I had worked on the plan. I told him that I started as soon as he said that thirty-plus men were coming. I told him that I would have tried it with just my three friends and me, but it sure would be easier and safer with forty men on our side. I also told him that the other way would have required explosive devices.

Walker said, "Get some sleep tonight. You can leave Sinbad at the police kennel to keep him safe."

We parted company. I'm sure that his mind was running on full steam as mine was. I dropped Margaret at her place and told her enough to keep her from being upset if she didn't hear from me for a couple of days. She looked like she was holding back tears. Now I headed home, hoping to get at least one more night of safe sleep.

The phone was ringing as I unlocked the door. It was Walker. He said that he'd be coming over with Al and Steve, who had volunteered. They would be coming with body armor and M-16's. I thanked him profusely and told him to flash his lights twice so I would know who it was.

The three men showed up in separate vehicles, which they used to block the road before it widened. Sinbad greeted them as long lost friends. Believe me, I was glad to see them too. I moved my van to the rear of the cemetery, no sense in tempting fate. We settled into the four bedrooms, which were at the four corners of the house. Each had windows on both outside walls, which gave us interlocking fields of vision and firing. Sinbad had the roam of the house. He could be our burglar alarm.

...

The night passed without incident. The next morning, Steve and Al went to their homes to await orders. I put Sinbad in the van and followed Walker to the station. After saying good-bye to my dog at the kennel, I went to the Chief's office to visit until it was time to go to the airport.

"So, Mr. Walker, what is your first name?" I asked. " We've been in so many scrapes together that I think I'm entitled to know."

"Walker is my first name. My last name is Archer. I thought that 'Chief Archer' sounded awkward, so I use my first name. Just say Chief Archer ten times fast and you'll see what I mean. By the way, I have good news for you. You passed the detective's test, Lieutenant Johnson. Your pay is retro-active from the day of the exam," said the chief.

"I appreciate all you've done to make that possible. I'll try to be a credit to the force," I said.

"You already are. You've taken more risks, killed or arrested more bad guys, and gained more public attention and praise for the department than I have in twenty-seven years, and I've been a popular chief," said Walker.

"You talk like I'm being groomed for your job. Does this mean that you're going after the mayoral seat next year?" I asked.

Walker said that it was a damn sight safer than what we're doing. After all, he was an expectant father. I congratulated him and asked when Mrs. Archer was due. He said to call her Eleanor, and she was due in mid October.

I asked him if we had time to go to the shooting range. I wanted to zero the sights on my M-16. He said that it would have to wait because the airport was in the opposite direction. He said that several of us would probably need to do that.

I threw plan B at him, the one with forty men instead of four. He nodded his head several times and said, "Now I know why you wanted to zero your weapon."

It was now the time to head to the airport to meet my friend's planes. Barry would be glad to avoid a little more winter. All of them would be glad for the excitement. I know that I needed it to feel alive. What better cause than to eliminate human predators who used terrorism to gain material wealth and whatever sick rewards they craved individually?

Travis and Ed arrived first on the same plane. We were all impressed when Barry got out of a small jet. He had Otto, the dog with him.

"Hey, Bro', looks like you managed to buy Otto after all," I said as I shook his hand. Otto gave me his paw. Barry was training him.

I informed him that I had acquired a dog too. I had to tell him that this operation was 'people' intensive, and that dogs wouldn't be used. He said that Otto had retired and was just along for company. I told him that after the meeting in twenty minutes, we would leave Otto at the kennel with Sinbad. Then the three of them could draw weapons and body armor and belt radios.

The meeting went smoothly. My plan was accepted. Not only did it make sense to all concerned. It seemed as if some of my ideas were on the minds of my hosts.

On the way to the station, I got a lot of ribbing from my three friends about them having to wipe my nose again. That's when Walker sobered them up by recounting my two previous encounters with the gang. Travis and Ed both had Harleys, but they were non-affiliated lone wolves. The three of them were impressed into silence upon hearing that I'd handled eight alone. I'd been trying to convince them that my biggest muscle is my brain since I met them. It was time wasted.

Otto and Sinbad were in adjacent cages. There was a lot of bristling and growling at first. My guess is that my smell on both dogs was the common denominator that led to their eventual truce. I let Sinbad out long enough to meet my friends. He expressed none of the initial animosity that he had with Otto. All three asked where I got the lion dog and how much he cost. The truth seemed to disappoint them, unless it was jealousy that I detected.

We made it to the shooting range and were allowed to go before the early morning shooters. Everyone knew that accuracy would count, for my plan to work. Haste was also imperative since we would have little advance warning.

I planned on our entire party to arrive in a 2-½ ton troop truck borrowed from the National Guard. This meant that we had only one vehicle to hide. My van would be parked out front with the hood up and tools out. I would also leave a portable radio out by the van to further the ruse that someone was home.

We would have ten men in the cemetery with eight more behind sandbags camouflaged in the trees nearest the cemetery. We would have the remainder of the men behind camouflaged sandbags in two more groups. There would be eight behind the house and ten in position to cut off escape. We couldn't fire on automatic because of the obvious danger to each other, hence the importance of accuracy.

A fire truck would be on standby to block the end of the road and to put out any incidental fires. The truck would move into place when all the turkeys were in the pen. There would be four uniformed County Police to protect the fire truck.

The noose at the house should be intimidating enough to produce almost total compliance with orders spoken through bullhorns from all four manned locations. The few fools who may have to be shot should provide all the show of force necessary to defuse the situation. Our early warning would come from the surveillance at the gang's clubhouse.

Now to set the trap and do something I don't like to do, wait. I used to tell my children that 'patience' means behaving when you have to wait. It was my turn to behave.

. . .

Since the airport had the largest and most convenient parking lot, we had the deuce-and-a-half delivered. I had requested enough hand flares and trip flares for every man to have three of each. The odds were greatest that the bikers would strike at night. There would be a one ton truck following with pre-filled sandbags.

Everyone boarded the truck when it arrived. I realized that my place might be under surveillance by the outlaw gang, and resolved to check this personally. I instructed the truck driver to let Travis and me out one block prior to turning down the road to my house.

We each grabbed a sandbag from the second truck and waved them on. We crossed the street and waited with our sandbags. Shortly after the trucks turned down my street, a motorcycle slithered out of his hiding place and parked on my road for a moment while the rider took out a pair of binoculars and studied the trucks for a while. Then he put away his field glasses and rode our way. This was our man. Before he realized that he'd been spotted, two sandbags went flying and brought his journey to a screeching halt. I dragged the driver out of traffic while Travis retrieved the motorcycle. My stunned captive was resisting arrest, so I had to stun him some more with a straight right. Travis was bitching that I should have let him hit the spy. He was only fooling, but it made cuffing the guy easier.

I radioed for a squad to come for our friend. Travis got the bike running and smiled, "So, Derrick, are you sure that you want to ride with me?" he asked.

"Why not? You haven't killed yourself on one of these yet, and don't try to scare me or I'll make it crash." I hoped that this warning was convincing.

I had taken the biker's colors, thinking that they might come in handy. The squad came and we loaded our man. The three miles to the house was the last time that I'll ever get on the back of a bike with that lunatic. He knew that I was bluffing about crashing the bike, so he took the opportunity to show me that he knew how to handle one.

Now, we had to gamble that Travis could pass for their lookout. He could put on the guy's colors and wait at the end of the road like a Judas goat. I truly expected them to come at night, and to come in a moving van or similar means of transportation. Thirty odd bikes were bound to attract attention and they knew it.

We set up all four positions and camouflaged them. Then I jacked up the van and put out the radio. I left it loud enough to be heard from forty feet away. It was supposed to storm tomorrow, so I expected them tonight, especially since they had a lookout posted today.

The existence of the early warning people allowed us to socialize freely. We all knew our positions and would have plenty of time to move into place. Barry, Ed, and I joined Travis out by the highway to shoot the bull. I told them that they were scheduled to be here a week with pay. I explained how this operation had screwed up my plan to visit the smokehouse today, and asked if they would like to waste some time in the woods across the river again. They all agreed.

Edwin said, "On two conditions; That we keep our M-16's out there, and we park on the dirt road instead of walking out from here and getting our feet wet." Those conditions seemed like good ideas to all of us.

The four of us stayed together, comparing notes, trying to conjure memories of scarier times twenty some years ago. Chronological order of events was a problem for all of us. Barry and I came in country together and we still had memory problems. The kind of trauma that we shared had to be experienced to be appreciated. The last deal we went through together with "Big Foot and the Mercenaries" (rock band for sure) was some heavy stuff, but it was so brief that it didn't have the same effect. Hell, none of those guys used camouflage or tunnels. They were easy prey for us because they never expected us to be out there. We were usually equal to or greater than any force that we opposed. That night on the roof with eight noisy fools surrounding the house was more annoying than frightening. They never knew that I was on the roof until I hollered after the last man fell.

The North Vietnamese regulars and their Special Forces, those guys were scary. They had been fighting for decades. They had tunnel systems to rival the expressways in this country. You might think that you were alone, when in reality, you could be outnumbered and surrounded. That was a long, scary year. Too many men never made it back from that trap. That was pretty much a synopsis of our conversation.

"Let's talk about something pleasant," I said, "like how easy tonight will be and how much fun we'll have walking to Camp Cannibal." Everyone seized on the opportunity to quit talking about Vietnam. We had several hours until dark, at which time I would turn on the yard lights and the rock station on the portable radio. Then everyone would put on their body armor and assume their positions.

Travis had the worst job as Judas goat. If his disguise didn't work, he could take a bullet in the head. He knew his job well. They couldn't see his face, just the colors on his back as he preceded the gang down the dirt road. If one shot were fired at him, he would snake through the trees and join me at the position nearest the road. Unless they were crazy enough to continue the attack anyway, the mission was scrapped. The next alternative was to confront them at their headquarters and bust them for conspiracy to commit murder. The truth was, I didn't anticipate any problems with the current plan.

Darkness settled in and people's moods changed. The joking stopped and we put on our business faces. I know, all the jocks would say, "game faces" but they'd be wrong. This was no game. We were cops and this was "business".

Everyone was in position. The yard lights lit what may become a kill zone. Should anyone shoot them out, we would toss out trip flares, saving the pop up flares for last. Those kind of flares make nasty weapons too. I saw one fired against a tree once and it exploded in a burning shower of white phosphorus.

Our surveillance at the biker's clubhouse radioed us that the gang was on the move. They were coming in a large Salvation Army truck. They were armed with AK-47's and shotguns. Their arrival time was estimated at twenty minutes. Travis saddled up and put the colors over his body armor. He was to come down the dirt road with his light off, then drive to the western side and make his way back to our position, on foot if necessary. We wished him "luck", and off he went.

The next minutes dragged by, probably more so for Travis. We radioed the fire station to be prepared. Soon I could hear the motorcycle coming cautiously down the road. As soon as I could see the dim bulk of the truck behind Travis, I told the firemen to block the road. Travis went slowly around the extreme western edge of the circle of light and the truck killed its engine almost directly opposite our position. For a brief moment, the rock radio station was the only noise to be heard. The roll top door opened and the bikers hopped out, keeping to the outer edge of light as Travis had done. The enemy moved in two columns, going in opposite directions until the house was surrounded. Then they crept out into the light as they approached the house. Two of them checked my van to see if I was there. Travis appeared next to me. We waited for them to make some hostile move before using the bullhorns. The lives of the bikers would be in their own hands from that point forward.

Four of their men appeared on the roof. Evidently they had spoken to their incarcerated brothers. Once assured that the roof was empty, they climbed down to join their idea of fun. They had thirty-one men, not the thirty-two that they thought. Travis had been smart enough to remove the colors before infiltrating our position.

All at once, they opened up. They were using the shotguns to blow out the windows and the AK-47's to shoot through the walls at floor level. We let them burn up a lot of ammo before using the bullhorns. "Freeze! Drop your weapons!" came from four directions at once, well outside of the circle of light.

These bikers were the hard core of the hard-core and surrender wasn't in their vocabulary. God, I wish they would have listened. They started shooting as they ran towards the bullhorns. They paid for their foolishness with their lives. After the shooting, we threw out some trip flares, but there was no sign of life.

I don't think a man among us felt good about what just happened. It was almost murder. Almost, but they would have over run us if we hadn't responded immediately. There wasn't much ground for them to cross. They would have been at the sandbags firing point blank. My only consolation was that these evil men had come out here specifically to kill me.

The lone biker that Travis had replaced would probably turn to Jesus once he got the news. Walker called the coroner and told him to bring thirty-one body bags. Then we sent the fire truck away and requested a pair of 2 ½ ton trucks, one for us and one for the bodies. The Salvation Army could claim their stolen truck tomorrow.

As I gazed at the wreckage of my home, I was trying to picture the new one that I was already designing in my mind. The chief said that the gang had assets that could be seized for compensation of damages. This time I wanted a brick home with bulletproof glass. I couldn't even sleep here tonight. I'd have to buy aquariums for all the snakes until a new home was built. That is where David and his local connections would save me again.

Hopefully my van would still run with all the holes and broken windows. I'd have to trade it in before the storms tomorrow. I wanted to thank all these men personally, but I think that they needed time to digest what they had just done.

For tonight, it would be motel rooms for my three friends and me.

...

People were going to start thinking of me as the grim reaper. Was not my white van just a modern day pale horse? As long as good folks realized that they had nothing to fear, I didn't care if evil people feared me. So far, including tonight's operation, death at the hands of evil still outnumbered deaths at the hands of the police. I distinctly remember only wounding the first eight men who had come to kill me. I could just as easily turned them to ashes and dust, yet I showed mercy. That was something that they or any of my more sinister foes never considered. That was the principal difference between good and evil. This last blow dealt to the outlaw gang had decimated 25% of their total estimated forces and the Montgomery County Chapter no longer existed, except for the baker's dozen behind bars. The man with the binoculars was from the Harris County Chapter. Old 'Sandbag' was lucky, and by now he knew it. News travels fast. Bad news travels faster.

These were my thoughts as I awaited sleep at the motel on the I-45 feeder road north near Gladstell Street. The van had been dropped at the dealer's waiting for major bodywork while I had been given a loaner. It was another white van identical to the last one. Mine was more likely to be totaled than repaired. The motorcycle that Travis scared me on was confiscated for auction, which broke Travis' heart.

The next morning, thunder woke us earlier than we wanted. The rain was hanging in the air, but it looked like it would rumble for awhile first. We decided on breakfast at the Kettle Restaurant before it poured. There'd be no walk in the woods today. None of us liked to get wet if we didn't have to. I whined over breakfast that every time I got any time off, some creep or group of same would cut my vacation short.

My friends told me that it would always be that way. "Criminals breed like rats and roaches," said Ed, who had been an MP in the Big Red One for a while. "You either deal with it, or walk away and let someone else handle it."

Barry said, "You're a natural at this stuff, just like walking point in 'Nam. You can smell trouble."

Now Travis put his two cents in, "Derrick, you are addicted to excitement. That feeling from the jungle will never leave you. You're good at this, and, just like we protected the weaker soldiers in Nam, you feel obligated to protect society from the bad guys. If you give up your job, some lesser man might step up and the bad guys will gain the upper hand again."

Edwin spoke up again, "He's right. If you quit, it will be like surrendering to the enemy. We will always be available as long as we're alive if you ever need us again."

That ended my whining before everyone's breakfast got cold. We had to find a way that wouldn't get them in trouble with their wives and me with my girlfriend. Margaret knew that I wouldn't be available until my friends left town. Oh my God! I'd be without a woman for a week! Not that Margaret was just any woman. She was the nicest, most trustworthy woman I'd known since my mother passed away.

Walker gave me permission to leave my twenty-five mile zone and we went to Houston. Sharpstown Mall was a good place to waste time, so that was our first stop. It was pouring when we sprinted from the van. At least it wasn't a cold rain. It turned out that there were too many pretty women smiling at the mall for us to hang around. That was good for our egos, but trying on our weaknesses.

We got on the 610 Loop and drove to I-45 south to head to Galveston. I wanted to see if they noticed the lack of trees as I had on my first visit. The hurricanes take out anything taller than four feet every year or so. My friends were just as alert as I had been. Travis had to explain the phenomenon to Barry. Flint, Michigan doesn't have too many hurricanes.

We drove as close to the beach as common sense would allow. Some waterspouts were visible over the Gulf in the distance. Hopefully they wouldn't come ashore as tornadoes. As it was, this rain would already cause flooding. The stormy Gulf lost its fascination as conversation ran out. We decided to go to Pasadena for one drink at Gilley's. One drink, in and out.

The place was as big as a supermarket. Too many pretty girls and mean looking cowboys. I hoped that my badge would give us enough room for that one drink. I went first with the badge opening a path. The last thing I wanted was a fight for several reasons. Mostly because of the 'kill first' tempers that the four of us possessed. We got a lot of strange looks, but no one pushed it.

As big as this place is, it was little more than an overgrown small town bar full of regulars with a sprinkling of strangers. If we frequented this place regularly, we'd be as invisible as the pictures on the walls.

If it was Saturday, we could have gone to the Astrodome to the flea market. That place was amazing. A man could buy literally anything there if he knew what questions to ask. Before the badge, I could talk my way into anything just with charisma. Now, I was proud and happy to wear the badge.

We wound up driving to the Wharf in the Woodlands to window shop. That place really came to life on Independence Day. I used to live in empty houses in that town when it was first being built. Rough times used to follow me around the nation. I felt like I was being groomed for some exalted position in heaven if I could manage to behave through all my trials.

The Wharf had covered piers between the buildings, but the wind driven rain discouraged lingering there too long. We decided on a movie back in Conroe.

I called dispatch to let them know that I was in town again. The movie 'Platoon' was playing. I'd wanted to see it since I first saw it advertised. A lot of it was familiar, even the napalm scene. It was not a place for faint hearts. All four of us had lived through napalm sorties. Three of us had been underneath 'wall to wall' napalm. Three men in our Platoon got horribly burned in one day.

After the movie, we all agreed that too much time was spent emphasizing atrocities. Now we could be baby killers again for the next ten years. Most of us who served over there were just brave kids doing what we thought was right. Most of us would never commit or tolerate atrocities. Now there it was on the big screen. Thanks for nothing Mr. Stone. It made me wonder what was being taught in the schools.

All four of us needed cheering up after that slap in the face. The place for that was the Kettle with a jukebox full of classic country and western with plenty of ZZ Top mixed in. Lots of coffee and breakfast twenty-four hours per day. Too, there was the company of other policemen and waitresses who could take a joke. There we would feel welcome.

The rain and wind were subsiding by nightfall. We could only hold so much coffee, so we headed to the motel to play cards and listen to the weather. First, I tracked Walker down on the radio. I asked if there was going to be an inquiry into last night's massacre. He said that internal affairs had put on their rain gear and checked the scene. They found all kinds of AK-47 rounds and double ought buckshot in the trees as well as in the sandbags. That coupled with none of the bikers being shot in the back satisfied their needs for justification for all the killings. Walker had volunteered to undergo a polygraph during questioning. That had put the cork in the bottle.

The rain was due to end by midnight, making the hike to the smokehouse a go for tomorrow. When the cards all started looking alike, we called it a night. We wanted an early start. Barry and I still had to get our dogs from the kennel.

. . .

The sun was a glorious sight in the morning. The weathermen were promising more storms for tomorrow. Oh well, it was that time of year. The first thing that I did was call dispatch and give her David's Phone number. I did not wish to live in a motel while my dog lived in a kennel. I told dispatch to confirm funding with Walker. Now we could go to breakfast before picking up the dogs.

. . .

With every man and beast loaded, including side-arms and M-16's, all we needed were some disposable cameras, dry dog food, beer, soda, lunch meat, rolls, and a kitchen sink. The good news was that the dogs had completely buried the hatchet. That had been one of my concerns. Otto was slightly larger than Sinbad, but I think they were evenly matched in ferocity and heart. I expected Sinbad to outgrow Otto in another year. My dog was still filling in.

When we were done at Kroger's, the next stop I insisted on was the mansion at the estate, which had served as headquarters for the human meat distributors. I wanted to look under that particular rock before returning to the scene of all those nightmares.

The closer that we got to the mansion, the more uncomfortable I felt. The dogs felt it too and the same uneasy feeling was on all of my friend's faces. I couldn't remain quiet any longer, "Before we pull in, I want everyone locked and loaded. We're undoubtedly off on another adventure. By the way the dogs are acting, and how we're all obviously feeling, this may even be a paranormal adventure. We could wind up meeting Satan himself. If anyone wants out now, speak up and I'll stop the van. My answer was the sound of rounds being chambered. I truly wished that we had a priest with us. I pulled up to the door of what appeared to be an empty house. We passed a "For Sale" sign on the way in.

All the drapes were closed, but the door was ajar. This looked like an invitation to our funeral. It was time to back up and regroup. We had to restrain the growling dogs from entering. I got on the radio to tell Walker where we were. He wasn't at all happy to hear what I was suggesting. He said that he'd muster a small army and join us. I told him to bring a priest and to look for us at the smokehouse if we weren't at the estate.

I pushed the door open the rest of the way, using the muzzle of my rifle. We let the dogs go ahead. They were bristling and growling at the room in general, like it had an invisible occupant. There was a note on the coffee table which read, "Derrick, I'm the one you've been after all along. You've killed too many of my pawns. It's time that we met." The note was signed 'Legion'.

What an ego! My brother knew a biker named Satan. He wound up in jail for armed robbery. I knew another man who gave me this uneasy feeling. I faced him in Calumet City. He later murdered both of his parents. That guy was captured and wound up on death row. He eventually died in prison. Even that evil bastard had to literally be in the room with you, to make you feel this uneasy. Whoever left this note had a strong enough aura to be felt nearly a mile away. It was very strong in this room. The dogs were already at the open back door. They didn't want to proceed without us. That was when I started feeling afraid. I couldn't feel my adrenaline other than as a racing heart. My friends were practically vibrating with energy. None of us had felt this alive since the jungle, where Satan had been more than just a spectator.

I asked again if anyone wanted out. They were actually grinning like wolves. "Let's get this over with," I said and went through the open door. The dogs came out last. That was a compliment for all of us. Now the dogs were bowing to our individual auras. There were six alpha personalities for Mr. Legion to overcome, and God was on our side. It looked like the odds were in our favor. We spread out on line rather than in a file. The dogs were shoulder to shoulder in the middle and proceeding at a brisk pace towards the cart trail. The only tracks readable on the trail were those of a hoofed animal, like a large goat. The dogs went crazy when they sniffed the footprints. They appeared angry rather than frightened which heartened all of us.

Now that we'd crossed the open yard and were under the trees, I felt more comfortable. I told my companions, "Gentlemen, these are the tracks of our foe. Whoever made these are probably wearing some cleverly designed boots designed to frighten us away."

Now Ed dropped to one knee and examined the tracks more closely. "Here's our answer," he said. "Look at this one."

Then we could see the smooth imprint in front of several of the tracks. It was like the man was trying to keep his weight on his heels, but would occasionally lean forward. What a relief! It was only the most evil person on Earth, not Satan. If our foe was flesh and blood, he would need the priest, not us. We followed the bold trail to the place where we used to cut down to the dirt road by the river. Here were three more sets of the strange tracks coming from the river to join our actor. It was time for us to compare notes.

I explained my theory to them. "The first set of tracks are those of their group leader. Either they insult our abilities by only opposing us with four men, or they have help waiting ahead. I've got some candidates in mind for the makers of these tracks. This will be our ultimate test even if they are alone. The egos of the men in front of us suggest that they are indeed alone. They must expect us to come ahead of the army that Walker is bringing. Also, they must have been aware of all of our plans from the beginning, including us going to the mansion before going to the smokehouse. That means that the van is bugged, phone lines were tapped, and every radio transmission was monitored. This has to be the work of the FBI or a more sinister organization like the CIA or a homogenized mix of both. Look at these tracks, the deepest ones, that's Tiny. He was one of their main players. The FBI has the power to gain custody under any pretext they dream up. The other two from the river path are probably those two creeps Smith and Jones. I think that we can rule out Schultz. My best guess is the local bureau chief or the headman from the houseboat. My money is on the bureau chief."

"That is my theory that I'm betting my life on. Here is my plan on which all of our lives depend. The trail will be booby-trapped. We also have to leave a message for Walker so he and his men don't fall prey to booby traps. We can no longer use the radio, so that will have to be in the message also. Walker's group will see our tracks leave the trail and follow us from there. We will be expected to move slowly once the first and probably only booby trap is detonated. They are hoping to delay us until nightfall. They almost certainly have night vision devices, giving them one more advantage. It is imperative that we move with haste and approach them from the rear. One of their men will have to back track setting three booby traps. One will be on the trail and the other two will be one on each side of the trail, closer to us. The man that back tracks will be on his toes to avoid leaving legible footprints. I will use the trail so I can find the traps. I want the rest of you to walk uphill from me with the dogs, close enough to where you still have me in sight. When I wave my arms, hit the ground so I can detonate the bombs and hold up our side of the charade. Then I will join you and we'll have to double time the rest of the way."

Travis spoke up, "You're not going down that trail alone. I'll walk your slack to watch for wires up high while you read the trail."

I told him that once again it was hard to argue with logic and thanked him for volunteering.

Barry, the artist of the group, wrote a clear message in the mud of the trail. "No radio traffic and stay off the trail. Follow uphill fresh tracks." He signed it, "Otto and Sinbad." Nice touch since the bad guys didn't know our dog's names. Walker and his bunch would know that the message was legitimate.

Ed said that one man and one dog should walk a wide flank on either side of the trail since an ambush was still possible. Again, I couldn't argue with sound logic. I certainly had the right team to do a tough job.

Barry and Otto flanked uphill, while Ed and Sinbad flanked downhill. When they were in position, I waved them forward. It was a long, slow process until I found the trap. It was a mechanical ambush. It was battery operated, with two Claymore antipersonnel mines, one on each side of the trail. We backed up and found the other traps, which were placed to catch anyone who tried to leave the trail on either side. I motioned for Ed and Barry to drop. Travis and I walked around to the far side of the booby traps before we detonated them. The force of the blast was all channeled the other way. The first one to blow set off the other two. All it took was to pitch a dead branch on the center wire.

I was deafened by the blast, but I could still see. I saw two tall men in tiger striped camouflage fatigues running up the trail from the direction of the smokehouse. They hadn't spotted Travis and me off the trail.

They were intent on getting to the kill zone of their booby traps to shoot survivors. It was Smith and Jones. When they ran past, Travis bellowed, "Freeze!" Of course they didn't, they instead whirled with their weapons firing on full automatic. Travis and I were still off the trail, so their firing was ineffectual. Their firing was brought to a stop as Barry and Ed dropped them with head-shots, creating the 'pink cloud' that snipers are familiar with. The dead men's belt radios were still working and a voice came over the air, "What's your situation? Over."

I answered, "Four down, we're coming in, over."

The reply was simply, "Roger." That meant that they, whoever 'they' were, would be waiting for Walker's group at or near the smokehouse.

Barry and Edwin were the tallest, so I had them pull the tiger stripes over their jeans and T-shirts. I was in SWAT fatigues, as usual, with the shirt tied around my waist. Travis was in camouflage pants and a green T-shirt. Now Travis and I were the flankers with the dogs. We agreed that we had seen the last of the booby traps, but I was sure that Ed would keep an eye out anyway. The combined smell of the blood and the exploded C-4 plastic explosives from the Claymores made for a bad trip down memory lane. Vietnam and the war were never more than a memory away. Sometimes, all it took was a loud noise.

With our two taller friends trotting down the trail, Travis and I flanked uphill with the dogs. That is when Otto and Sinbad saved some lives. Otto alerted and Sinbad stopped and snarled. When Walker heard Sinbad's unmistakable growl, he said "Don't shoot, it's me." He had Steve and Al with him along with three uniformed cops. I told him everything, especially not to shoot the two men in tiger stripes on the trail.

The remainder of the trip was covered in less than an hour. I remembered to watch for Tiny in the tree. Using a borrowed belt radio from one of the deceased, I called the smokehouse, "We're coming in." Then Ed and Barry strolled into the clearing. The door to the smokehouse opened and the bureau chief came out at an excited run. "Are they really dead?" When he got close enough to realize that these weren't his men, he made a move for his sidearm.

"Don't do it!" Barry ordered him.

The bureau chief raised his hands, counting on his ace in the hole up in the tree fort. He was shocked to hear, "Freeze!" from eight voices to his left. So was Tiny, who froze like a good boy when he saw that he was covered as well. Tiny had to drop his machine pistol and do the rope trick again. Once we had him and the FBI Chief cuffed and on the ground, we left a uniform on guard while we spread out looking for their backup. The dogs were roaming freely and showed no signs of danger lurking about. These egomaniacs really thought they had us covered.

Once we'd established that the grounds were deserted, we spread out security. Walker and I approached the open door of the smokehouse with more than a little apprehension.

The table was still in place with various forms of listening and communications devices on it. There was a cable running out the door, which we traced to a satellite dish hidden in the brush. I'm sure that the FBI would like to know whom it was that their stray sheep had been chatting with.

We went back inside to explore the many boxes and crates behind the table. One had LRRP rations in it. The rest were full of weapons, cash, explosives, and antitank weapons. The cash amount could only be estimated at several million dollars. I wondered how much had come from the motorcycle gang's seized funds. The rest was probably siphoned from all the cults and other illicit goings on ever since this guy held his position as local bureau chief. It looked like he was getting ready to leave the country. He sure had some creepy friends. We would have to let the FBI take over from here. Walker said that he'd call the bureau in Washington to watchdog the local people.

We found their boat moored at the usual old spot. Walker volunteered to wait for helicopters with his team while one of the uniforms ferried us to the dirt road. I reminded Walker to have the bodies on the cart trail picked up. Then we were off on our boat ride.

. . .

We found a fancy crew cab pick-up truck with a boat trailer at the dirt road. The trailer was obviously designed for the boat that we were in. It was my obligation to check it out. The windows were tinted, so we treated it like there was someone inside. We set up security prior to searching for explosive devices. Next I tried all the doors. They were locked. I had already located their hide-a-key box in my bomb search, so entry was easy. There was a briefcase in the front seat and four passports in the glove box.

The sniper rifle behind the back seat was equipped with a night vision scope. There were four expensive looking men's suits in a zipper carrier, plus various little items like bottle caps, cash register receipts, and credit card receipts.

We sent the important items back with the boat along with the spare keys. Then we locked the truck and I radioed Walker. I told him that there was a truck full of clues waiting to be searched. The big items were already on their way.

Finally, we could finish our sunny day off. The Kettle for lunch was our next move. The food in my bugged van would be spoiled by now. We walked up the hill to the mansion and looked for the bug in my vehicle. I had some questions about how and when it was placed. This was a loaner. They must have tailed us to the dealers and bugged it at the motel, or at Sharpstown Mall, or Gilley's or any of just about a dozen other places. I would hate to think that it was bugged when I got it. The dealer was a friend as well as my banker's brother. It was a possibility that could be checked out with an eye to eye conversation. His reaction to my still being alive would be readable in his eyes. We threw the food in the woods for the animals to eat and squashed the electronic bug in the driveway. Then I got behind the wheel and asked Walker or anyone if they could read me. I took the lack of response to mean that there had only been one bug. I explained to my hungry friends the need to see the auto dealer ASAP.

I parked down the street and the four of us walked in with me in the lead. He showed only the normal response one would expect from a friend. My first van had been "totaled" by the insurance company. The loaner was mine, but I had to reimburse the insurance company when I got the money from the biker's assets.

We fed Otto and Sinbad and took them for a walk before going to the Kettle. All that I could think about now was food. Radio traffic had preceded us and once again we were heroes. It was embarrassing to be so popular. I really preferred to keep a low profile. So far the other police were just respectful, no sign of jealousy or animosity. That was good, because I had my eye on being the Chief when Walker challenged the current mayor. I wanted unanimous support and a smooth transition when I took over. I was sure that Walker would support me.

We had to relate the story to everyone in our little audience. They were shocked at learning that the local FBI chief was the organized crime boss in the area. It was devastating news, but the logic was there. Who better to have his finger on the pulse of every operator and player in the region? Who better to bring the kind of pressure that would guarantee cooperation or else? And, who would have better cover? He was probably grateful for my efforts on wiping out his subordinates so he could liquidate everyone's assets and shut down his house of cards prior to disappearing overseas. If he had that much in cash, he might have more stashed in Swiss banks. Who the hell needed more? Still, that satellite dish intrigued me. There were still some sleaze bags in the world providing a market for all the ghoulish nightmares that this one man pedaled. To think that once, Sergeant Donald had joined us in prayer led by our friend Jimmy from the First Cavalry.

When we killed the headhunter and arrested Tiny, he was left with Smith and Jones as his enforcers. They must have been quite efficient. That was no small pile of cash at the smokehouse. My question is; "Is it over yet?" Smith and Jones claimed to get their orders straight from the president. I hoped with all my heart that they had been lying. Time would tell if we healed the wound in the Earth that Satan had rent. I anticipated a long period of peace. After today, I felt that we had truly slain the dragon.

I felt confident in my future. I pictured myself gaining custody of my three children. I saw Margaret and I married, raising Nikolas Ryan with his brother and two sisters. I wouldn't rest until I made all these dreams come true. I couldn't wait to get back to my peaceful home with the quiet neighbors.

# Part Two

Mayor Walker opened his mail from the Johnson's. It was a simply printed invitation that read; "Chief and Mrs. Johnson request your presence at their first anniversary celebration to be held at the Conroe VFW hall at 1:00PM Sunday. Food and beverages will be served. Children are welcome. RSVP."

Back in the crowded Johnson house, everyone was in high spirits. Rebecca and Annie were giving baby Ryan a bath. Nikolas Ryan, or Ryan for short, was seven months old. My son, Travis, named after the man in Florida, was walking Sinbad around the border of the property, which was now surrounded with a cyclone fence. Today was the last day of school and he and his sisters had been free for the summer for nearly an hour.

Rebecca had graduated, Annie was just entering sixth grade, and Travis had two years of high school left. Margaret had quit her job at my request to be a full time mother. Right now, she was baking in preparation for Sunday's party. I was only at the office about a half of the day and spent the rest of the day monitoring my radio. As would be expected, I was on call twenty-four hours per day.

Conroe was once again a peaceful community. I remained somewhat of an enigma. I managed to pass a mandate requiring polygraphs and drug testing for the existing police force and anyone wishing to become one of Conroe's finest.

We had easy access to backup from the county and the state. The area had a new local FBI bureau chief and he was a family man. People on the street gave friendly waves to passing patrolmen. Block Watch was a citywide endeavor so effective that street gangs fizzled out before they could take root. Church attendance was up as were community activities.

Conroe had become a magnet community. The street that I lived on was now paved and had the rather catchy name 'Derrick Place'. The cemetery was still next door, but now it had flowers and wreathes and the grass was kept mowed.

All the ingredients for happiness were present, but I wasn't happy. I was a man of action in a peaceful environment. The bad guys stopped for gas and kept right on going. Our community was too clean and well policed for them to blend in.

I needed some new bogeyman to make me feel alive. At present, our biggest problem was poachers with would be counterfeiters coming in second. Speedboats with telescopes and machine guns kept Lake Conroe free of poachers. The woods were patrolled by the Forest Rangers. They also patrolled the San Jacinto River and its streams. Backup for the Rangers is always as near as a helicopter ride away.

The town was so well run that it was boring for the likes of me. The excitement that I craved was not to be found in Conroe. I was proud of our crime free streets, but it left me feeling useless. What I needed was a vacation in a less docile environment with my army friends. Right after this anniversary party, I would do that. They must be as bored as I was.

My oldest son, Travis, was bigger than I. I treated him like a man, respectfully. There were no doubts that I was still the father and head of the house. I always hated the bullying that I got from my now deceased father as I tried to grow up. My father's favorite expression used to be, "You'll do as I say until you're twenty-one or big enough to whip me." God how I hated that. He always had a hundred pounds on me since I was a frail, hungry youngster. At any rate, when I was eighteen, I told him a thing or two and he had no legal recourse. I was paying room and board since I was fourteen and he needed my income. I wanted no such animosity between my sons and me.

Rebecca was already a woman at eighteen. I let her and Margaret run the house as they saw fit. I seldom stepped in. I was grateful that they lived in such harmony. It was a rare home that had two women in it who got along so well. Soon Annie would be Margaret's right hand as Rebecca went off to college.

Our street now had nine houses with families and six more under varying degrees of construction. David was finally enjoying the prosperity that he'd been denied for so long.

. . .

Time passed and the anniversary party came and went. We moved the outdoor activities to the City Park for all of those who wished to participate to enjoy. The kids had made a lot of friends since they had moved to town. The whole thing was a scene from a Norman Rockwell painting. That only made it more boring. My life had been spent in an infinitely more exciting mode. It had not been a pastoral scene from some post card of Americana. Don't get me wrong, I was happy to raise my family in such a safe town. I'm sure that the whole town felt that way too. Travis from Florida was right. I was addicted to excitement. I needed it to feel alive. This serenity would make me old.

That is why I was letting Detective Washington take over when I took off.

. . .

I decided to drive to the Tampa area where Travis and Edwin lived near each other. Barry got a vacation from the auto plant in Flint, Michigan. He was flying down. Edwin was on his own time since he was diagnosed with 100% disability from PTSD and basically retired. Travis arranged some vacation time from his foreman's slot at the iron works in Palm Harbor. The superintendent was at the job site dotting "I"s and crossing "T"s.

Travis had a big boat that he was dying to take on a cruise to the northern coast of South America. That sounded like trouble, which is exactly why we decided to go. He said that our government gave handsome rewards for leads on marijuana shipments and the location of plantations. The four of us would split the rewards after expenses. We only had twelve days to make it work. Then we had to return to our families.

An aggressive approach was the key to success. First, we had to obtain suitable armament. I make it a rule to never go to a gunfight without a gun. Travis already had that covered. He said that guns were cheap twelve miles out. He knew the main man in that field. Naturally the guy was a Vietnam Veteran and a former arms sergeant. He had six tours in Nam without ever setting a foot in the jungle, a damn black-market thief. I asked Travis about bringing this guy down on the way back.

His response was that the guy was working for our government as well as himself. Who better to keep Uncle Sam informed as to 'whom' was purchasing 'what'. As far as bringing him down, it would take a torpedo since half of his crew kept watch in five smaller boats in an aquatic perimeter. This guy covered all the angles. "Besides," Travis said, "this guy is squared away." That was a compliment that Travis didn't give out lightly or often.

So, after a big breakfast, the four of us made a trip to Paladin as the arms dealer was known. He knew Travis' boat and we had no trouble pulling alongside. Once the boats were secured to each other, boarding was simple. Paladin's boat had a dozen or so tires fastened on its side to accommodate frequent visitors.

Paladin was a burly, full bearded man about a half -a-head taller than Barry was. He was covered with colorful tattoos. He had what we wanted at a price that was affordable and he didn't ask why. I'd call that squared away. Travis got an M-60 machine gun like his old one in the jungle, Barry had to have one too. Ed and I opted for M-16's, and everyone got .357 combat magnums for side arms. A good revolver won't jam like some automatics. I still had my bottom line .38 special in my pocket plus a folding lock-blade knife on my belt. All of us carried knives. At this point, we were all armed to the teeth and would use those too if need be.

We had to return to shore to secure edible provisions and backpacks, plus emergency medical supplies, something none of us wanted to have to use. After one last night ashore, we were to leave on our new adventure.

I hated not being in the driver's seat, but the boat and the idea belonged to Travis. We four considered ourselves equals anyway.

We left the dogs at home. Otto was at one of Barry's brother's houses and Sinbad was in the care of my oldest son.

Travis stayed with his boat while the rest of us went shopping. Backpacks first, then water purification tablets and dehydrated food. Then we bought the perishable items, beer, soda, lunchmeat, beer, bread, cheese, and beer. Barry said to get whiskey and Tequila in case we didn't get enough beer. Hell, it was a vacation first, adventure second. We got fresh fruits and vegetables and a bottle of vitamins too. The last stop was for ice and beer.

When we got back to the boat, Travis asked if we had remembered to get some beer. That got us all laughing. As we passed the provisions to

Travis to put on board, he figured out what he'd said that was so funny. We all slept on the boat that night in case someone tried to steal our beer.

...

Our trip would take us between Cuba and the Dominican Republic. We would pass Jamaica on the eastern side and enter the Gulf of Venezuela, to pass into Lake Maracaibo. We ran out of friendly faces once we passed the US Marine base at Guantanimo Bay. We were definitely on our own now.

Travis planned to anchor in the big lake out of sight of land. We would rubber raft it in from there. His plan ended with the landing of the raft. We would wing it from there, sort of adlibbing the rest of the adventure.

If we wanted excitement, this open-ended romp would surely provide plenty of opportunity. Fuel would be available along the way, even though his tanks were oversized. Travis even had a scarecrow remedy against theft of his boat. He flew a medical quarantine flag with warnings in English and Spanish. This trip was dangerous if we never left the boat. Pirates were as common as fish in the waters we would traverse. We didn't look like scientists or tourists. We looked like competition.

Knowing this made the adventure more appealing. I didn't like water, especially large bodies of water, but I'd learned to face my fears long ago. In my mind, we were always surrounded by hungry sharks. In reality, it was surrounded only about half the time. The rest of the time, there were only a few.

Thank God the weather held through the night and the next day. We passed through the Gulf of Venezuela on the second night and continued our journey south into Lake Maracaibo. At sunup, we anchored just out of sight of the southwestern shore. Travis hoisted our bogus medical flag. Then it was time to load the inflatable raft. For me, this was the worst part of the journey. That raft rode mighty low in the water. We shot an azimuth and each of us kept a copy of the back azimuth just in case.

That sure was a long trip to shore. I'd as soon walk back through Panama as go through that again. All that paranoia about pirates was wasted so far. I could handle that. With both feet on the ground once again, my self-confidence rose to its usual mountainous proportions. Anyway, I was braver on shore where I couldn't get beaten up by a fish.

We carried the equipment a little way into the jungle. Then we carried the raft under the trees and camouflaged it. Branches dragged over the trail hid our footprints. We rolled a boulder to mark the spot and to shoot our back azimuth from.

The beach was an inviting place, but we didn't know who our neighbors were. We used our azimuth as a guide inland. We walked fifty yards and performed a two-petal cloverleaf exploration, meeting back at the boat. There was no sign of man in that short reconnaissance. We walked three hundred paces the next time and did a four-petal cloverleaf with the same results. This, coupled with the fact that there were no footprints on the beach when we landed, gave us the secure feeling that our immediate environment was deserted.

Now I walked in front while Travis guided me with the compass as Ed and Barry flanked us at eight o'clock and four o'clock. Fifteen yards out was as far as they strayed due to the density of the jungle. Any farther would have meant loss of visual contact.

We came across a dirt road after about ¾ of a mile. There were signs of fresh traffic. We decided to watch it for a while as we sat and ate breakfast in the cover of the jungle. We sat in a close group, all eyes on the road. The only sound to be heard was our chewing and swallowing. I decided not to bring up the fact that we were aliens without passports, visas, or even a note from "Mom". Normally, I operated within the close confines of the law. This time, the integrity of the local lawmen might be questionable. We couldn't afford to be spotted by anyone.

Other than our families and Walker, no one had any idea of where we were or what we were up to. We weren't even sure. All we wanted to do was make some easy reward money and experience a little excitement again.

From our knee-high vantage point twenty feet off the trail, we were invisible to anyone over two feet tall. As long as no elves came along, we were safe. So far, all the traffic had been pedestrian. The volume suggested that there was at least one town nearby. Most of the traffic was going in one direction. I pointed this out to Travis who said that they were probably leaving town and going to work. Food crops would certainly be grown close to the village. The bulk of the people were almost certainly going to a farm with a different crop. This near the Equator, the growing season was all year long.

Our first vehicle finally passed. It was a small truck loaded to the gills with the unmistakable sight and smell of marijuana. Bingo! This was what we were after. We would have to pinpoint the town and plantation. The next question is who to report it to? We would have to raise the DEA on the boat radio. The local police might be in on the operation.

It was decided that short, dark skinned me would go on the road, rather than my three tall friends with their fair skin and light hair. Removing my military shirt and taking only the .38 special in my pocket, I first walked towards the village that was visible to the west. Even at a mere 5'6", I felt large and bulky compared to these people. They didn't even give me a second glance. This was one of those places where questions just weren't asked. The nearby village only had a few dozen huts with one fairly modern looking building that looked like hotel and bar and café and trading post and maybe even police station. No sense tempting fate, time to look for the pot farm.

Here came the first test of my masquerade. A Jeep with four soldiers was almost upon me. I kept my head down and moved out of the way. I dared not look back, but it sounded like it stopped at the hotel. My feet wanted to fly, but I forced myself to walk. A five-shot pistol is no match for four automatic rifles, except of course in Hollywood.

I couldn't stop to talk with my cohorts on the return trip due to the volume of pedestrian traffic. I walked towards the pot farm as if I had a purpose there. Two more trucks full of the stuff went by. The packaging and shipping end of the operation must be on the other side of the village.

The plantation was as organized as anything you'd find in Napa Valley, California. The big difference was that there were huts and guard towers abundant, acres and acres of pot like a cornfield. The individual fields were in various stages of development. No plant was taller than five feet. All were cropped to make them bush out and produce more of the desirable tops.

Finally I saw what I was looking for. People in nice clothes relaxing in the shade instead of working. These were fair skinned aristocrats who avoided the sun so as not to look like the peasants. On the pretext of relieving myself, I wandered into the brush and squatted down. After crawling into the jungle, I made my way back to my friends.

We all agreed that we were too few to take over this camp. We would have to return to the boat and radio for backup. We returned to the concealed raft. Barry and I stayed with the provisions while Ed and Travis headed for the boat. Within the hour, they were back with the news. We stumbled onto a farm that the DEA wasn't aware of.

"So what about the reward?" I asked.

Travis said that it worked on a ratio of dope seized, with a bonus for every honcho arrested. The dope was only five grand per ton, but the honchos were worth ten grand apiece.

Now I had a plan that I ran by everyone. Since DEA wouldn't be at our location for two hours, we needed to kidnap the four palefaces in the expensive clothes. That meant taking out the guard towers quietly, unless we could be so fortunate as to catch them on their way to the village. It was nearing the noon hour. I'd be willing to bet that our aristocratic friends ate their lunch at the hotel. "We had better hurry, or we may miss a forty thousand dollar opportunity," was my advice. Hiding the raft again, we went to set our ambush. With two machine guns to brandish backed up by two automatic rifles, we shouldn't have to fire a shot. We hurried to the road in time to see that our well dressed friends had just passed in the Jeep on their way to the village for who knows how long of a lunch break.

"Travis," I said, "those boys may move on after lunch. I say that we should go get them. The bulk, if not all the guards are at the plantation. The men in the Jeep had no heavy weapons in sight. They may even be unarmed."

Travis replied, "I doubt if they are unarmed, but you're right about them moving on after lunch. Let's go get them."

Everyone was happy to be doing something other than waiting. We kept to the cover of the jungle until we were across from the hotel. Our four movers and shakers were plainly visible through the front window as they sipped their drinks. Other than the bartender slash cook and one waitress, the foursome seemed alone. We waited until their food was brought out and the hired help was out of the way.

Once again, short, suntanned me had to initiate the proceedings. I entered the café portion of the hotel and walked right up to their table. I said, "Mire a la ventana," which means, "Look at the window."

While their attention had been on me, Barry and Travis had approached the window with their machine guns. Those two look scary when they're unarmed. As the honchos stared in disbelief at the two big men with the hardware, Edwin walked in carrying two M-16's by their pistol grips. This was my cue to frisk the diners. Relieving them of their pistols and cell phones, I retrieved my own M-16 and we escorted our prisoners across the street and into the jungle. We tied their hands with their own shoelaces and marched them to the raft.

We had to play leapfrog with the raft to get the four of them and all of our equipment out to Travis' boat. Now all we had to do was wait for the DEA boys. I hope that they brought their checkbooks. The money for the tonnage of pot could be mailed. I felt like we had just pulled a rabbit out of a hat. I was ready to return to familiar shores. That last operation was a miracle whose time was probably used up.

...

The DEA finally showed up and removed our guests. I turned over their pistols making sure to tell the agents which pistol went with whom. They promised us an additional bonus if we would pose as bait for some particularly vicious pirates who were bound to hit us on the return trip. All that we had to do was carry some bales of hay on deck. That was like a magnet to the pirates. We had no objection to making some extra money, especially since the pirates were bound to hit us one way or the other.

Now we had two dozen bales on deck, loosely covered with a tarpaulin. It looked good to me. A helicopter would be scrambled to assist us once the pirates made their move.

"How many men do the pirates have aboard?" I asked Travis.

His response of "Two dozen, give or take a few" made me grateful for the backup.

"Travis, just how did you expect us to overcome two dozen men?" was my very appropriate question.

"I didn't," he said. "I expect to overcome their boat. I have six antitank weapons aboard, any one of which is capable of sinking their craft. Hell, if you hit them in their fuel tank, they cease to exist as anything but smoky little pieces of flotsam."

I apologized to my dangerous friend and asked him just how long he'd been looking forward to this trip.

"Oh, I'd have to say 1970," he said through his grin. That date happened to coincide with the year we had left Vietnam.

So, off we went looking forward to some more excitement and even a bonus if we lived. The four of us discussed that part about living and decided to hit the pirates with the antitank weapons before they got close enough to be a danger.

We said "Adios" to the DEA and steered a course for the Gulf of Venezuela. About halfway between there and Jamaica, we picked up a shadow. The telescope showed at least twenty Rostifrarians with AK-47's on deck and who knew how many below. Time to hit the maritime equivalent of 911. We called the DEA and radioed our position and heading, then we broke out two of the light antitank weapons and kept an eye on our shadow. Travis said that there was a second ship ahead of us on a collision course. If we veered, both of the two strange boats would have a broadside target.

Travis got on the radio to raise the ship in our path. "Fok you mon!" was their response which led to their boat trouble. The trouble came from the large hole in their prow and the interior explosion. They gave the wrong password.

I had no desire to rescue the few survivors from the boat that we just hit. The sharks are kinder than a Rostifrarian posse anyway. Possees killed slowly for fun. Sharks killed to eat.

The ship to our six O'clock started firing a large caliber machine gun at us. We gave them the same trouble as the first boat. As an animal lover, I couldn't bring myself to shoot any of the sharks that were just doing what came natural to them. The chopper was above us now and some guy on a bullhorn was asking us if we were alright. I got it. It was a joke to buy more time for the sharks. I played Mr. Bullhorn's silly game and shouted, "We're a little shook up, but we're OK."

He said that they would look for survivors in a little while and to keep the hay until we docked in case more pirates developed boat trouble. It was pretty obvious that they didn't like the brand of pirates in those waters. At any rate, I never heard anyone shooting the sharks. The screams were awful, but they were the screams of devil worshippers who had less mercy than the sharks. I saw the chopper lower a Penetrater to pick up one man who could tell his friends ashore what happens to pirates.

Before we headed to Tampa, we dropped our hay bales at the Coast Guard station on Key West. I hate open water, but we made a bundle of money. Without the pirate bonus, we cleared about fifteen thousand apiece. It could have been us swimming with the sharks as easily as the posse. Whatever the pirate bonus was, we earned it.

It was time to play hero on shore to anyone who would listen while we waited for the rest of the money to show up. Hell, we'd been so busy that we barely made a dent in the beer and we didn't even open the Tequila. We loaded the cooler in Travis' pickup and went to the beach. On the way, we bought a large tarpaulin to make a first rate Vietnam style hutch. It was big enough for the four of us. We got so drunk and made so much noise, that we had a sizable area to ourselves. Some stray women were attracted to the noise, like moths to a flame. As good as they looked, we had to send them packing as all of us were married.

The next morning, one of Travis' daughters found us to let us know that Western Union had the rest of our money. My head hurt. I needed sunglasses and lots of food in that order. We all got dark glasses before we had breakfast. We looked like unshaved FBI agents at the restaurant. If there weren't so many of us, we could have passed for the Blues Brothers. As far as that went, Barry could even play a guitar.

There was about five grand more apiece. I guess that pirates aren't worth very much. At least the sharks seemed to like them.

Now we had a choice, either we went to Travis' house and got him in trouble with his wife, or we went to Ed's and did the same to him. Or, and we liked this one best, we rented a room on the beach and didn't upset anyone's wife. That's what we wound up doing.

The lucrative vacation was over too soon. Barry and I both had to mosey. Neither of our wives had a chance to be mad for a while, so we'd just go home and give it to them. (Good!)

...

Of course I missed my friends, but naturally I missed my family more.

I had been driving all night as is my custom on long trips. Conroe felt different when I got back. I assumed that it was just me. After my trip to South America via Florida, the town seemed smaller. The feeling that I was getting was not about the size of the town. It was more of an uneasy feeling. It was like the town missed me or more like it needed me. Margaret could tell me what had changed. It would be good to hold her again and mess around with the kids and Sinbad.

I switched on the citizen's band to catch up on the latest. I was three days early and no one was expecting me. I was coming in from the eastern side of town on FM 105. That's a highway, not a radio station for all of you not from Texas. It was unlikely that I would be spotted coming home. Radio traffic was routine. No aliens had landed while I was away. Still, my instincts told me to keep my eyes open.

I turned into Derrick Place to be greeted by three more foundations awaiting homes. My friend David wasn't letting any moss grow under his feet. I'd have to purchase two more acres as much as an investment as to protect my privacy. I planned on giving the children an acre apiece. They would welcome the extra acre buffer zone for their own privacy.

About halfway down the road, I ran into David with his surveyor. He gave me a handshake on two more acres at the original price, with two more on option at current market value, which was already considerably higher than when he had first broken ground. I thanked him for his generosity and the options.

Now, just a few blocks more and I would be home. I could already hear Sinbad barking. He knew the sound of my van. As a matter of fact, everyone was waiting on the porch. Darn David and his cell phone. So much for surprises. It was great to be home, yet the strange feeling didn't go away, even after all the hugs.

"OK, Margaret, what's wrong with Conroe?" I finally asked. She seemed to be holding little Ryan a bit too tightly.

My older son Travis spoke up when she hesitated with her answer. "The Rankin twins are missing. They've been gone almost a week. Steve and Al have been running the search efforts in your absence."

The twins were only four years old. Those girls were the Rankin's first and only children.

Travis went on, "They were stolen from their home during the night. The Rankins didn't have a dog. They only know that it was after ten PM since that was the last time that Mrs. Rankin had looked in on them. Their bedroom was on the second floor. Bloodhounds were brought in, but the trail ended in the street in front of the home. The police believe that the girls were carried off in a vehicle. No one has called asking for a ransom. No clues have surfaced. It appears to be a random act with no motive beyond the possession of the girls. No blood was found in the vicinity. There is still hope that the girls are alive."

"Travis," I inquired, "Were there no tire tracks or footprints?"

He said that it was pouring rain. It was the kind of night that even a barking dog would be ignored. It sounded like the kind of night that criminals love. He said that Sinbad had been sleeping inside while I was gone. I already knew that Sinbad would go through a window to get someone that he didn't like. He was up to a lean 118 pounds and was more than a match for all but the best-trained men.

With the greetings over, I had to respond to the call of duty. My family understood. All they had to do was picture Annie or Ryan gone. I radioed the station and got dispatch. She said that everyone was out looking and circulating photos. Even the off duty personnel were out covering every patch of woods bigger than a breadbox.

I left Travis the M-16 and the .38 special. He had long since learned to shoot both accurately and with confidence. I took the .357 and Sinbad. I was able to meet Al and Steve at the Kettle. They said that it was very likely that the missing children were no longer in the area. I asked if there were any similar disappearances within fifty miles.

Steve said, "Yes, unfortunately. There were two in Houston, one in Tomball, one in Kingwood, one in Spring, one in Grangerland, and two in Pinehurst."

"What is the time lapse on these ten missing children? What are any other similarities? And what are the other departments doing?" I asked.

Al said that our department seemed to be the only one to consider a link. The others were treating them as separate and isolated incidences.

"Okay," I said, "Let's go to the station and plot these on a map. Then we'll list dates and times, days of the week, weather conditions, race, sex, economic factors, ages, sizes, hair color, everything personal about each one. Then we start looking for common denominators."

It took over four hours to gather all the necessary information to try solving this puzzle. All were girls between the ages of four and seven years old. All were Caucasian, blonde, blue eyed, economic background not a factor. Crime scenes were similar, stormy weather, no family dog, all taken from their homes during the night, all during the last two weeks, no signs of blood or violence. The perpetrator was either storing the girls or selling them as quickly as he picked them up.

Looking at the map, the town of Spring was at the approximate center of our monster's area of operations. The center was still Montgomery County. I was not only chief of Conroe, I was also SWAT team leader for the county. That gave us jurisdiction down to the Harris County line.

"How much sleep have you all been getting?" I asked my partners and friends. Steve said that he hadn't had any and Al had less.

"Sleep in the van on the way to Spring, then eat some Dexedrine like I'm going to. Don't be shocked. Special forces in Vietnam and some unnamed presidents had to do it all the time. I'm providing it and I'm authorizing it. Just be sure to drink plenty of water or you'll become dehydrated and may hallucinate. Now pass out, and that's an order.

Neither one managed to fall asleep. I stopped at Speedy Pack and got three gallons of drinking water. I told them that if Spring was a wash, we'd try the town of Tamina.

Armed with recent photos of all ten girls, we started cruising towards the western side of Spring watching for anything out of the ordinary. Sinbad had his nose glued to the window. I wondered if he could sense misery as well as he sensed evil. I voiced my thoughts and both men agreed that it was possible. We were already at a point where any input was welcome, be it divine or canine. Cases like this produced more survivors if they were solved early.

We were cruising slowly, not really knowing what we were looking for, just praying for some clue to jump out of the woodwork. We definitely could have used a miracle. It was near dark on a night that promised rain. We were all on tip-top alert, having consumed twenty milligrams of Dexedrine and a quart or so of water. There was already heat lightning in the western sky.

As far as hiding places go, this side of Spring seemed to have an outbuilding on every piece of property. We finally parked in a schoolyard and killed the engine. This was going to be one of those rains that made sensible people stay home. If it rained hard enough, people would have to pull over unless they had Rain Dance on their windshields. I swore by that product, and I'd be willing to bet that our kidnapper did too.

My instincts told me that he would be out tonight. The roads in Tamina tended to flood worse than streets here. I had a feeling that we were in the right place. It was full dark now, and a heavier rain was upon us. It would probably be after ten o'clock before the kidnapper went prowling. He may have already passed us on his way out. We were dealing in unknowns and uncertainties. I wish that my van wasn't white. We'd have to move to a less conspicuous spot. The parking lot at Gunny's Shack would do. There had to be some die hard drinker's vehicles to camouflage our van at least a little.

The tavern was crowded despite the weather. I backed the van into an open spot in front. There were only a few homes between here and I-45. I knew some of the people in those homes because I'd worked for them years ago. I was gambling that the abductor lived deeper into the community. Two cars crawled past before a flat black van pulled in. It looked like it belonged to a thief of the night. Sinbad didn't like the driver one bit.

The man ran into the bar. I hopped out to peek into his windows. They were tinted too darkly to see anything. I tried the back door and it was unlocked. There was an unconscious girl in the back who was bound and gagged. I closed the door quickly and ran back to my van. I couldn't believe our luck. The owner of the black van came out at a run and got behind the wheel, pausing only long enough to light a cigarette before backing out and driving deeper into the subdivision. He never even glanced our way.

I gave him just enough lead to make him think that he was alone. Then I pulled out with my wipers on maximum speed. I was able to follow his taillights this way until he turned left. Then I was able to put my lights on and speed to that corner. I already knew that this was a dead end road from studying satellite maps of the area. He was ours now if we played carefully. Dousing my lights before turning the corner, I saw headlights bumping down a rutted driveway at the end of the road. We parked where we were and ran the length of the street to the driveway in question. Sinbad had long since learned to follow me unless I told him to "Go get him!"

We arrived in time to watch the suspect unlock a garage at the back of the property. His headlights were illuminating the inside. The interior was lined with bunks that were mostly full. When he started towards the back of his van to retrieve his latest victim, I let Sinbad go. We caught up to the dog before he killed the creep. I called off my dog while Al called an ambulance and a paddy wagon. Steve carried the little girl into the garage while I found a light switch.

The ten other blonde haired little girls seemed to be unharmed. They were handcuffed to their bunks and wearing diapers. Their mouths were duct-taped, but they appeared in good health. I got on the radio to have dispatch notify the families that eleven seemingly healthy girls were on their way to Children's Hospital in Houston.

A squad car picked up our prisoner. After we arranged for and supervised the safe transport of the children, we all climbed into the van for a brief meeting.

Steve said, "Welcome home."

Al said, "The town missed you. Everyone missed you."

I told him that it was good to be home. I meant it too!

. . .

That kidnapper was an awfully busy man. I wondered what his purpose had been for so many little girls. They had seemed healthy and unmolested. They could have been intended for someone else who only paid for undamaged goods. I had a hunch that a buyer lurked in the background somewhere. It was decided to set up a sting at the creep's home. We would have to put a lid on the press until the sting netted our next catch.

The kidnapper apparently lived there alone. The house was small and dirty. The garage was better kept. We ran a phone line to the garage and used it for a base. The house, when searched, revealed an extensive collection of child pornography. There were magazines as well as videos. The minor subjects were all girls ranging from preschool age to early teens. Some of the teens appeared to be pregnant. Whoever masterminded this affair was bound for prison or worse if I had anything to do with it.

Steve and Al were in desperate need of sleep. I was still tired from driving all night the night before. We picked out three bunks in the garage because it was cleaner than the house. Sinbad could rouse us if there was any trouble.

Sleep is what we did until the birds woke me up at sunrise. Feeling bad, but knowing they would understand, I woke my partners up. We had work to do.

There were twelve bunks in the garage. Last night's victim was number eleven. That meant either a delivery or a pickup soon. Steve and Al would help me on this one. I needed their extra firepower just in case. I found a number tacked to the wall in the house near the phone. Our prisoner was named Mike, but his tattoo said "Indio". I didn't know if that was a nickname or just the town in California of the same name where he got his tattoo.

I decided to take a chance and call the number. An answering machine picked up on the first ring. I identified myself as Indio Mike and said that the bunks were full. Then I hung up and held my breath. The phone number was a Woodlands exchange. They could be here in no time, or they might call back. If they called back, they might smell a rat. I wondered if the pickup crew was the end of the line, or if there were people higher still up the ladder. It would make sense that the brains would be reluctant to get their hands dirty.

It would speed things up if the adults in the videos could be identified. It might also speed things up if we offered the creep who performed the actual abductions a deal. One frightening thought that was bothering me was whether or not similar operations were in action in other or all large metropolitan areas. When I was through here, I'd be sure to share this theory and provide a copy of these files.

It wasn't long before a black stretch Lincoln pulled in like they'd done it more than once. The driver got out first. He was a monster, the kind of steroid freak that lurked around the gyms where professional athletes worked out. The lights were on in the garage, so the gorilla let his sissy friend out of the back and they walked right to the door and us.

They had no guns in sight, which gave us the advantage since ours were. When they knocked, we unlatched the door and read them their rights. All that we had them on was suspicion, but I was sure that creep number one would drop the dime on the high rollers to lessen his sentence. I'd be sure to mention that to the judge when he was setting their bails.

A search of the limousine provided us with a link to this place. There were more of the same kinds of videos and magazines along with a briefcase full of cash. I called the FBI to sort out the mess.

The problem with the Houston area was that there were so many people coming and going from all over the world, they couldn't be kept track of. Well, there were three who could be kept track of for many years to come.

When the Feds showed up, we bowed out as soon as possible so I could take my two tired friends home to get some more sleep. I told them to take tomorrow off, just to leave their radios on.

I would also have to reign in the press a little. Nothing short of a miracle kept these latest two creeps from hearing about yesterday's arrest. They were probably too busy watching child pornography on the TV in the limousine.

...

I got home that afternoon with a satisfied feeling. Police work can be gratifying. Sinbad greeted me when I pulled in the driveway. Margaret was waiting in the door. We had all barely said "Hello" the last time when I had to run.

My son Travis wanted to be a cop like his dad. He said that he wanted to be a hero. Now there's a compliment. They were all astonished at how quickly and happily this last case had been solved. Me too. I would do this job for subsistence wages just for the satisfaction of helping people.

Something that I consistently failed to do was follow up on each case. It would be nice to know who the Feds put back on the streets and why. That damned crooked Bureau chief would have opened my eyes sooner if I'd known that he had Tiny released.

The collective efforts of all the local law enforcement agencies had taken a considerable bite out of crime in the area. A follow up on the past few years' crimes would tell me which players were back on the outside. I made a promise to myself that I would start taking preventative measures instead of always reacting to a crime after the fact.

I was hoping that both of my sons would decide on a career in the military or law enforcement. I was old fashioned enough to hope that both of my daughters stayed out of harm's way. What I wanted most for all my family was happiness and a Christian lifestyle.

It was good to have both of my teenage children at home before curfew. We plugged in an old Chuck Norris video. He always had happy endings. He taught the ill mannered bullies a lesson and made the world safer for Mom and the girl who was left behind. I don't think Sinbad understood the movies, but he seemed content just knowing that we were happy.

We hit the hay that night in our respective bunks. Travis had taken over the attic. Together, we had made it quite livable. Only half was storage. That left him with the largest room in the house. He had room for his weights and bench plus the few odd pieces of furniture needed to keep everything neat.

We got the brick home with the bulletproof windows that I requested. The home lost a little of its country charm, but it was safer this way. The gate across the drive was left open during daylight hours. There was a regular attendant taking care of the cemetery weekly. My pet snakes had been released after their eggs were laid. The big rat snake had laid twenty-eight eggs. All turned out to be fertile. I hatched twenty-one king snakes from their eggs. We hadn't seen a Cottonmouth in many months.

Margaret had turned the place into a storybook home, a pleasure to come home to. It was a place that we were proud to entertain our few friends. We had considerable playground equipment for Annie and Margaret's nieces and nephews. Soon Ryan would be playing too. He already liked the swings. Whenever the sun was out, we had a yard full of kids mostly from the new homes on the street. The dead end no longer held the dread that it once did. The stories of the headhunter and the infant graveyard were hard to fear when the sun was shining and children were laughing. We didn't, however, have many children hang around after dark.

Tonight would take care of itself. Tomorrow would mark my new approach to police work.

. . .

Sinbad started growling shortly after midnight. It had started to rain. Travis came down the stairs and handed me the M-16. I pulled on a camouflage shirt and black pants and rubber boots. I told Travis not to let anyone turn on any lights. I asked him to stay inside with the family while Sinbad and I slipped out the back door.

Sinbad's attention seemed riveted to the cemetery. I got my five-cell flashlight from the van and we went over there. Travis waved from the window as I walked from the van. I didn't turn on the flashlight yet. That would make me too easy of a target in case of an armed enemy. I followed Sinbad to the top of the hill by the fancier headstones. One of the stones had been toppled. Sinbad sniffed at the hole beneath where it had been standing, but he didn't enter. The toppled stone was the largest monument, more or less the centerpiece of the hilltop. It would have taken several men if not a vehicle to move it.

I played the flashlight into the hole. There was just an empty concrete coffin in the hole. Sinbad was growling furiously, but he made no move to leave my side. We walked around in the rain awhile until I found some tracks. They looked like a copy of those goat tracks that Smith and Jones had left. These were much larger and appeared authentic. Of course they couldn't be, yet what in the hell had tipped that massive stone?

I figured that now would be a good time to call for backup and send my family away. The tracks actually went towards the house before they veered north and entered the swamp through a hole cut in my fence. I went inside and roused the rest of the family.

I had everybody dress and pack extra clothes. I gave Margaret money to check into the motel at I-45 and Gladstell Street. I told them that I'd be in touch to let them know what was going on and when to come back. I called for two patrol cars, then I saw the family safely off. I had Travis follow them in the van to insure their safety. I instructed him to return ASAP.

The warm rain was still falling steadily. Sinbad and I waited under the porch overhang until the prowl cars showed up. Mayor Walker was in his own vehicle followed by Steve and Al.

When I showed them the monument, the eight of us managed to struggle it back upright. Travis returned in time to witness our efforts. I showed them the tracks and gave them my theory. "Gentlemen, what I am about to say is the only sane explanation for what we have before us. It is my belief that someone used a rope tied to a bull to pull the headstone over. The person was riding the bull and rode it into the swamp. If we wait for the sun to come up, our bull rider will be long gone. I'm going after him tonight to prevent his gaining an impossibly large lead. I would gratefully welcome all your company, but I will not order any of you to join me."

My son was the first at my side, but to a man, everyone there was willing to take up the pursuit immediately. Sinbad would be an immense help once we caught up to the bull.

Whether it was a lone vandal or a group waiting to take me out was a mystery. I suspected a group. To make the night more exciting was the fact that it was summer and all manner of beast and bug was out.

Talking time was over. Now we were supposed to track the bull through the swamp, at night, and in the rain. This deal of always going into the damn slough at night was getting old. It occurred to me that only the most desperate, fearless people would be out tonight. There must have been something very important in that concrete coffin beneath the headstone and the time to retrieve it had become urgent.

I suspected that the bull would be found wandering loose now that his services were no longer needed. It occurred to me that the bull could be leading us in the wrong direction. The logic of the situation dictated that the bull was brought out in a trailer and that the trailer would be at the dead end nearest to mine.

The nearest farm with livestock was several miles away and belonged to the former mayor who bred bulls, but had no horses. That was why he hadn't ridden a horse. This moved our search from the swamp where all that we would find was a bull, to the dead end just east of here. I told everyone my thoughts as quickly as possible and we made a beeline for the vehicles. Travis and I rode with Walker, Al, and Steve. The uniforms followed and off we raced to the next road east that went north from Highway 105.

There we found the trailer that I expected, but the truck that towed it was gone. The fastest way to the ex-mayor's house was the shortest way to end this mystery. We killed our lights before going up his driveway. The former mayor was alone and packing for a trip. He came out the door with a suitcase in each hand.

"Police!" I announced, "We'd like to ask you a few questions." I was trying to be polite.

The man dropped his bags in surprise. The larger suitcase burst open scattering hundred dollar bills onto the wet ground.

"I can explain everything," he said.

I told him that he'd have his chance but we needed his truck to pick up the trailer and his bull. "A bull is a dangerous animal. I'm afraid that I'll have to arrest you for releasing it in a residential neighborhood. Further charges will follow, I'm sure."

Mayor Walker was looking into the other suitcase while the other officers were putting the wet money back into the larger suitcase. Walker was still a policeman at heart. He found printing plates for several denominations of US currency.

We took the former mayor inside of his home to confirm if he was truly alone and to see what else His Honor was packing. The first thing that caught my eye was an 8x10 photo of the recently arrested local bureau chief in an exalted position on his mantle. When we entered his office, we found an extensive library of videos that I'm sure the FBI would be interested in. According to the disgusting titles, it was a felony just to possess them. They certainly linked him to all that nasty business with the mercenaries that I thought we'd cleared up.

His flight was probably due to his concern that someone was going to implicate him from behind bars just to get a reduced sentence. The former bureau chief was the most likely candidate for that honor. I felt that with the arrest of the former mayor, we had the last piece in a very old and complicated puzzle.

It was now after two AM and way past all of our bedtimes. The bull would probably wander back to the trailer for a sense of the familiar and security. That would make our jobs easier.

The former mayor was escorted off to jail by the uniforms. Al drove the pickup and the rest of us followed him to the dead end where the trailer was. The bull was hanging around the trailer as expected. Sinbad convinced him to climb aboard and all was well in his little world once the gate was closed. We hooked the trailer up and Al drove it back to the property that would be up for auction soon.

I thanked my friends for their loyal support. Travis and I drove them back to my house to pick up their vehicles. We decided to let the rest of the family finish their night at the motel.

My last call of the night was to the FBI to tell them that we'd left the door unlocked and the lights on at the former mayor's house. "Wake somebody up and get a search warrant." I told them not to open the trailer unless they were 'real' cowboys.

...

I called the motel in the morning and asked Margaret to meet us at the Kettle for breakfast. Travis and I walked Sinbad over to the newly righted monument to read any tracks that hadn't been washed out by last night's rain. The bull hadn't stayed in the swamp very long. His trail came out of the swamp just east of my property and followed the hard ground in the direction of the dead end where the trailer was parked. His trail coming and going was still plain where the hoof prints didn't overlap. I had seen enough for now. It was time to go to breakfast.

The girls and little Ryan had gotten there ahead of us. Ryan was being carried around the restaurant by one of the waitresses. All of the ladies were making a fuss over him. Travis said, "What about me?" That got him a few embarrassing pecks on the cheek from a couple of waitresses. He loved it.

I clued the family in on last night's adventure. The town cops drifted in and out for their staggered breakfasts. Only the newer cops showed any surprise at the former mayor's arrest. The old timers said that the ex-mayor had been too chummy with the former FBI local chief and those two creeps, Smith and Jones when they appeared on the scene.

We hung out until past lunch. The only thing that I had planned today was to use a strap tied to the van to move all the larger monuments in the cemetery.

...

That search, aided by Travis, produced nothing. I refused to believe that the counterfeit plates and cash had been stored in such an inaccessible place. It was my belief that he was going after some long hidden secret that had nothing to do with either. At any rate, it was my mystery to solve.

Starting at the start, I decided to topple the largest monument once more. We hadn't spent much time with it last night other than the superficial examination that concluded with the assumption that it was empty. What if Sinbad's growls had interrupted the grave robber before he had really gotten started?

So we put the strap on the big marker and toppled it again. Once it was moved, the daylight revealed what couldn't be detected in last night's gloomy rain. The floor of the concrete coffin was just a false bottom. The rain had temporarily filled a depression where a man might insert four fingers and raise the lid.

I sent Travis to fetch the M-16 and the five-cell torch before raising the lid. As I raised it, a counter balance started moving and made the task easier. The apparatus reminded me of the trapdoor beneath the couch in the Satanic Cult house. The counter balance also served to hold it open. A narrow set of stairs was revealed descending to God knows where.

I didn't think there was another exit simply because the ex-mayor had chosen this route next door to the chief of police's home. Had he another choice, he certainly would have used it. The possibility existed that we may have trapped an accomplice in here last night. This didn't seem like a time for backup, just a flashlight and the company of my son. I took the M-16 and gave Travis the .357. We started down the staircase that spiraled counter-clockwise to the floor twenty feet below.

There was another set of counter balances for the monument, but time and rust had taken their toll on the already strained mechanism. The chains had snapped. The room was too vast for flashlight exploration. We ascended into the fresh air again. I left Travis to guard our rabbit hole while I ran for extension cords and lights.

Rebecca and Annie volunteered to go to town for the extra cords. I had fewer of both than I remembered. I also put fifty feet of ½ inch chain on their shopping list so I could repair the larger counter balance. I told them not to mention our new find to anyone. I had a feeling that many of Montgomery County's unanswered secrets were about to be answered. I rejoined Travis at the top of the hill. He said that he was pretty sure that he had heard something below. I told him that it was probably just echoes of exterior noises like the effect of holding a seashell to one's ear. Then I heard it too. This was certainly no 'seashell' noise. The sound was stealthy and yet it gave the impression of great weight behind it. For all the world, it sounded like a very, very large snake. When I laid that idea on my son, he said that he had thought the same. It was possible for a snake to live down there. It could eat any burrowing animal that made its way down there.

My daughters were back in a little while. The whole time, Travis and I were listening to that ominous slithering. We were convinced that it was a snake. We agreed that it was best to wait for the lights. Rebecca hooked up the extension cords while Annie brought us the lights. I sent Travis for the chain. He wound up half-carrying and half dragging it. I let him do it alone. It would make him strong.

If that was a snake, it was a giant. I didn't want to face it alone. I also thought that it was time to share our secret. I called Walker. He was a man whose wisdom I had great respect for. Also, I trusted him implicitly. I doubted if Al and Steve were home since I gave them the day off. I told Walker to check out two more M-16's for the exploration. When I got back to Travis, he was pointing the rifle in the hole.

"Whatever is down there is making its way towards the light," he said.

We watched, as the head of a monstrous, Reticulate Python, came into the little circle of sunlight at the bottom of the spiral stairs. It definitely wasn't afraid of people since it started up the stairs immediately. I told Annie to call the nearest emergency vet and tell him to bring a tranquilizer gun with enough juice for a hippo. I didn't know if there was more than one snake and I wanted to be prepared. This seemed to be a prudent time to close the lid and sit on it. We were about four hundred pounds together, add that to the weight of the chain that we put on first, and we made a pretty heavy lid. Now, to wait for Walker and the veterinarian.

...

Our nervous wait was a short one. Walker preceded the vet by only moments. The mayor trotted up the hill like he missed police work. "What did you find?" were the first words out of his mouth. "Is it like the tunnel house? Why is the vet here?"

"Do you want those questions answered in order, or should I run it all together like you did?" was my response to his enthusiastic questioning. He laughed at that. Then I told him of our fruitless search beneath the other large stones, and finally of the second search of the largest monument and our subsequent findings.

The vet was approaching with his tranquilizer rifle. It was time to unveil our latest find. "Don't shoot this thing until it is all the way out on the ground. I don't want to have to carry it up those winding stairs," I told the vet. I opened the lid and stepped back as the python crawled slowly out into the sun. The animal was over twenty feet long with an average girth of twenty some inches. It had a head large enough to swallow a basketball. The beast, once it was all the way out, sat there warming in the sun that it had been denied for who knows how long. I wondered what it's diet consisted of over the course of its lifetime. The spurs present near it's tail marked it as a male, thank God.

I figured that the Houston Zoo might like to have so large of a specimen. Getting it there would be the chore. The thing must have weighed three hundred pounds if it weighed an ounce. We got the traveling kennel from the vet's pickup and placed it as close to the snake as we felt safe. It looked like a good place to hide so the snake naturally crawled inside. We closed and locked the cage door and the vet tranquilized the monster for safety's sake. It took all four of us to lift it into the truck. I upped my earlier estimate to three hundred fifty pounds.

The vet wanted to come downstairs with us. I recognized him and his tranquilizer gun as valuable assets should we find any more living surprises. Now we could resume the fun part of the day, exploring our man made cavern.

I took the lead, as usual, with my son close behind, followed by Walker and last, the vet. The artificial lights proved unnecessary. The auditorium, we soon discovered, had it's own lighting system. A flick of a switch bathed the room in ample light. The power source was probably pirated from the power pole outside my home. My bill hadn't been outrageous, so I assume that the place hadn't been used since I moved in, at least, and probably longer since the main counter balance was non-functional.

The illumination gave us a better idea of the vastness and shape of the chamber we were in. It wasn't fancy at all. It was like a movie set in some old horror movie. The floor and walls were concrete. There was a pre-stressed concrete ceiling with the only hole of any consequence being at the stairwell. There were several other smaller holes, I presumed for ventilation, scattered about the ceiling. Critters falling through these holes must have kept the snake so well fed. These holes would look like gopher holes to anyone mowing the grass above. The overall effect was like being in a cave. The perimeter of the approximately thirty foot square theater was lined with wooden bench type seats. Forty people could have been seated in here comfortably. Once upon a time, this must have been a very popular arena. It probably existed before the rest of the cemetery grew up around it.

Closer scrutiny of the seating revealed hinged lids cut into about three foot sections. Wiping the dust off the first seat that I came to revealed the number 'twenty three' on the lid. I dusted off the seats on either side to reveal what was probably sequential, assigned seating. I raised one of the lids to examine the contents. Besides the expected cobwebs, there was a black hooded robe made of what felt like silk. This particular seat also contained several candles.

The four of us had spread out, lost in our own explorations. I wondered to myself if the big snake had been an escaped pet who had entered through one of the holes in the ceiling, or if it had served some more sinister purpose. I suggested that we search every seat well, leaving the lids up after each was looked into. The ex-mayor must have thought that there was something down here that couldn't be found out, even at the risk of his capture.

Each of us took a wall and started raising seats. We piled the hooded robes under the stairs. There were some newspapers dating back to the early seventies. Travis found a purple robe, the only one so far. Next to it was a large zipper type bible. Upon opening it, he discovered that it was hollowed out and filled with Polaroid photos. The pictures were of forty different people, women as well as men, all with their hoods off. Walker recognized several of the people right away. I even knew some of them, including the ex-mayor. What made the photos so horrible was that in each one, the person was hand feeding a human baby to the great snake. The snake wasn't as big in most of these pictures, but still a formidable reptile. The infants were either freshly killed or still alive, as the blood looked shiny and wet.

When these human monsters abandoned this site, they probably assumed that the snake would perish and their secret never found. It almost wasn't found. It was too bad that the mayor hadn't gotten down here that night to receive his just reward. The snake was easily large enough to kill him. At least we got the photos before he did. The pictures in that bible would change politics around here forever. Other than a few more newspapers, the bible was by far the most significant find.

I wondered aloud why all these people had allowed their unmasked pictures to be taken in the act of committing the most heinous crime imaginable. Walker suggested that it must have been a binding ritual to show their dedication to this cult. The photos would probably show a connection to the tunnel house.

We were all glad to reach the sunlight after our awful discovery. My son did a lot of growing up this day. He handled it all very well. Once again the FBI would be called in to match people to the photographs. Walker and the veterinarian left while Travis helped me repair the counter balance for the monument. We worked in virtual silence in light of our gruesome knowledge. I guess that truth is stranger and more horrible than fiction.

...

Once again my home looked like Grand Central Station, or Union Station if you're from Chicago. The agents were coming and going from the subterranean theater. They photographed every aspect of the place, from the monument to the counterbalance and the auditorium itself. They were intrigued by the elaborate affair. Since I'd replaced the chain, the monument could now be moved by one strong man. It was a piece of cake with two people.

The FBI insisted that the only reason that these monsters could operate under our noses so long was that people in the 'Bible Belt' couldn't conceive that anyone would behave in such an abominable manner. As for myself, I started out in the projects in Chicago. I held the belief that the worst thing that you could think of has already happened, it can happen again, and it can happen to you. That outlook kept me alive. The agent who said that didn't know much about me. To me, he was the bumpkin.

When the last of the agents left, I let Sinbad run loose. This was a dead end that really earned its name. It occurred to me that if the largest monument crowning the hill was fake, there could very well be other fakes hiding more secrets. A mass exhumation seemed a bit radical, but cemeteries had been moved before to accommodate right of ways for freeways, this wasn't the case here. I didn't expect much luck in that direction. The peace of mind of the community was at stake. That had to carry some weight. I would present the idea to Walker and have him test the waters. In light of our recent discovery and the very age of the cemetery, it might not be so difficult for the community to swallow.

I'd be willing to bet that none of the hilltop markers had people buried beneath them. The graveyard was on my property. I should have some say so in the matter. I would run an ad to suggest moving the cemetery after the news of the underground chamber got on TV and in the papers. I expected my request to be greeted more amicably once the community heard of the latest atrocities and the place of concealment.

Finally I could spend some time with the family. They all wanted to see the chamber. I expressed the thought I had of filling it in. My family thought that it would be a waste. Rebecca and Travis thought it was a cool place. I have to admit that I agreed with them. I told them that if it didn't get wrecked when they moved the cemetery, we would leave it and find some use for it.

Pizza for supper and a rented video filled in the rest of the day. Time for me to call the station for a situation report. The news was that everything was placid, which meant a good night's sleep.

Sinbad slept in Ryan's room. 'Doggy' was little Ryan's first word. Maybe when he grew up he would say "Daddy".

...

Travis came to the station with me in the morning. The reports on my desk were all routine matters. Thank God that the FBI took over that mess at the graveyard. The paperwork would be monstrous not to mention the man-hours chasing down the participants who were still alive.

The mayor called to say that if I advertised for one calendar month, I would be able to have the cemetery moved. He also said that a nearby church was volunteering some land to relocate it. He said that they had suggested the re- interment to him in light of the news. I found that rather odd. It was still good news as it would facilitate the relocation process. He also warned me that there would be a lot of visitors looking to confirm that their relatives might be there. I'd have to keep Sinbad on his leash until the sightseers were gone. I would ask my family to keep an eye out for shady behavior when I wasn't home. There may still be more mysteries surrounding my quiet neighbors in the cemetery. The Jones' had been full of surprises since I moved in.

All was under control at the station, so Travis and I went out to visit the mysterious and generous minister who had volunteered the land for the re-interment. He was just up the road in Willis. I thought of the old adage about kids and dogs being the best judge of character so I stopped at the house to pick up Sinbad and Annie, then all the bases would be covered.

It was only a ten-minute drive to his church. I didn't call ahead because I wanted his unrehearsed reaction for all of us to read. The premise for my visit was to look at the final resting-place for the nearly fifty of my quiet neighbors.

We drove north on Frazier Street and turned east on an unpaved road very similar to the way Derrick Place used to look. I made the mental note that this road ran in the general direction of the smokehouse. It was too soon to tell if that was just a coincidence. The church was at the end of about three miles of dirt road, another coincidence? If I had any sense of direction or perspective, I'd say that we were less than a mile through the woods to the smokehouse. I was becoming very suspicious.

We pulled into the front of the parsonage, thinking it the most likely place to find Preacher Quinn. There was no answer at the house so we went to the church. The doors were open and we walked in. The building appeared empty at first. The preacher came from behind the drapes in back of the pulpit. At least I assumed that he was the preacher. He was dressed the part, but he looked more like a professional wrestler.

Sinbad was growling instantly. The big preacher tried to stare down my dog. I grabbed Sinbad's collar as he made a lunge for him. I asked Travis to take the dog outside while I spoke to the minister. Annie went with him. I could tell by her face that she didn't like the big stranger.

He looked instantly familiar. He wasn't as big as Tiny and the headhunter, but the family resemblance was unmistakable. I'm not one to beat around the bush, so I asked him up front if they were his kin.

He denied that he had any brothers or cousins. Then he introduced himself and said that he recognized me from the Chevy commercials on TV. As hard as he was trying to be cordial, I could see that it was a strain on him. I told him that I wanted to thank him in person for volunteering his land and assisting with the smooth transition of the re-interment. I asked him if he'd mind showing me the plot that he had in mind. I knew that it was hard for him to be nice to me but he maintained his cool. I asked him how he knew the Mayor. He said that he'd bought this land from Walker many years ago. He was only recently able to build his church.

I was still trying to digest the fact that Walker knew this man for many years but failed to see the resemblance to Tiny and his very big brother. The simple answer to that was that the Mayor Walker had never seen the other two men. He had no reason to since the FBI was in charge of that investigation. Walker would have no reason to view every prisoner or body from that blood bath.

I followed Quinn out a side door to a piece of flat ground that would get a lot of sun. "Will there be enough room for all of them?" was my innocent question.

"With frugal use of ground, I'm sure that this plot will accommodate everyone," was his strained answer.

There was no need to push for a confrontation now. I desperately wanted to know why he wanted that cemetery in his back yard. Time was on my side here. I figured that he and his brothers were loose cannons like Smith and Jones. They served no real master other than greed. Let's explore the adjective 'greed' here. First, let's divorce it from its most common application, money. Let's substitute power, or sex, or a closer personal relationship with Satan or ad infinitum. The possibilities are endless. This small time preacher could be the last surviving honcho in a once powerful organization. It had already been established that the organization that we thought we had wiped out had international affiliations. Quinn could very well know someone abroad who might help him re-establish the diabolical business that was going on for so long.

At present, I couldn't raise his suspicions about me anymore than I already had with that question about his kin. I wanted him to see me as a hick lawman that was eager to get a lot of dead bodies off his property as soon as possible. At this point, I was so ingratiating as to light a spark of contempt in his eyes. That was my cue to part company, I had finally covered my tracks.

Once we were off the property and going south on Frazier, Travis asked me, "Didn't that guy give you the creeps?"

"Of course he did, son, but my job is to take creeps like him off the streets, dead or alive, as long as it's done legally. Timing is everything. He will go out in cuffs or in a bag, it's his choice. First we set up surveillance.

Then we get rid of the cemetery in our backyard. Mr. Creepy will do the rest for us. All we have to do is wait," I answered.

. . .

It was pretty obvious that the beast up in Willis was the wrong person to practice Christian duties. My current task was to convince the sheriff's department to perform surveillance on Pastor Gorilla. My judgment was widely respected. I anticipated immediate cooperation. We sure as hell couldn't have a couple of Keystone Cops eating donuts in his driveway. We'd need some men to set up telescopic cameras like we used by the bridge when we brought the headhunter and his buddies down. Walker was just the right man to lure Quinn into town for lunch while the cameras could be placed.

I set up a meeting with Walker at the station where I was to receive faxed pictures of Tiny and the headhunter. Walker saw the family resemblance immediately. Assuming that I had a plan, he said, "What now Chief?"

I told him about the cameras and we called a judge for a court ordered surveillance. Walker called the preacher for a late lunch. I had my daughter Rebecca go to the restaurant and sneak a photograph of Quinn that I could have the FBI run through their data banks. By dark, we had our cameras in place.

Now that my plan was in motion, I took out a map and started plotting some places of interest between north Frazier Street and the 105 bridge over Peach Creek. First I located the recently named Derrick Place, then the road to Quinn's church. Two lines following the general direction of these roads intersected at the approximate location of the smokehouse. When I continued his road straight across, it met the estate where the snuff films and the drugs were found. These interesting discoveries led me to believe that Quinn may have been the puppeteer all along. He was the Teflon one with his 'man of the cloth' routine. His face never appeared in any of the videos or in the Polaroid's from the chamber next to my house. Foolishness and greed would eventually trap him. Moving the graveyard was probably the key to this mystery. The two hunters whose bodies were found in the cemetery might have been killed to protect more than one secret. He should be all out of puppets unless he'd been recruiting overseas. It would be interesting to discover who was netted in this next operation.

It would be a good idea for Al and Steve to sleep over at my house until this was cleared up. The four of us should have enough firepower, especially with 911 at our fingertips. At any rate, we had to wait for the expiration of the ad about the re-interment before the Jones' could be relocated. On the off chance that something could happen before the ad had run it's course, I decided to send the family to Galveston on an indeterminate vacation. Travis and I could stock the house with food and play cards with Steve and Al until Quinn made his move. Sinbad would have to go to the kennel. I wanted the house to appear empty.

When Rebecca returned with the film, I sent Travis to drop it at the FBI headquarters. Then I told Margaret about the trip to Galveston. That was an easy idea to sell. She said that they would leave tonight. She said that her sister could look after little Ryan.

The cameras would give us plenty of advance warning. My question was, "Would he come by road or through the swamp?" In either case, he would be closely watched and apprehended or killed. A lot hinged on how clever and aggressive he was. Suddenly I was angry. I could handle this guy alone. I'd been through more than he had ever dreamed of even if all he ever dreamed were nightmares. He was just a man like me, only I was the better man. I decided not to call Steve and Al and I would send Travis to Galveston with the girls. I'd just sleep with the windows open so I could hear while I slept.

When my son got back, I told him about going to Galveston with the family. He immediately responded with, "No way Pop! You're not facing the preacher and God knows how many others alone. I'm staying even if I have to sleep in the chamber!"

Instead of stomping his guts out, I shook his hand and told him how proud I was of him. So that would be the plan. Cameras, open windows, and just me and Travis. Naturally I would procure an M-16 for my young lion.

. . .

We didn't get the girls loaded and off to Galveston until the next morning. After that, we dropped Sinbad at the police kennel using Margaret's car.

She had taken my van to Galveston. I checked another M-16 out of the arms room. Then we went to the shooting range to zero the sights for Travis. Our next stop was the Kroger for some microwave meals and some fresh fruits and vegetables.

Now, to test the waters at the home front before unloading the groceries. I parked the car at the nearest house under construction on Derrick Place. It wasn't as distinctive as my van and would be more likely to blend in. The workmen all knew me and didn't make a big deal when Travis and I entered the woods with our rifles. We were on the western side, away from the cemetery as we circled the house. We were careful to stay in the cover of the trees, which meant getting our feet wet in the swamp behind the house. It was pretty dry this time of the year, but still muddy. We completed our swing around the cemetery, staying out of view beyond the cyclone fence. It appeared that we were alone. Truth be known, I missed the keen senses of Sinbad.

My instincts told me to unload the groceries pronto and ditch the car at the cop shop. We took our muddy feet back to the car and I unloaded speedily. I sent Travis to drop the car and catch a ride back in a squad.

The squad eventually showed up out front and I radioed them that it was all clear for Travis to hop out. Once we were safely inside, the waiting began.

My son and I had a lot of father-son time to catch up on. At sixteen years old, my task was going to be a challenge. As much respect as he professed for me, he had grown used to being his own man. He had practically raised himself. He had a stepfather that set a worse example than I had when I was a wilder, younger man. The time that I did spend with him, I tried to fill him in on the mysteries of life.

When he was little and scary movies intimidated him, he asked me if there were such things as werewolves and vampires. I told him that lions, tigers, bears and gorillas were real. I told him that the scariest thing on Earth was man, and when he grew up, he would be the scariest thing on the face of the earth. Then his mother and I got divorced and I had to renege on that statement. I told him that women were scarier because they would break your heart and wreck your life, while most men would be satisfied with just killing you.

So here we were face to face and it was father-son time again. We were in a situation that might require him to kill a man. I started the conversation like this; "Son, killing a man is a permanent thing. You can't bring him back and you can't forget that you did it. You must save killing as a last resort. You may be confronted with the act only to find that you are unable. At that moment, he may kill you. You must be clear in your mind when it is necessary and believe that God is on your side. That is a lot to run through your head in a millisecond, that is why you have to think about it before the time comes."

"Dad, I know that you have killed many men. I also know that one day you wounded eight men that another man might have chosen to kill. How can you know when it's right?" he asked.

"Son, the Lord is my shepherd. I gave him the steering wheel of my life a long time ago. The decisions that I make are guided by His wisdom. That makes my whole life easier. I'm never afraid because I'm never alone," I said.

Travis inquired further, "Is that what got you through the war, just relying on God? Didn't training or ferocity have anything to do with it?"

"Son, as important as those things are, they are only preparation. Execution depends upon the man inside. We all need a guiding light. Make yours Jesus and you'll never stray. Someday you will lose your life. All of us do. More importantly, you'll never lose your soul."

The conversation got a little lighter after that. I felt that I had reached him. It was training time for my young soldier slash son. We had all the windows open as well as all the interior doors. The house was the catcher's mitt for all the sounds that nature threw at us. We could sit at the table in the center of the house without speaking and listen to our environment in all directions. First, the nearby noises are all that are noticed. Once you filter that cacophony to its origin, you learn to hear beyond it to the next circle of sound. Then, if you're blessed with good hearing, you can distinguish the individual sounds and assign them a relative distance and direction.

He and I sat there while I explained all of it to him. The cicadas and katydids up high are almost incessant. The crickets are nearly as constant. Bird noises are generally an evenly distributed punctuation. The thing to listen for is silence. It won't be a blanket, more like a blank spot in the chorus of natural noises. That is an indication of an intruder. Crows, Blue Jays, and squirrels are also vociferous indicators of intrusion. Even a

Robin conveys a sound of annoyance. The trick is to figure out why they are scolding or why they are silent.

Once you get used to listening to all these natural sounds, you are locked in for life. Few people ever develop this talent unless they are raised in the woods. Even many of those who are never figure out this puzzle. The ones that do are excellent hunters. They are invaluable as scouts or Point Men.

The insects and animals can be fickle too. They can become used to the presence of a man who has lain in hiding for a long time, and resume their natural pattern of sounds. That is when instinct and The Lord must take over. The thing to do if one is to read their environment well is to get out in it and pay attention.

We decided to go on a reconnaissance patrol. First we went to the rear of the house and listened. All of the natural sounds seemed to be in harmony. We slipped out the back door in camouflage fatigues carrying our M-16's. We covered the open ground to the fence by the swamp quickly and quietly. Hopping over the fence and entering the cover of the summertime foliage made me feel more secure.

Travis was smiling. He must have noticed the commotion that our entry made. The insects at our feet were silenced, the droning overhead ceased momentarily, and several sparrows chirped noisily away.

I had him squat down while I whispered some instructions. "Be light on your feet, fewer insects are disturbed. Watch the trees for deer stands and men. Travel in the natural openings in the foliage and try not to wreck spider webs. Avoid soft ground that will leave distinct footprints. Speak only when absolutely necessary. Keep your eyes moving and your ears open. Wind your way through the brush rather than moving branches. Moving branches is like waving a flag not only to animal life, but also to anyone that you may be sharing the woods with. Memorize the position of the sun, the moss on the trees, and look for unusual landmarks. Skirt large open areas staying in the cover of the brush."

Then I told him to take me for a walk about twenty minutes, ending up right back here. I had my belt radio on low, just loud enough to hear if squelch was broken.

Travis must have been listening well. We moved no branches, left no footprints, and wound up in the same spot. "Travis," I told him, "You're a natural woodsman. Keep that a secret or you could wind up in the infantry." He smiled at that remark.

We waited in the brush awhile before hopping the fence and entering the back door. Once inside, I complimented him again, "What you just did is something that most people never get right, even after years in the woods. I believe that you could walk in a circle and sneak up on yourself."

"Oh, that's a good one." That was my son's way of acknowledging my joke. Now, to slave over a hot microwave for a few minutes. Nothin' like home cookin'. It made for fewer dishes too.

Just then the radio crackled, "We have company in Willis, three men in a Jeep Wagoneer. The preacher is getting in and now they're heading southeast on a car path through the brush. The preacher had a rifle with him. We'll keep an eye on them from the chopper at a high altitude, over."

"Roger that, out," was my response. Was this a dry run or some preparatory move? I'd assume the worst and be ready for it. The helicopter would keep us apprised of their location. If Quinn and his friends parked the Jeep and proceeded on foot, the chopper would be noticed. I warned my airborne friends to abandon their tail if that happened so the bad guys wouldn't abort their mission.

My theory was that the preacher and company would drive as close to the cemetery as the car path allowed, then conceal the Jeep and hoof it across the stream and through the swamp. My plan was to set up on the eastern side of the cemetery where we would be least expected. We could observe and act if necessary. We wanted the goods on these guys with no loopholes in the law for them to squeak through.

Travis and I gathered plenty of ammo and some water. Then we set about finding two suitable observation posts. The near one would be used only after the intruders completed their own re-conning. They may not bother, but it was safer to assume that they would take their own security precautions.

Radio traffic informed us that the Jeep had parked near the smokehouse and the passengers were exiting the vehicle. They lost sight of the four rifle toting men once they crossed the stream. I gave the chopper a "Roger and out."

The nearer observation post had to be a standing one in a clump of palmetto. The farther post was specifically a hiding place in the event that our friends did any re-con of their own. It was only about a forty-minute walk from the smokehouse to here. They should be in sight soon.

Travis and I were standing in the clump of palmetto. The birds and insects announced the approach of our quarry. Before long, a tall man appeared at the fence behind the house. He was wearing a knapsack that was obviously empty. It wasn't the preacher. He was too cautious to walk first. The second man in line was practically a clone of the first, tall, dark haired, and sturdy, with an outdoor tan. They seemed alone, that meant that they had flanks out. The first two looked to the west and another clone appeared followed by the preacher. At least one, if not all of these men, had been in the military. Someone taught them well.

Quinn motioned for them all to duck down. First, he threw a stick at the house. When that got no response, he bounced a rock off the back door. After a brief pause, he whistled like he was calling my dog. With a wave of his hand, all four hopped the fence and rushed the house. They were positioned with a man at each back corner and a man on each side of the back door. The men at the corners made their way to the front of the house. The one that I could see was staying below the windows. I distinctly heard the front doorbell ring. Then we watched the two strangers let themselves in and check the interior. At last, they let the preacher and his partner in through the back. The open windows let us watch nearly every move they made.

All were in tiger striped fatigues and carrying AK-47's. They made a big deal out of booby trapping the front door. This alone was just cause for arrest. I still needed to find out what they knew about the cemetery that I didn't.

Two of them and the preacher exited through the back door while one of the clones took up a guard position at a front window. I gave Travis the field glasses and had him watch the goon inside the house.

The other three men went straight to the cemetery never bothering to see if they were being watched. Once again, I was being underestimated. They walked to the movable monument at the top of the hill. Then the preacher walked an 'L' shape on top of the smaller stones. Every stone that he stepped on was flipped over by the other two who used the three cornered bayonets on their communist guns. When Quinn was through marking the stones, they had a Swastika shaped pattern of stones overturned. Now they were removing plastic wrapped objects from the holes left by the overturned stones. Soon all had full knapsacks with an extra for their man on guard. Now they took the trouble to replace the stones and cover the traces of disturbed earth. Satisfied that everything looked natural, they resumed their positions at the back of the house. The big preacher easily carried the extra backpack. A simple knock at my back door summoned their guard who immediately donned his pack.

These didn't look like the kind of men who would surrender without a fight. Travis and I were outgunned here and our clump of palmetto only offered superficial protection, nothing that would stop an AK round. I suppose that my son and I could have opened up on them on full auto and wiped them out, but it would have been an illegal act of excessive force. I had a reckless plan that would have worked if I had my body armor, but neither of us was wearing any.

I clued Travis in on my hasty plan that he damn well better adhere to or else, period. I would literally dash out into the open and holler "Freeze" like in the book. My son was to fire a single shot into the ground at their feet to let them know that I wasn't alone. There was no time to argue since they were saddled up and heading for the fence.

I ran out and shouted, "Freeze!" before hitting the ground to make a smaller target. To say that they were surprised would be an understatement. To say that they were impressed would be an overstatement.

They were a little more impressed as my son moved up behind the big monument, fired a round at their feet and shouted, "Freeze!"

If they had frozen, they would have lived. We had just enough of an advantage to smoke them when they opened up. God, it hurt to get shot by an AK-47. I took one that passed through my left arm and into my left leg. At least I was alive, thanks to Travis who emptied his magazine while I fired mine off. The bad guys were in a classic crossfire situation, designed to produce casualties, not survivors. We both switched magazines unnecessarily since they were already dead or rapidly dying.

My arm wasn't serious, but my leg was screwed up royal. Travis tied it off with his shirtsleeves while I pressed the rest of the shirt against the hole. I called an ambulance, the bomb squad, and the FBI chopper. I sent Travis to guard the front door so no one would fall prey to the bomb. I wanted to see what was in those knapsacks. I hopped painfully down to the bodies to have a look. Damn bars of gold wrapped in plastic. Each pack had twenty-four bars of one kilogram each. I did some mental gymnastics and came up with a conservative estimate of 1.2 million dollars. Next I hopped into the house to look at the booby trap in case it was something simple that I could disarm, rather than having the bomb squad blow it in place and wreck my home.

It turned out to be a typical mechanical ambush disarmed by removing the battery wires very carefully so as not to generate static. Travis was happy to see me hop out the front door. I called off the bomb squad and asked the ambulance to speed up. I was getting dizzy and had to sit down. I came to briefly in the back of the ambulance with Travis sitting across from me.

...

I was treated and released from the hospital. They gave me a pair of those wrist type crutches. I could darn near fly on those. I had to use a pair of them earlier in my life following a construction accident.

That was as close to death as I'd ever been including the many times during the war. It was the first time I had ever been shot. I wasn't happy, but I was grateful to be alive.

The FBI never found anything illegal in Quinn's past. He was a brother to Big Foot the headhunter and Tiny, the guard in the tree at the smokehouse. He had been in on something since he knew the exact location of the gold. His three fallen friends were as squeaky clean in the legal department as Quinn had been. That made me wonder if they were new players from abroad. They looked like brothers to each other, and there was some resemblance to Quinn and his brothers.

...

When the thirty-day publication of the re-interment expired, we went ahead with the move. It turned out that only eighteen of the forty-odd graves actually housed any remains. The Swastika as well as all the large monuments held no remains.

Now that the move had been completed, the Montgomery County Historical Society became involved. Even I was interested in who was laid to rest in such a God-less place.

We didn't fill in the chamber. Instead, it became a favorite play place. Finally, I could close the driveway gate at night. I built a style over the fence in front. I now had eight acres fenced and two more acres outside the fence in front. Sinbad was pretty good around people, but I put up bad dog signs every twenty feet along the fence to warn off any strangers.

The wound on my arm healed to a conversation piece of a scar. The other as yet unhealed scar wasn't a topic of much conversation, except between Margaret and me, since I seldom wore shorts.

My son Travis aged now that he'd killed his fellow man. He'd aged an eon in ten seconds. He knew that he'd done the right thing, and I hoped that his conscience wouldn't eat away at him. Going back to high school would be different this year. Now he knew that he could stand up to the worst that life had to offer. His act was not comparable to some cowardly drive by shooting or the murder of an unarmed innocent. We were outnumbered and out gunned. In the military, he would have earned a medal.

...

My two acres outside the fence were the last two remaining parcels that hadn't been sold to outsiders. Sinbad had the run of the yard and never crossed the style without me. Rebecca had a boyfriend that I sincerely liked. Travis had a few girls that he saw, but he didn't seem overly attached to any of them. Annie was discovering boys too. For this problem, I enlisted Rebecca and Margaret to warn her about everything that she needed to be warned about. Ryan was walking around in training pants. He looked like he was going to get big. In a nutshell, my life was getting boring again. No bogeymen meant no excitement.

I had a plan involving something that had been bothering me forever. I let Detective Washington take over as acting chief one more time as I planned a camping trip for Travis and me. I told him about the smokehouse and the mysteries that must abound there. Twice now I'd found subterranean chambers connected with this diabolical crime wave. I'd always suspected something similar at the smokehouse, but I'd never taken the time to explore the possibility. Every time I got near that place, something happened to distract me. This time, I was going straight there and take a week to search it if necessary.

We would take LRRPS and water purification tablets. I'd carry a PRC- 77 to stay in touch with everyone. I would leave my belt radio with Margaret so she could stay in touch. I'd leave Sinbad at home to protect the family and borrow a K-9 from the station to come with us.

I planned on leaving after breakfast tomorrow. We were promised five sunny days in a row. Today would be a family day. We would go to the lake to swim and have a picnic. There was always a uniformed policeman at the beach to prevent trouble. It made more sense than sending them out after the trouble was already in full swing. People at the beach generally had beer in their coolers and sometimes that provoked altercations. There always used to be a group with a Frisbee or a football terrorizing the family groups. New rules were posted and the uniform was there to be sure that the rules were adhered to. His belt radio meant backup a call away. The armed cop was a good idea too, in case a stray alligator came hunting.

The day at the beach was just that, a day at the beach. The unhealed wound in my leg kept me out of the water, but I enjoyed watching my family have fun. At least I wasn't on crutches any more. Little Ryan was a fish. He had to be watched constantly to keep him from trying to swim too far out. Rebecca's boyfriend was there to help Travis with lifeguard duties. Annie was making goo-goo eyes at him. I don't think Rebecca or her beau took it seriously. Travis damn near got whiplash looking at all the girls. Finally he coaxed one over to join the family group.

Lunch was grilled hot dogs and hamburgers with chips and cold beans. Nothing too complicated. Today was supposed to be fun, not work. Naturally I was the chef since I couldn't go in the water. No problem, I liked to eat so I liked to cook.

The day was over too soon. The beach closed at sundown for safety reasons. Rebecca left with her boyfriend in his car to meet us at the house. The rest of us squeezed into the van. We beat Rebecca home by fifteen minutes. I was worried until they showed up with pizza. Annie gave her "goo-goo eyes" a rest just long enough to eat.

I was already thinking about tomorrow's trip to the smokehouse. That place had been bothering me for a long time.

...

Margaret sent us off with a big breakfast. We picked Spike up from the kennel and got a PRC-77 for me, and an M-16 for Travis. Our packs were necessarily heavy, but the hike was only about a mile on flat ground, even if it was a little muddy in places. We had to pass the backpacks over the fence. I hadn't built a style here for security reasons. We hopped over easily enough and began our adventure.

I didn't have any premonitions one way or the other about this trip. I only hoped to dispel a few demons that had been haunting me since my first discovery of the meat locker/smokehouse. Preacher Quinn may have beaten me to the secrets out there. It's not like the place was under any surveillance. All the wrong people had access to that grisly cabin.

The entire route between Quinn's church and the estate where the mercenaries used to meet was state forest. Why weren't any rangers aware of that joint? Were they in on the operation or simply asleep at the switch? None of the people picked up in any of the operations were forest rangers. I tended to think that they were spread so thinly statewide that they had overlooked this stretch of Peach Creek. The East Fork of the San Jacinto wasn't too far off. That waterway was more traveled and poached. The rangers in this area probably had their hands full just patrolling that stretch of river.

I pointed Travis in the direction of travel and let him lead the way. We reached the creek at a shallow place, which meant lots of mud, which means lots of footprints. We traded packs so he'd be heavier than I. Now I walked first with him walking in my footprints. His feet were bigger and they made tracks that obliterated mine. We created the impression of a large, heavy man traveling alone. I really didn't expect anyone to be out here, I just liked the edge that caution gave. Once we gained the higher, grass covered ground, we were able to walk normally again. I hoped that the dog prints would be dismissed as coyote tracks.

Now I did something that I had wanted to do ever since Bigfoot had pulled it on us. I circled around to watch our back trail. We walked to a point inside the foliage that gave us cover but allowed us to view the stream. I couldn't believe my eyes. Two men in tiger striped fatigues were walking southeast along the river and they stopped to examine our trail. This in itself was not a crime. We were close enough to hear their conversation.

"We'll have to warn the congregation that someone else is going towards our cabin," said the older man.

"It looks like only one man. I say we should kill him now. These tracks are fresh. It's probably that cop Derrick who's been so much trouble. We may never get a better chance," said the younger of the two.

The older one said, "That sounds like a plan. If we're lucky, he will have his back to us."

They were carrying AK-47's. I hated those damn communist weapons. Once their minds were made up, they wasted no time trying to track us, which led them right past our present hiding spot. As soon as they passed, I stood up and shouted, "Freeze!" They practically jumped out of their skins but they were smart enough to freeze.

"Police! Drop your weapons, lace your fingers on top of your heads and back up slowly." When they were far enough from their weapons, I ordered them to lie face down while Travis gathered their rifles. We bound their hands with their own bootlaces. I called for a helicopter to pick up the two prisoners who were to be held on conspiracy to murder an officer of the law. The chopper appeared overhead after about an hour and hovered above the stream bank long enough to pick up the trash and deposit three ghosts. The ghosts were Barry, Travis, and Ed who paid a welcome visit. Barry had driven to Florida and picked up his two friends for a surprise visit to Texas. Their timing couldn't have been better. They were armed with M-16's and revolvers and were wearing backpacks full of LRRP rations or dehydrated meals.

I explained to them how we had found the prisoners and pointed out that the two might have friends come looking for them when they didn't return to the church. I assumed that it was Preacher Quinn's old church since the men had referred to a 'congregation' and his was the nearest church.

The two men we had arrested had been wearing empty backpacks similar to the ones that Quinn and the clones had worn. That could mean more gold or something of equal interest. At any rate, when those two clowns didn't return with the goodies, the congregation was sure to send someone looking. We didn't know who or how many might come, but five of us provided a more formidable force than I had hoped for. We had very little time to plan since we didn't know how long the church would wait before sending the search party.

Our best bet was to trot the last seventy-five meters to the smokehouse since that was the most likely place for searchers to show up. We couldn't let them control the cabin and we couldn't get trapped in there ourselves. First we had to make sure that the cabin was unoccupied. Barry and Travis pulled a John Wayne on the only door. The interior was empty. Now my son and I began digging frantically with our entrenching tools to make a trench all the way around the cabin. We passed the shovels around and everyone had a hand. It looked like a Chinese fire drill with too much coffee. Anyone not on shovel duty was on guard duty. Between the depth of the trench and the piled up dirt, we had a fighting position with a four-foot vertical protection and two feet wide to crouch in. We took the time to pack down the dirt to give it better bullet stopping capability.

With five healthy men digging, we were finished sooner than I had hoped. We had a man at each corner giving us overlapping fields of fire plus an extra man to reinforce as necessary. Then I remembered the tree fort. It surely must be empty or we would have known by now. I put the PRC-77 on my back and climbed the knotted rope while the others covered me. Now the waiting began.

That congregation was a trusting bunch. They didn't send anyone to check on the clowns until about three O'clock. Four men with the traditional AK-47 assault rifles approached from the river trail. That meant that they saw all the footprints. They came on in a comical version of stealth. They obviously had no military training. When they heard the mandatory line, "Freeze! Drop your weapons!" coming from two directions, they complied without a fight.

My son knew the drill. Grab the weapons and bind them with their own bootlaces. Big Travis and my son Travis hog tied them and wrestled them into the cabin. I'll bet that the next bunch wouldn't take as long to arrive.

I was right. At 4:45, six more men came from the river more cautiously. We held our breaths until all six were in the little clearing. After I shouted the mandatory, "Freeze!" the six newcomers started shooting at the tree fort. Thank God that Tiny had built it to withstand just such an assault. I couldn't even raise my head at first. The four men at the cabin opened up enabling me to rise up and contribute some lead when the six men turned to face this new danger. There were no survivors among them. We took their bootlaces and dragged their bodies into the cabin.

I sent my son up the tree to man the radio and keep watch. I figured that the sight of six bodies would loosen the tongues of our four prisoners. I wanted to be at the interrogation to read body language and voice inflection.

The four live ones all knew my face from television. They also knew that my personal body count was astronomical. They had no real reason to expect mercy, so I thought the questioning would be easy. Well, not one of them would say shit even if he had a mouthful. Nobody dropped the dime. So I told my silent captives that I would be leaving them alone with the door open. The smell of blood was bound to attract all sorts of wild animals that they knew were out there including bear, feral hogs, and cougar.

Even that threat didn't work. They sure as hell were afraid of someone even more than the thought of having hogs gnaw on them while they were alive. That made me mad. There was still someone out there scarier than me.

I climbed up by my son and called for an extraction of six cold ones and four live ones. I also requested six men to man our position in our absence. It was time for us to go hunting. The dog would help now.

I hated the thought of taking my son with, but he'd already proven himself and we needed the firepower. I told the chopper pilots that we were going to walk up the river towards the church. I requested every bit of backup that could be spared to meet us at the church. I told them that the helicopter landing lights would be needed if the operation went beyond sundown. "Have the backup on the road to the church ASAP. Listen for my radio message before storming in."

Now began one of those long marches where a man's imagination is his worst enemy. I was sure that the remainder of the congregation was not expecting trouble to come to them. It was a small church. I had already killed the preacher and his three best men. This afternoon we had accounted for twelve more. They had to be running low on manpower soon.

The idea of someone so intimidating to keep our prisoners silent was cause for concern. He was a flesh and blood man so my fearless crew and I would deal with him as we'd dealt with everything and everybody that tried to kill us. At least I wasn't bored anymore.

I found the church easily enough. That jerk of a preacher had left a good trail with his Jeep. The building was built with three blind sides. The windows were so high up as to be useless to look out. They were just a light source.

We rushed from the trees to the back of the building. I left the radio with Barry, who stayed with Ed and my son at the rear of the building. There was still the possibility of someone in the rectory trying to make an escape.

Big Travis and I were going to John Wayne the front door as soon as I radioed for the backup to move in. This was the big moment, maybe our last moment left alive. First I had Ed and Barry make a human ladder so I could look in the rear windows. It was a good thing that I did. All the pews had been used to construct a barricade, which was manned by four men, armed with assault rifles, all pointing at the front door. These men were in black robes like you'd expect a priest to wear. It looked a little out of place in a supposedly Baptist congregation.

Behind the four men was what I first thought was a large statue of Satan. It was the traditional characterization with the massive horns and the goat's legs and feet. The statue was seven and a half feet tall and as big around as a three hundred-year old oak tree. It would have taken two men to get their arms around this statue.

When the statue sat down, I fell off the human ladder. There was no way that what I saw was possible, but I did see it. I convinced my friends and my son that what I saw was real. I said that it must be a very large human in a very convincing disguise. They all took turns peering at the abomination and they all came away shaken. None of us were certain if it was a disguise or the real thing.

I radioed the approaching police army about the four armed men and the giant mutant or thespian or whatever it was. "The riflemen aren't in a surrender mode. If your bullhorn demands of surrender aren't complied with, destroy the church," I told them.

My group moved to a safer distance that still allowed us to watch for escape attempts from the rear. The backup could see us now. I thought it rather unusual that the church didn't have a back door, which made me suspect a hidden or underground entrance.

There was an impressive show of force out front, surely more than enough to make five men want to surrender. The man on the bullhorn was

Lieutenant Washington. "Throw out your weapons and come out with your hands up, all five of you!"

We watched the miraculous surrender of the four would be priests, but the ogre didn't go out. Another demand from the bullhorn brought no results. That had the human ladder in place once again as I peered over the windowsill. The place was empty. The ogre was nowhere in sight. My group went to the front of the church. I radioed the men at the smokehouse to watch for a nightmarish figure to show up at their location. My group entered the church to look for the exit that must be there. I walked cautiously around the barricade to where the monster was seen last. There was an outline in the floor that suggested an opening of some kind. We could find no means to open it, but when all of us stood upon it, the piece of floor began to descend. Naturally we hopped off immediately. I went and collected enough five cell torches for all of us.

The FBI agent in charge wanted to know the details of my hurried plan. When I described the missing fifth occupant to him and told him about the weight-activated elevator, he was as excited as we were.

The four prisoners were brought into the church with their hoods off. All had shaven heads and pale, cadaverous appearances. Their surrender only bought time for their master to escape. I asked the agent to send reinforcements to the smokehouse, where I was sure that the ogre would show up. I also told him to check out the parsonage while my group explored the elevator.

"You'll have to let me come with you on your subterranean hunting trip," he said.

Naturally I complied. So after the two aforementioned bases were covered, it was time for the six of us to get on the elevator to hell. We tested the weight activation level. It took four of us totaling approximately eight hundred pounds to make it work. That ogre was one big dude.

With the six of us on the elevator platform facing outward, our rifles at the ready, we had all torches on and the dog in the middle. The elevator descended about twenty feet to the bottom. Down here there were controls for the elevator. There were three tunnel entrances to choose from. Here is when Spike earned his money. He alerted in the entrance that appeared to lead towards the meat locker cabin.

If we entered this passage in a group, we would be easy targets with our torches lit. One man with an automatic rifle could wipe us out. I suggested that we pretend to choose one of the other passages, then proceed along the dog's choice in the dark. No one offered a better plan, so that was what we did. With the dog on his leash, I went first, Big Travis second, followed by Little Travis, the agent, Ed, and Barry.

Our eyes never adjusted. There was absolutely no light. The dog must have had his nose to the ground. We stayed linked by placing a hand on the shoulder of the next man in front. We did our best to be quiet, but our rapid breathing and pounding hearts seemed extraordinarily loud.

The luminous dial on my watch showed that we'd been walking at a snails pace for fifteen minutes. If the smokehouse were the destination, it wouldn't be long now.

Finally the dog froze causing a chain reaction along our ranks. I turned to gather the group in a face to face whispered meeting. I told them to lie down along the left wall head to foot, still maintaining contact by holding the man's foot to the front. Once we were in position to make the smallest target possible, I raised my flashlight above and away from me at arm's length. Then I turned it on. Ten feet in front of me was another platform like the elevator at the church. Like the other, this one had controls. Now what? I said that we should send it up empty to check our reception.

As it started to ascend, I hopped on before any of the others could stop me. It did come up in the smokehouse, which was empty, thank God. I wasn't heavy enough to activate the elevator but my angry friends retrieved it using the controls below. Soon they were all with me.

I had forgotten to bring the radio, so we were liable to be shot by a dozen of our own men. This was not a problem. The FBI agent used his belt radio to try to contact the friendlies, who were supposed to be right outside the door. We couldn't raise anyone so we pushed the door open and called, "Police," but there was no response.

I slipped out the door followed by Big Travis. The ditch that we had dug had a few M-16's in it but no people. They must have fled when the ogre had made his grand entrance from the seemingly empty cabin. It was almost dark now and we had panicked friendlies in the woods. Most were still armed and frightened enough to shoot at noise. I borrowed the belt radio and called for a chopper at the smokehouse. We tried to raise any member of the security force that might have ears on. Finally we heard a voice over the air.

"We have an armed friendly element at the cabin. Bring in your men ASAP." Soon, six men came straggling like they were shell shocked. We rebuilt the perimeter around the cabin, leaving the doorway open, but guarded.

When the chopper appeared overhead, I radioed them to use their PA system to round up our men. Eventually, all were accounted for. They all asked the same question, "What came out of the empty cabin?"

I said, "Gentlemen, I'm not too sure myself, but it must be a creature of this earth since it is subject to all the same laws of gravity and locomotion that we are. Did anyone try to shoot it?"

No one responded in the affirmative. The general consensus was that each man believed that they were looking upon Satan and everyone fled.

I told them, "Satan wouldn't need armed guards and an elevator. We will treat this creature as one more suspect and give it the chance to surrender if it approaches. Kill it if it becomes violent. My team and dog will track it before its lead becomes too great. Keep your radio on and your wits about you. This creature *can* be killed."

With that last statement still ringing in the air, I let Spike cast about until he looked like he was on the right trail. Even on the relatively hard ground, the cloven hoof prints were visible. As darkness descended, the forest became as frightening as the tunnel. No sir, boredom was no longer a problem. The creature, man or beast or some combination seemed to be headed to the mansion on the highway. The agent called his men to have a welcoming party choppered in at the estate as we were driving the suspect in that direction.

With the dog for early warning and the belief that our quarry was unarmed, I let the dog go and we trotted after him trying to overtake our prey before it reached highway 105 and the possibility of gaining wheeled escape. This was our chance to nab the beast that all the nightmares emanated from.

...

The dog was trotting along rapidly. We were doing the airborne shuffle to keep up with it. In the gloom ahead I could make out a moving object that resembled a large, horned bear. It too was running, but it was obvious that we would overtake it. I could smell the thing now. It reminded me of a hot day at the zoo. The smell was akin to large, sweaty beast. It reminded me of a horse that had been ridden too hard.

I couldn't help but feel that this was just another bad man that we were closing in on. Worse perhaps than any criminal that we'd brought to justice so far, but still a human that experienced childhood and maybe knew childish fears once upon a time. What could drive a person to such depths of behavior? People dabble in deviltry. Many of them don't believe in the existence of Satan. Then the devil heaps them with earthly rewards and they never realize where their luck comes from. Luck comes from Lucifer. Everlasting life comes from the Lord. Earthly rewards are a poor trade for eternal life in heaven. It's a fool's choice to follow the wrong path.

The fool in front of me was running out of time. We were on the cart trail near the ruins when the ogre finally quit running. His time was up. We formed a semi-circle facing him. The sight of six automatic rifles backed by six determined faces told the impostor that he was at the end of his journey.

"So you're the famous Derrick?" he said in a surprisingly gentle voice, almost hypnotic. "Do you feel like David in his battle with Goliath? Or perhaps you're an agnostic or atheist who could be tempted with gold? There is still plenty of gold."

My speech began, "You have the right to remain silent..." This seemed to infuriate the bully and he made as if to attack. Everyone held their ground and weapons could be heard coming off safeties. This united front took the wind out of his sails in a hurry. He gave up on his effort to intimidate us. I read him the remainder of his rights and he shut up like a clam. He relieved us all by removing his skillfully constructed helmet. We watched him closely as he unbuckled his fancy leggings in case he had any hidden weapons. He was still a monster of a man, but much easier to look upon with his convincing costume off. Handcuffs would never fit him. We were forced to transport him unrestrained.

I radioed in the news and requested a flat bottomed boat with three armed guards and nylon rope to bind the prisoner. We marched down to the creek, which was barely deep enough for boat traffic this time of year.

When the boat arrived, the agent gave me his belt radio and joined the boat crew. They took the helmet and leggings along as well.

The five of us walked back to the meat locker. All the guards had been extracted when news of the capture filled the airwaves. They had left our backpacks so we at least had food and coffee. There was no pressure to hurry back, even though I felt a nagging desire to explore the tunnels further. I radioed the church to confirm the safety of the PRC-77. It had been recovered. It turned out that we had enough canteen water to avoid a trip to the river in the dark.

We built a fire and enjoyed a good visit. This was the first time that my son and Big Travis ever met. Big Travis had nothing but praise for his namesake. He thought that my son was at least eighteen since he handled himself so well.

After we had eaten and cleaned up our small mess, we decided to take the tunnel back. We planned on sending Spike back with whoever was left at the church. We decided to pick up one of our vehicles and operate out of the church, which seemed to be the hub of this particular wheel. Tomorrow would bring many answers.

. . .

We crashed at the motel for convenience. Breakfast at the Kettle then back to the church. We were armed to the teeth, hopefully for nothing, and we each had a five-cell flashlight. A search of the church turned up nothing new. Back on the elevator, we used the same outward facing formation for 360-degree security. When we reached bottom, we used the tunnel leading in the direction of the parsonage.

Ed and I walked abreast, my son Travis next with Barry and big Travis in the rear. It was only about five hundred feet to Quinn's former home. This tunnel ended in stairs. I reflected that these cedar-lined tunnels must have taken years to build. The deep-seated evil that we were systematically rooting out probably began before I was born in 1948. If the dates on the tombstones were legitimate, this evil was brewing since before the turn of the 20$^{th}$ century.

I started up the stairs to listen at the door. When thirty seconds passed without my hearing a sound, I motioned the others up. The door had no handle. It was a traditional pocket door that slid sideways. Pressing my palms against the door, I moved it easily aside. We entered the room and spread out to search every room and closet. Big Travis boosted my son up to search the attic crawl space.

I heard my son say, "Holy cow!" Then money started pouring through the trap door. Bundles of cash. It had to be counterfeit. There were twenty's, fifty's, and hundred's. Travis kept throwing the stuff down like a pecuniary blizzard. About ten minutes went by before he finally stopped. He dropped down and we took a closer look at the currency. It looked real to all of us. We were faced with a moral dilemma of epic proportions. We had to turn it in, period. The question was; "Where did it come from?" If it was stolen bank funds, there might be a reward. I didn't know what a million dollars looked like but I had a feeling that this was a lot more.

You could have heard a pin drop when I made that radio call, the one that left us in relative poverty, while higher authorities decided the fate of our newly found fortune. Maybe no one would claim it for a year in which case, we could split it.

First I wanted to count it, then have someone sign for it. We spent over thirty minutes with all of us tallying and we came up with a total of just over three and a half million dollars. That meant seven hundred thousand plus for each of us.

We put it in pillowcases and loaded the stuff in Barry' trunk. The mood was pensive on the way to the bank. I would have to check into the law on the waiting period this afternoon. We deposited it into an account with all of our names on it.

It was an excited ride back to the church where we still had a job to do. We re-entered the parsonage and exited the sliding door to the tunnel. Back to the labyrinth of darkness where our torch- light was an intruder. Before we left the stairwell, we examined the woodwork thoroughly looking for other possible secrets. Finding none, we retraced our steps to the elevator and the three-way junction. The third tunnel went due west, and our flashlight beams were lost in the distance.

We assumed the same traveling formation with my son in the middle. Thank God that there were no forks or side tunnels. Little Travis was our pace counter. At 2,030 paces, I called a halt.

"We've come about one mile now and our lights are still lost in the distance. Just in case the mile mark has some significance, lets do some exploring here."

Now we had all five torches on and the psychological lift was welcome. I was fighting claustrophobia and just barely winning the battle. We were busy at our task. I was checking the low ceiling as the others checked the walls and floor. The floor was dirt throughout the tunnel system. The walls and ceiling were cedar. It was like a fancy mine shaft. I wondered to myself if that was how the tunnels started, just some mining operation that had been abandoned and later improved upon.

"Kill the lights quickly," whispered Barry who had wandered the farthest west. The sudden and total blackness was frightening. Now Barry whispered, "I distinctly heard a noise from this direction."

We all stood there in the dark trying to hear what Barry heard. It sounded like another elevator. We watched in the distance as Lights descended to ground level and started moving in our direction. We had company and all the myriad questions that went with it. Were we outnumbered? Outgunned? Surprise could make up for either of these problems.

I whispered a plan to my men. By sitting shoulder to shoulder, the five of us started digging a fighting trench by scraping with our heels. We had to work fast to finish before our sounds would reach the approaching group.

Soon we had a deep enough trench to afford protection. We slid quietly in and waited. The strangers were coming at a leisurely pace as if they weren't expecting trouble. They must have been players who weren't aware of yesterday's arrests. We allowed them to come dangerously close before halting them.

"Drop your weapons and proceed with your hands above your heads. No sudden moves if you want to live," I ordered.

Now we turned on our superior torches to see just what we had. It was four more bald headed monks in those stupid robes.

Ed and Barry frisked them while my son and I covered them. Big Travis walked several meters past them for security. For armament, the monks had pistols and mace. Thank God they hadn't sprayed that stuff in the confines of the tunnel. They claimed that the mace was for the wild animals that sometimes found their way into the tunnel.

After we bound their hands with bootlaces, we made them walk ahead of us. When we reached the elevator, Big Travis and I borrowed a couple of robes and rode up with two of the monks.

It was a good thing that we did it that way. There was a limousine parked topside with two more monks and a big ugly driver leaning against the side of it. They sure looked disappointed when Travis and I produced M-16's from beneath our robes and pointed them their way. Travis disarmed them and we made them lay face down, spread eagle and motionless. The car was empty. We bound their hands with their shoelaces.

This lift was set in motion with the weight of two men. Once we had it going, Travis hopped off to guard our newest prisoners. I went below to retrieve everyone.

Soon, all of us were above ground. I called for a paddy wagon to pick up our guests and a tow truck for the limo. When the elevator was up, it was practically invisible. If a man didn't know where to look, he would pass it a million times and never guess what it was.

Since Walker Archer sold this land to Preacher Quinn, how could he not know about these tunnels? The parsonage and church were fairly new, but the tunnels were ancient. I felt certain that he was unaware. At least I hoped so. He and David were my best friends in town.

The paddy wagon arrived and we retrieved our bootlaces in exchange for handcuffs. With the trash picked up and gone, we searched the limo before the tow truck arrived. There was a .44 magnum in the glove box and a trunk full of AK-47's. We called in that information and went back down the elevator.

That particular elevator platform was only marked with two boulders. One of which could have been used in a pinch to help activate the elevator by rolling it onto the stage. Why hadn't the monks driven up to the church? They were certainly headed that way. Their car had been parked out of sight of both Frazier Street and the parsonage. Were these monks part of a renegade faction? Were their sights set on the cash in the attic, or maybe the gold alluded to by the ogre? They weren't wearing packs. Maybe they planned on using pillowcases as we had. Their driver was waiting so they didn't plan on a long stay.

We continued west along the tunnel in our same formation. My son paced off another mile and we started another search of the area. Barry moved forward for security. It had been his keen ears that warned us last time.

I had a hunch that the elevators were a mile apart. The pace count could have been off because my son was in the middle where his stride might be hampered. We moved forward with our search and finally spotted the next elevator. There was no reason to exit, so we just started a new pace count with Big and Little Travis up front. That way, my son could step off a yard at a time. Concentration was not a problem since we were being as deathly quiet as our surroundings.

At the end of the third mile, we came upon another elevator, which we boarded. It came up near Frazier Street as I expected. We were still on the eastern side of Frazier, just inside the woods. We descended and continued our search of the seemingly endless tunnels. I never would have dreamed that the tunnel would go west of Frazier. Was there another house or church at I-45 North? I wondered aloud why they hadn't used the electric carts like between the smokehouse and the mansion. No one ventured an answer.

I vowed that at the next elevator or stairs, we would use the radio to send for lunch. After the next mile, the flashlights illuminated another set of stairs. That should mean a house. We climbed the stairs as quietly as possible, expecting the worse. I had my ear to the door for what seemed like ten minutes without detecting a sound. I finally mustered the courage to slide the door aside. We entered a large walk-in closet. Walking to the closet door, I put my ear to the door again. Nothing stirred. It was unnaturally quiet. The chauffeur and monks had been arrested, that meant that they were allowed one call. It was possible that one of them had called this very house. We could be in an empty house or a deadly trap. Opening that next door would tell all.

. . .

In Vietnam, this is where they put the scout dog on a leash and the point man moves up. We didn't have a dog, so that should speed things up. That door looked like a booby trap or an ambush waiting to happen. It could have an explosive device or just an electric doorknob. There might be a dozen men with automatic rifles pointed at it. The devil himself could lie in wait. That's the fun of being on point. The mystery of not knowing which step would be your last.

The first thing that I did was gather all the clothes from the closet and pile them in front of the door. Now we went back to the stairs and descended until mine was the only head still sticking up. Now I hurled a shoe at the doorknob. The explosion sent all those ties and sport coats flying back at us. The force of the blast is up and out. We were pretty safe where we were.

The monks who stormed the door after I triggered the blast weren't as safe in their standing positions as Ed and I let go with everything that an M-16 is famous for. The closet floor was choked with bodies as we were up and running to mop up while we still had momentum. Ed and I covered the right side of the house while Barry and Big Travis covered the left. My son ran up the middle and through the front door where I heard him yell, "Freeze!"

We wound up with eight dead monks and my son had a driver at gunpoint out front. He got the shoelace treatment while we waited for an ambulance and a couple of patrol cars. So they evidently were waiting for us. I had to mention the fact that at least some of the prisoners were using their phone calls to make our lives miserable. There must be some legal way to control where their initial phone calls were made.

This modest home was at the end of a long driveway just east of Interstate 45. There was nothing distinguishing about it except for the limo and it was parked out of sight from the highway.

The good news was that this was the end of the tunnel. We had covered all three completely, if somewhat hurriedly as far as their destinations. Now the FBI could come down with dope and explosive sniffing dogs and metal detectors to tear the walls apart. The ogre dressed as Satan spoke of more gold.

We bummed a ride back to the parsonage so we had our own vehicle at our disposal. I asked the rest of the group if they wanted to look for the gold after we had lunch. Everyone liked that idea, especially the lunch part.

This whole operation had blossomed out of the simple desire to look for secrets at the smokehouse. I wanted the entire length of the tunnel, the mansion, the meat locker, the church, the parsonage, and the house at I-45 searched and destroyed. Then I would ask the state to supply a special task force of forest rangers to aggressively patrol the entire route. We would wrestle control of our national forest from the unwholesome element that had ruled it for so long.

First, lunch at The Kettle, then back into what might indeed be a gold mine. We all fit in Barry's car for the trip into town. There wasn't much conversation. We had all spilled a lot of blood recently. It was like a never-ending nightmare. I was wondering if I wanted to go on being this county's executioner. I couldn't say within ten people either way just how many I had killed. Once again, I had to look at the caliber of people that I was killing and all the innocent lives I was saving. If not me, then who? It was like Big Travis said a long time ago. If I quit, a lesser man might step up and give criminals the upper hand again. Too much ruminating is bad for digestion.

Barry was driving like we all felt. The car could have been on automatic pilot for all the effort he was putting in. We were all in our own little worlds, reflecting on the past few days, years. For the older members of this group, the job of killer was assumed over twenty years ago. I was sorry that my son, even though wise for his years, was thrust into such a heavy role at only sixteen years old.

Lunch was more cheerful with the jukebox going and the waitresses flirting and cracking jokes. The people around us sensed that we didn't want to discuss the recent events surrounding the church and tunnel. Hell, for all we knew, it wasn't over yet. Besides that, the newspapers and TV would display all the gore in graphic color.

We turned lunch into a two-hour affair. Our spirits were buoyed sufficiently to tackle another trip to the tunnels. We would have to warn the FBI of our presence. The tunnels might be too crowded for safety, in which case, we could go to the Gulf on this sunny day. We radioed ahead to the group that was at the scene of the last killings. They said that the dog teams weren't due until tomorrow. They had men at every location except the smokehouse. I said that we'd enter there and radio as soon as we'd gained access.

I was having second thoughts about sharing the tunnels with other armed men. An accident could easily occur. What if there were hidden rooms in the walls? It would be easy to get us shooting at each other. I voiced my thoughts to the car in general and we unanimously agreed that it was too real of a danger. I radioed the FBI again to tell them that there would be no additional friendlies in the catacombs. We were going fishing in the Gulf. Once again, our spirits lifted.

...

We hadn't even gotten as far as Highway FM-1960 before the belt radio started crackling. I had Barry pull over and I turned up the volume. There was some sort of blood bath going on in the catacombs. Every available unit was ordered to respond and report to the church parking lot.

Barry got back on the freeway looking for a turnaround. I had a premonition about hidden rooms and too many friendlies spread out at once. We picked up Spike from the kennel and sped towards the church.

I assumed command when I arrived since the FBI seemed disorganized and leaderless. They had several men wounded or dead below. Someone had started shooting from the direction of the house on I-45 and the group at the church had returned fire. The fire that they were receiving was so intense that they fled to the parsonage and went up the stairs.

"Here's the plan," I said, "Unless our men try to contact us, we are to assume the worst. I want every one of the six exits covered from outside. No one is to enter the catacombs unless called to do so. The password is 'Airmobile'. You may call backup as needed to insure six men minimum at every entrance. When Lieutenant Washington arrives, he will assume command above ground unless the FBI sends a higher ranking agent."

Then I told my son over his protests to take Barry's car to our house and see to the safety of the family. I reminded him that the smokehouse was little more than a mile from our home. I told him to call 911 if any strangers showed up.

"Now, gentlemen, we four and the dog will catch a ride to the house on I-45 and enter the tunnel system there. We need body armor and silencers for the M-16's and the .357's plus extra ammunition for both weapons. We will need first aid kits and extra bandages. Have your chopper drop our gear at the far house and start by covering the exit by the meat locker first. The paired boulders on the dirt road to the church mark two more exits to be guarded. Remember the password. It will be dark here soon. If we should use any of the exits for any reason, we will be very vocal with the password. We may have to evacuate wounded. Pray for us and keep your eyes and ears open in case there are more than six exits." Those were the orders that I issued at the church.

We drove to the small house on I-45 and I sent my son Travis on his way. The chopper was there moments later with the gear and extra ammunition. It was time to enter. I couldn't imagine doing this with anyone else. Hell, I *wouldn't* do it with anyone else. We were entering in total darkness and relying on the dog. Flashlights were to be lit only in extreme emergency. This was a lights out mission.

We entered the house as quiet as fog. I was in front with Travis close behind, then Ed and Barry on drag. I radioed the six-man team outside to enter quietly and observe extreme light and noise discipline. I pointed out that they could be shot through the floor with an AK-47. That should keep them quiet. I made my way through the shredded pile of clothes that I'd used to cushion the blast earlier. The sliding door was still open. Making my way downstairs reminded me of a dozen horror movies. None of them had happy endings.

There was a little light coming from the open door. We were all on the tunnel floor waiting for our eyes to adjust to our immediate surroundings. All too soon, it would be pitch black. There was a body near by. The man was in a suit. One of ours? We crept closer to investigate. The man had a pulse as well as ID marking him as FBI. We plugged his worst wound and Travis took him up the stairs in a fireman's carry. I called the team upstairs to watch for our man and to send for a silent ambulance.

When Travis rejoined us, we crept forward on our hands and knees, shoulder to shoulder with the dogs tail in our faces. Soon it was pitch black and I had to leash the dog. I figured that we'd know when he alerted because the leash would go slack. I decided that we could take the chance of walking erect now. As long as we walked abreast, we wouldn't get separated. Shortly, I heard a noise like bees far off. I stopped for a whispered meeting.

"I think I hear muffled voices. I doubt if it's our men. They are probably in a room off to one side or the other. We should be able to determine that easily enough when we get closer," I said.

Ten yards or so later, the dog alerted. The sound was indeed voices, which were clearer now. We crept up to a door faintly outlined with dim light. It looked like it opened inward. The voices inside were harsh. It sounded like they were interrogating one of our men. It also sounded like they were abusing their prisoner. Time for another whispered meeting.

I whispered, "Choose your targets, we may have at least one friendly in there. Make all your shots head shots in case they have armor too."

Travis and I crashed the door stepping to the sides. We popped four robed monks in the blinding light. The man being questioned had been beaten badly, but he could still walk. Ed was walking around with his silenced pistol putting an extra round in each monk's head. We couldn't afford to have them making any noise behind us. Barry had pulled the door closed behind us. The monk's prisoner had FBI identification on him. We burdened him with every gun in the room except for ours. Then we killed the light and held a quiet meeting in the dark.

The dog wasn't as effective as I had hoped. I decided to send him back with the agent. I radioed the house to expect another agent. I told our friend the password and pointed him in the right direction when we re-entered the black corridor. The dog could lead him easily enough and would lend the poor man some measure of comfort.

We resumed our seemingly endless mission in the haunted blackness, shoulder to shoulder once again. We stumbled onto the platform of the first elevator. I radioed up that we were passing beneath. "The tunnel is secure to this point," I advised.

Walking in total blackness is not as easy as it sounds. Depth perception is hampered. The two men on the outside would alternately bump the tunnel walls. The effect was more like staggering than walking. This time, Ed picked up the 'bees' first. As we drew nearer, the conversation behind this new door grew clearer. The unseen men were bragging about their victory and what they would do to me and my big, tough, Vietnam Veteran friends.

There was no indication of any friendlies inside, still we had to be careful. This time, Barry and Edwin crashed the door and sidestepped. After the shooting stopped, there were six dead monks and no good guys present other than us. Travis applied the coup de grace to each monk with his pistol. We killed the lights and held a whispered meeting. We needed to know how many more agents and uniforms might be down here. Our job would be easier if we didn't have to worry about accidentally greasing a good guy. I radioed up top and got the welcome news that all were now accounted for. The other casualties must have evacuated under their own power before we returned.

Back to the long, dark road. Sooner than I expected, we stumbled onto the platform of the second elevator. "All secure to exit three," I radioed up.

As we drew nearer to the church, it got steadily brighter. That could work against us. I didn't want to be silhouetted and become a target of opportunity for some atheist in a robe. We halted and sat along one wall for another meeting. I called the church and asked them to raise the elevator if it was safe, or at least to turn off the lights. I remembered that the controls were at the bottom. As soon as it got black again, we proceeded as before.

When we got beneath the church elevator, we had a problem. The main tunnel went on, but there was also the short tunnel to the parsonage. Rather than splitting my group up, I requested the agents to open the sliding door and put a lamp on the stairs. Meanwhile, we all laid down to make the smallest target possible. We had our rifles trained in the direction of the stairs to the parsonage.

Before the agents even put out the lamp, we saw the ambush waiting in the short tunnel. The group of monks had hoped to catch us in the light of the church elevator. There were about a dozen men lying in wait. They had no cover and made easy targets when the lamp was put on the stairs. The opening of the sliding door distracted them too, which made it easier for us. When the last body stopped jerking, I ran up for the head shots.

I called the agents in the parsonage to come and clear the tunnel. The agents were dumbfounded at the carnage. The stairs and tunnel were littered with dead. "Airmobile," I said. I left my friends long enough to get more ammunition.

Upon my return I said, "The tunnel is secure to this point. Leave a skeleton crew at the exits and push the surplus men to the smokehouse. We will take a ten-minute break here while you implement that strategy. Let me get past the bodies, then lights out again."

I found my men in the semi dark of the stairway light. They were still safely in the entrance of the short tunnel. I dispersed the ammunition. Empty magazines were left behind. This was the last leg. It could be a cakewalk or the end of the road. We all knew this and we eagerly took up our marathon swim in an ocean of adrenaline.

This was what we all lived for. Not a ski jump or a roller coaster, no kid games, just man against the monsters from the ID. That inner dimension that magnifies your worst fears until you feel like you are about to be swallowed by the whale of fear in your mind as you go forth confidently. Yea though I walk…Sound corny? You just had to be there.

Fear builds to a plateau that few men can walk upon. All four of us camped on that plateau many times while lesser men wept and hid. We strode about that plateau as warriors doing warrior's work and living to do it again and again. This was our plateau. Anyone who dared tread upon it would die like the rest.

...

This last mile was measured in inches. We were walking at a cautious pace, concentrating on staying abreast. The sounds of our breathing seemed loud. I had a bad thought that I pushed from my mind. "What about booby traps?" The answer to that question lay in the fact that the enemy had to travel these same corridors. They wouldn't take the chance of killing their own people.

I had another unpleasant thought. It was of running into an enemy patrol in the dark. That ditch that we had scraped with our heels had been filled in. The monks may have learned from this tactic. We could only hope that it was the FBI that had filled it in. I hated the thought of training my enemy. This thought was eating me so badly that I called a halt.

We sat down and leaned against the tunnel wall. I whispered my fears of ambush and the possibility of our tactic being stolen and used against us. We decided to scrape a new trench and have the FBI illuminate the meat locker end of the tunnel. We should be able to see any ambush if we were within a quarter mile. I wished aloud that we'd been keeping a pace count. Barry said that we'd traveled just over eleven hundred meters. Bless his heart for foresight. I said that we'd scrape the trench in another four hundred fifty meters, then have the tunnel illuminated. If there were indeed an ambush waiting, we'd have the advantage. Even if they had superior numbers, our cover in the trench would make up for that aspect.

So, four hundred and fifty paces later, we sat gouging at the floor with our heels. We had an eighteen inch deep trench with another twelve inches of loose dirt in front that we quietly began packing down. Our little fighting position gave us a small measure of confidence, hence some relief from the stress. We had two men tight to each side with the center open. It was time to call for the light.

When the tunnel light came on, I felt like General Custer. There at the end of the tunnel was a group of about twenty monks in the chamber to accommodate the elevator. The light really threw them into confusion. Some were firing up through the floor of the elevator. Most were ineffectually expending their ammo in our direction.

We were a lot closer than I anticipated. Aiming was no problem. We wiped out all in the center, but the chamber gave some cover at the sides. We did our best to skip and ricochet bullets but the dirt floor and the soft cedar walls absorbed most of them. I called our men upstairs to concentrate their fire along the sides of the elevator floor. Grasping the problem immediately, they sent down so much lead that we got our first surrenders of the day. Two men stood in the light with their hands raised. We radioed a cease-fire. Then we leapt to our feet and stormed the last hundred meters.

The two with their hands up were the only two still moving and even they were both wounded. I got on the horn again and told them that all was secure down here. I watched the two shocked prisoners while my friends dragged the bodies free of the elevator.

"Airmobile is sending up the elevator," I told the men upstairs as I rode up with the prisoners. I went back down to send the rest of the bodies up. It took three more loads to get the rest of the dead out of there. We got on the last lift and I warned the FBI that there were twenty-two more bodies down there to be extracted tomorrow.

"Make that ten bodies. We already got the twelve from the stairwell at the parsonage," said their headman.

I advised, "Leave all night guards at every exit so no more men can get down there and cause another incident like today. The search has to be completed tomorrow so this place can be destroyed.

Time for supper at the Kettle and a call to Margaret that we were all okay. Then maybe we could finish that fishing trip to the Gulf.

...

We spent the night at the motel on the feeder at Gladstell Street and I-45. Breakfast at the Kettle and then off to Galveston.

Fishing in the Gulf this time of year was like going to a lingerie show and trying to play poker. There was just too much scenery to concentrate. We had to give up on that idea just to stay out of trouble. My son had no one to be faithful to, so naturally he didn't want to leave. The rest of us were too jealous to let him stay.

I knew a place on the Brazos River where the snakes and alligators were too thick for bathing beauties to venture. We fished a while and wound up catching alligator gar for the most part. We still had our squid bait and the gar loved it.

Blotched Water Snakes were breeding on the banks and White Egrets were doing some fishing of their own. I kept waiting for an alligator to grab an egret but our presence must have made them wary.

I got bored with fishing and started catching snakes. That didn't last long. Those water snakes will make you a bloody mess if you don't use gloves.

I spoke up, "Do you all realize that once the tunnel is searched and blown up, it will be the end of an era? We'll just be aging heroes with nothing to do."

Big Travis said, "Don't underestimate human nature. There's still plenty of creeps out there who will find your quiet town appealing. They'll organize some vice or cult and we'll have to bail your butt out again. You owe us plenty for the cost of tissues for wiping your nose so often."

"I didn't call you this last time, you just happened along. If it wasn't for me being the brains of the outfit, all y'all would be pushing up daisies and bluebonnets," was my quick response.

Barry said, "We need to take apart that ruins where the snuff films were made. That would be a logical place to find clues. It might even turn up the gold that the ogre spoke of. We could take some beer and sandwiches and waste the rest of the day there."

So, that was the plan. We would stop at the 7-11 for some party fixin's and go party. If the cart was still at the mansion, we could drive to the ruins. In a pinch, Barry' car would fit between the trees.

I felt guilty about being this close to the house and not stopping in, but the girls and Ryan could be anywhere on a sunny day. Besides, Margaret knew that I was always scarce when my friends were here.

With our spirits high, we rode out to the mansion on 105. There was a modest crew of FBI taking the walls apart. They wanted to be sure that nothing was overlooked before razing the joint.

We informed them about our plans at the ruins. They said that the cart had been too shot up to be usable. We drove around to the back and cut across the yard to the cart track. The Camarro had no problem fitting between the trees. This sure beat the hell out of walking. We walked so much on the first operation that it was like being in the army again.

The ruins were easily found from memory. We started with the sandwiches while our hands were still clean. Beer made the job seem like fun. We had to remember to watch for scorpions and black widows. We literally tore the ruins apart for nothing except the satisfaction that one more evil place no longer existed.

We built a fire and talked about forming a national task force to root out evil. Not just 'beer talk,' but a serious commitment to eradicating the type of evil that we'd run into out here. The telltale signs were clear. There would be frequent missing person reports, especially infants, women and children.

We kept the fire burning until midnight. I was starting to get a bad feeling about being out here. I had a pistol and Big Travis had one. Other than that, we had no real weaponry. We had dropped the heavy artillery at the police arms room.

We put out the fire and walked to the Camarro, then sat in the dark car for a while, talking. The woods didn't grow any less spooky as time went by. Prudence dictated that we return to civilization at the mansion. The drive back was creepy. I had grown used to having my M-16 with me when I was out here. I gave my son my .38 special to hold until we were back. Pistols don't stack up too well against AK-47's. Those weapons were as abundant as mosquitoes out here.

I expected that the wrecking crew at the mansion would be long gone when we got back, but the lights were still on and we could hear pounding. I decided to visit the G-men who were literally burning the midnight oil.

As we drove across the back yard with our lights on, the pounding stopped and the lights went out. We drove around front in time to see a Bronco or Blazer speed away. Barry said that we were on empty, so we couldn't give chase. We went inside and flipped on the lights. Our three friends from the FBI were nailed to the wall, upside down with their wrists slashed. It was already too late to save them. There was a message written on the wall in blood. It read, "Give up. We outnumber you!"

Personally, I thought that this was the work of the last of a dying breed. Unfortunately, it was the good guys who did the dying this time.

How could they be caught so unaware? It was a sad message that I radioed to all stations. I requested an evidence team and body armor and M-16's for all of us so we could spend the night. Then I woke Margaret and told her to take the kids to some brightly-lit motel and stay until further notice. "Drop Sinbad at the police kennel. We'll pick him up in the morning."

It looked like this international bunch of heathens had chosen our back yard to make their stand. We had no way to be certain how many of these pagan savages were left to make our lives miserable.

...

We got our weaponry, body armor, a PRC-77 Radio, and even some sleeping bags that we didn't expect. We also got a small refrigerator, a microwave, some instant coffee, and some microwave-able food. Besides all this, they sent out Spike and another three man wrecking crew to continue the work that had been interrupted.

My only request above what we had already gotten was that they bring out Sinbad as soon as he showed up at the kennel. The FBI was very grateful for the fact that we saved two of their men earlier even if we couldn't save the three tonight. The general consensus was that the three had let down their guard, thinking that they were wrapping up a closed operation. We, on the other hand saw it as what it was, a never ending battle of good against evil.

With that thought in mind, the FBI circulated the radio message that all parties to this investigation were to treat it as an ongoing and very dangerous mission. The new man in charge was a man named Schultz who had an excellent memory of the success of any mission under my leadership. This was the first time that I felt that the FBI was in tune to the music that I'd been hearing since the first snuff films made in our back yard showed up.

The small bit of good news was that the three slain agents were dead of gunshot wounds prior to being nailed up and bled.

I decided to send my young son to stay at the motel with the rest of the family. I wanted to spare him further nightmares.

We eventually settled into two, two man positions, one at each end of the house, each with a dog. We slept with the windows open so the dogs, and we, could be most effective. No pulling of guard was necessary with the dogs and our natural radar constantly on. The FBI wrecking crew was as well armed as we were and mercifully went to sleep when we did.

That night passed without further event. Barry borrowed the FBI car to fetch a five-gallon can of gas. When he returned, he took the Camarro out to fill it up.

We set up this morning's guard positions in the shrubbery at each side of the driveway. We were invisible unless we stood up. Travis and I had Sinbad on the western side. Barry and Ed had Spike on the east. We had the PRC 77 radio, and Barry had the belt radio.

This could be a very boring job or a very dangerous one. I tended to think that the bad guys were spread too thinly in the area to mount an attack in force. The men in the Bronco had just caught our men napping last night and took advantage of the situation.

This was turning out to be a working vacation for all of us. At least we weren't nailed to the wall with our blood running out. Now I pondered a question that just occurred to me. Maybe the G-men weren't caught napping. Maybe they knew their visitors and didn't see the danger. The Bronco was reminiscent of last year's blood bath and the gathering of all the mercenaries. Still, that make of vehicle was for sale to anyone and were, in fact quite popular. Travis and I discussed this possibility, then called across the driveway to plant the same thought in their heads.

The vehicle type was not the question, familiarity was. Were they expected, like a pizza delivery? That happened after midnight. Who would still be open and deliver that late? I radioed Lieutenant Washington to put someone on that question and call back with the results.

Now to think beyond that possibility in case no one was delivering that late. Let's suppose that the three-man crew found something worth reporting and did so. This created two possibilities. #1 that there was a bad apple at FBI dispatch and #2 that someone was monitoring their transmission and their find required immediate attention.

If the latter were true, someone at FBI dispatch would know what that find was. This was getting complicated. I thought it was time to call the new local bureau chief to arrange a personal meeting. All of his men and my little band of four should appear as pins on a map. Without revealing my location, I could request his presence. After all, he had to be wringing his hands in anguish at the recent deaths of his three men.

I got on frequency and made my request, which was granted. The new man must have cared about his losses. Then the mansion's front door opened and Schultz stepped out and stretched. He looked around awhile like he was admiring the beautiful day. Then he strolled up the drive as if to check the mail. When there were no cars going by, he pushed through the shrubs and sat down.

"You wanted to see me?" he asked. "They had me take over the day the last chief was found out."

"Congratulations! I should have expected it. It was only natural," I said. After handshakes, we got down to business. Schultz was taking notes.

As if on cue, my dispatch called with the message that no deliveries were requested or sent to this address. I explained what that last transmission meant to Schultz. He did say that an undisclosed find had been radioed in and that it would be brought in when their replacements arrived in the morning.

I said, "This means that once again, someone on your side is working for the enemy, or there was a colossal coincidence. Can you find out if there were any calls made from any of your men in the area during the hour before midnight?"

"That's a tough one, but I'll work on it myself." Schultz waited until there were no cars going by, then he slipped in the house.

With him gone, I realized that my position had been compromised. There were two houses across the street. Neither one was close by, but both were in sight. "Was Schultz cool? Could I afford to trust him?" I decided that my life and those of my friends were too valuable to take chances. I called vocally across the drive to Barry and Ed to head to the house ASAP.

We no sooner exited our positions than several B-40 rockets exploded where Travis and I were just sitting. We stormed the house and forced the FBI team face down on the floor. We disarmed them and cuffed them with their own cuffs. I called for police backup.

"If I'm wrongfully mistreating anyone here, let me apologize in advance. Until I'm sure that there is no connection between any of you and the rocket attack, you shall remain our prisoners," I said.

We left Edwin and Spike with the PRC-77 to guard the agents while the rest of us took Sinbad and stormed the house where the B-40 attack had been launched from. Travis flattened the front door as Barry and I crashed through the windows on either side. Sinbad was right with me as we made our way through the house and out the open back door. We could see several men running in the distance with the rocket launchers on their shoulders.

We had to drop them before they got in among the trees. We fell to the prone position simultaneously and started cutting them down. None of them escaped our fusillade. We sprinted across the field hoping to save at least one life to answer questions. We arrived at the bodies in about thirty seconds. All were dead or beyond saving. We had put out an awful lot of lead to prevent their escape.

One was conscious and Barry was trying to save him. I knelt next to the dying man and asked, "Who pulls your strings? You are dying. He can't hurt you any more. Telling us may help save your soul, but you'd better accept Jesus right now."

His face went through a metamorphosis as he paused quietly before speaking. This lost soul looked almost human again. I hope that meant that he took my advice about Jesus. The dying man's words implicated a wealthy preacher in Huntsville. When asked about Schultz, he said that Schultz was on our side. They were supposed to kill Schultz that night after they had located and killed my men and me. We were considered the more immediate threat. The preacher only wanted Schultz dead to prove that his power was greater than either the police or the FBI.

The sirens on 105 told us to hurry back. I radioed Ed to free Schultz and his men with all speed before the uniforms saw them with cuffs on. Then I got on frequency with my men and told them to stand down until I joined them from across the street.

We reached a very orderly group of police who were facing the house in a semi-defensive mode. I felt sure that had we seen them just prior to my last transmission, they would have been in a more formidable stance.

I told Steve to call a meat wagon and supervise the removal of six bodies that would be about a hundred and twenty-five yards behind the house across the street. Then I dismissed the rest of the patrolmen to their regular duties. I asked Al to stick with Steve and join us at the mansion when the bodies were removed.

When I was done apologizing, I explained why I had behaved as I did. Agent Schultz claimed to understand completely. He said that he would have assumed the same thing and behaved similarly himself were he in my position. He went so far as to say that he was embarrassed not to have checked the security in those two houses already.

With that thought in mind, I volunteered to ring the doorbell on the other house personally. Another unanswered question was; "What happened to the residents of the house that the rockets were fired from?" Last year, there was a family living there. We moved them temporarily for safety. Surely they would have moved back.

Neither Schultz nor I knew the status of the families from either house. He said that checking the other house was more of a task than four men could handle. I told him that Al and Steve would be with us as soon as the ambulance across the street left.

When the ambulance left, the six of us approached the house stealthily and I literally rang the doorbell. It turned out to be a loud one. I should have suspected a booby trap. It was a small blast, meant for one man. The body armor helped, but I hit the sidewalk pretty hard with my head, plus I had a face full of glass and wood.

I could still walk, and I did, right through the newly opened door as the others crashed through the windows. We filled that empty house within seconds of the blast. The place appeared deserted at first pass. We started a methodical search. I pulled down the stairs to the attic and found the bodies up there.

This was sad. They didn't appear to be dead more than twenty-four hours. They died hard. The parent's arms were cut off and the children showed signs of being brutally molested. It gave me an idea of what to expect in the first house.

The family car was in the drive, and the Bronco was in the garage. "No one touch the Bronco! It may have a bigger bomb than the front door. Call the bomb squad before anyone goes near either vehicle," I warned my friends.

We left Steve and Al at this house to greet and warn the bomb squad. The rest of us took the dogs to the first house and as before, the bodies were found in the attic. It was an elderly couple. They had been beaten to death.

I really felt no mercy for people who could kill other innocent people like we witnessed at these houses. I no longer thought of our foes as human. They were simply *things* to be killed as quickly and efficiently as possible. We didn't know yet if the six dead things with the rocket launchers were the end of our problems, or the beginning of a new wave. The dying man indicated a preacher in Huntsville as our new symbol of evil.

We needed to find out if all the people from the two houses were accounted for. God forbid if there were any children missing. Schultz, Walker, and I needed to put our heads together.

...

We had a hot lead to follow in Huntsville from the dying man with the rocket launcher. The news of today's events couldn't be released to the public until we had a chance to act on that lead. We had to leave a smoke screen at the mansion and raid the preacher's home and church with sufficient forces to induce mass surrender, rather than produce mass slaughter. We had more than our share of the latter lately.

My plan was to walk into the church in civilian clothes, then have the National Guard show up as soon as I had the preacher in custody, or at least at gun point. I figured for the six of us to enter with concealed revolvers and just grab the head man. We could only hope that no children were present. To make this work, we had to act immediately.

Schultz wanted to be in the church with us. I wondered if we could use the monk's robes for camouflage. If so, we could smuggle in our M-16's. We would have to observe the church for a while to determine the location of our primary target.

It was Schultz' excellent idea to fly over first in the helicopter, taking me along to observe the personnel and activity. We discovered that monks in limousines were common sights there. The limousines seemed to be generic from any available company. The bulk of the activity centered at the church.

Our best guess was that the preacher could be found at the hub of the most activity. Getting robes to match and a limousine would be a snap. Our end of the operation should be executed about the time the National Guard was ready to move in.

The chopper took us to the back yard of the mansion, which was to be the staging area for our part in the charade. Robes were donned and weapons concealed. The limo' drove around back and the seven of us crowded in. We went west on 105 to north on Frazier, rejoining I-45 north of town. We were about five minutes ahead of the National Guard which should work out fine.

We concocted a hasty but feasible plan as Schultz picked glass and wood out of my face. Schultz was going to contain the preacher with the rest of us surrounding them in a natural perimeter.

The National Guard would be coming up the driveway in trucks and inserting behind the church and parsonage via helicopter. If this compound used tunnels, we would flood them with riot gas. I thanked The Lord that there was no damage to my eyes as Schultz continued to remove shrapnel.

The FBI chopper was flying below the guard helicopters. They were our eyes as to the status of the situation. They were reporting a static condition. The parsonage had no traffic while the church looked like an anthill.

Meanwhile, back at the mansion, the bomb squad found plates for counterfeiting but no bomb. That was probably the discovery that the agents died for last night. I was surprised that they were left behind.

The big dance was about to start. Our limo' was turning into the driveway of the church in Huntsville. We drove right up to the front door and hurried inside. It looked like the man we wanted was directing traffic from the stage. The bustle was concerning two large stacks of money. The monks would put money in one pile and load from the other, presumably counterfeit pile. The preacher worried over his money like a mother hen. He was so engrossed that he paid us no attention until we were on the stage with him.

Schultz had knocked the preacher's feet out and had him cuffed in the blink of an eye. I fired a three round burst into the ceiling and yelled, "Nobody move!" That got everyone's attention. The sight of seven automatic weapons kept everyone motionless but us. We could hear the military trucks in the driveway and explained the new noise to our captive audience.

To our relief, twelve soldiers came through the door to assist with the securing of our throng of prisoners. I stayed on stage with Schultz while my larger friends took off their robes and moved among the crowd collecting weapons. The Guardsmen had plenty of disposable nylon wrist cuffs to go around.

There was a surprising amount of weapons in such a docile crowd. We must have taken out most of their heavy hitters in earlier operations. Once all the prisoners were rounded up, Schultz went outside to run things while we searched the church. Carefully, we looked for hidden rooms and tunnel entrances. When this search turned up fruitless, we wrapped the money on stage into our discarded robes and took it outside by Agent Schultz.

Next we searched the parsonage. We found a false wall in a closet revealing a set of stairs going down to a library type room. The shelves were full of bundled money and videos. We put everything in pillowcases and took it outside. This had been one hell of a day for the FBI and us.

. . .

The least charge that any of the prisoners would face was distribution of counterfeit money. When the videos could be matched with faces, other charges would follow aided by the inevitable squealers now that the headmen were rounded up or dead.

Now it was time for INTERPOL to go to work. We had killed or arrested nearly everything that walks, crawls, or flies. It was time to use our leads and go after offenders hiding on foreign soil. If we had missed anyone locally, chances were that their faces would show up on the new batch of videos.

We had hopefully dried up the source of bogus money, at least for the time being. I was looking forward to a time when murder was non-existent or at least a rarity instead of the local pass time. This was a totally different breed of people than I was accustomed to. They ranked right up there with the most awful of the awful. The vast number of participants was appalling. It was bad enough knowing that anyone was capable of committing such crimes, but to think of the army we faced was sobering to say the least. Here was truly a fine argument for getting prayer back in our schools.

Huntsville and Walker County had their own very capable police forces. It was time for us to bow out and leave the FBI to do what they did best. We could return to our town knowing that it was a safer place. We could also notify the holders of any bogus money that there were now funds to buy the counterfeit stuff back. We could also hold a brief news conference to explain all the shooting and explosions.

. . .

We bummed a chopper ride back from the National Guard. They dropped us at the mansion where we could squeeze in Barry's car. It was time that my family heard from me. The dogs needed some down time too. I'd keep Spike at the house overnight. He could run around the fenced yard with Sinbad.

I told Margaret and crew to meet us at the Kettle for chow and some ZZ Top on the jukebox. We dropped the dogs off and fed them. Then we took turns in the shower and put on clean clothes. I felt like a new man even if my face looked a little used. Steve and Al bought out their families and we pretended that we weren't cops for a while.

My son got over his disappointment at being left out as soon as the waitresses started flirting with him. I wanted him to be a soldier or a cop or both. That didn't mean that his nightmares had to start at sixteen if it wasn't already too late.

Mayor Walker had a home in April Sound with a nice beach. It was nearby and private. Walker was only too happy to let us use his backyard as a retreat. He said that we shouldn't go home before he got there at five. He said that at suppertime, pizza was on him. Family time had been scarce lately. It should be easier to come by after today. Shame on me for being bored when my neighbors were living in peace. I had other, more productive ways to fight boredom.

One thing that I could afford to do at my house was put in a swimming pool. That was something that all of us could enjoy. I could also turn the underground chamber in the former cemetery into a movie theater. There were other little jobs that I could do to entertain the family as a group.

We needed a screen house and plenty of bat houses and martin houses to keep the mosquitoes under control. There was room for Horseshoes, Bacci Ball and Croquet. We could also play Volleyball and Badminton. The more that I thought about all these domestic activities, the more I realized how much I would miss the excitement of dangerous missions. I liked Volleyball, but sticking my head in the lion's mouth was what I did best.

So, for now, I would build all my pseudo entertainment, and maybe even enjoy most of it. But until the dragon once again entered my now peaceful town, I would be a knight awaiting assignment.

. . . . . . .

. . . . .

. . .

. .

.

Five years had passed since they had blown up the long tunnel that ran from the house on I-45 to the smokehouse. All the buildings associated with the infernal goings on had been burned with the exception of the house on I-45 and two houses on 105 across from the mansion. All three had been repaired and eventually sold.

Rebecca had married her boyfriend. I helped them finance the building of a house on one of the lots by my gate. They had a little one on the way.

Ryan was in first grade and had a new girlfriend every day. For a while, he was going to marry the teacher until he was told that she was already married. That broke his heart for nearly one full day. Then it was on to the next girl.

Travis was 21 and in the army. He wanted to be Infantry like his dad. I guess that I didn't complain enough about the downside of being a grunt. He summed it up pretty much the way I had felt about it all those years ago. He said, "A soldier is either Infantry or just someone who wished they were." The Infantry builds character, and like Policemen, they keep people safe.

Annie, at 17, was a handful. She was a good girl, but every boy that met her seemed to fall in love. Boys were literally fighting over her but she hadn't found a special one yet. (Thank God!) Margaret and I still got along like newly weds. Annie was a big help around the house whenever she was home. Margaret wasn't too strict, but she didn't have to be. Annie knew the rules and had no problems obeying them.

Now we get to me, the Chief of Police, still the head of SWAT. We had our own six-man team. As I expected, we got the last three men through the VFW. They were all Desert Storm infantry veterans, good men, dependable and easy-going. They got along well with Al and Steve. As a matter of fact, it was those two who introduced me to Eddie, Joey, and Stack. Stack volunteered for sniper duty if the need arose. We were all awaiting that next dragon in need of slaying to arrive.

...

The dragon finally came under the guise of a men's club, strictly private, membership by invitation only. It started as a small affair. Neither Walker nor I or any of my men were asked to join. I just figured that it had to do with money. None of us were paupers, but none of us were wealthy either. It was quite by accident that I discovered that money or social status had little to do with membership. We stopped a couple of speeders that were under the influence. The patrolmen brought them in because the speeders were uncooperative and unruly, and then resisted arrest.

Neither man was local, yet both claimed membership to the men's club. That must have been some club for members to come from as far away as La Porte. These two piqued my curiosity. I wondered where this club advertised or from where it solicited its members. These men weren't lightweights. Both were sturdy enough to be cops and both had violent priors, one for aggravated battery and the other for felonious assault. They made bail and left our town with a court date.

I didn't make a big deal out of their membership only because I didn't want to set off any alarms. What I did do was mimeograph all the information from their cards hoping to get a man inside. Eddie and his friends didn't know anyone at the VFW who belonged. It was so exclusive that after a week of discreet questions, we could find no one locally who belonged.

The police had never been called to the club. Either they had no trouble, or they took care of it themselves. At any rate, the two men from La Porte were the only two people I knew who had been inside. Private clubs were allowed and they were handed a list of rules along with their charter. We left them alone unless some hint of criminal activity connected with them found it's way to police ears.

Since only strangers were members, our information pool was empty, limited to the likes of the two speeders who resisted arrest. Their doormen would discourage anyone from crashing the party. Those two looked like defensive linemen. On my side was the fact that as a lawman, they couldn't deny me entry.

After a week of prying with no success, I decided to walk right in the front door and look around. The parking lot was packed. Some of the plates were from Louisiana, Florida, and Arkansas. The doormen reluctantly allowed me to pass. The bar was practically deserted. There were seventy or so cars in the lot, but only five people at the bar. Five carbon copies of the bums awaiting a court date.

My badge may have been a rattlesnake around my neck. The bar accounted for only about ten percent of the building's space. The rest was behind several closed doors that ran along two walls of the club. I asked the bartender slash Godzilla what was behind the closed doors.

He got right in my face and said that that was a question that had to have a search warrant attached. That's when I told him to get the hell out of my face unless he liked the smell of pepper spray. He was determined to make something of it. He said that if I sprayed that sissy juice on him that he'd rip my face off. That's when I vaulted on top of the bar hoping that some vague law would make my action legal. Threatening or intimidating a peace officer rang a bell.

Before I dropped to the floor next to Godzilla, I kicked him in the face so hard that it split the stitching on my boot. His head hit and broke the mirror and bounced back and hit the bar. He may have been dead. At least he was easy to cuff in his current condition.

The five bums at the bar were amazed to speechlessness. How could the midget with the badge take out their hero with only one kick?

I said, "You men are needed as witnesses whether or not you saw anything. Don't try to leave." I called for every available unit in case the other ninety-percent of the customers should all come out at once. When the backup started coming in, I called an ambulance for Godzilla, hoping that he was still alive. I kicked him harder than I wanted to, but he made me mad.

I assigned two men to get names and addresses of the five patrons and get their statements before releasing them. I also told them to check for warrants and priors on the five.

I knocked on the nearest door. I wouldn't have bothered but it was locked. No one answered, but I heard a scream on the other side. That was my probable cause. I crashed the flimsy door to find a dark room with only the stage illuminated. There were a dozen men seated, their eyes riveted to the stage where a man was in the act of strangling a young Spanish girl who was impaled on his phallus. Shades of Rasputin! It was a snuff movie in progress.

I flipped on the light and yelled, "Freeze!" before leaping on the stage and putting my pistol to the actor's head. "Let her down gently, then get dressed." I left the arrests to the officers who followed me in.

I radioed the street crew to arrest the doormen and to have someone watch the back door. "No one here is to escape arrest. Hold everyone on complicity and accessory to attempted murder charges."

We went down the line breaking down doors as uniforms flooded the place. Unfortunately, we were too late to save three of the victims. Every closed door produced spectators and a film crew except for one, which was used for a prison for the girls. Most of them were Spanish, but no nationality was ignored. When they were questioned, the English speaking ones said that some of them made other kinds of movies. They only killed the girls who had been beaten so badly as to deteriorate their beauty.

The five men at the bar were still in custody in light of our findings. Now, to unravel this whole bestial affair. This club had been open for months. The number of bodies must be astronomical. This sad and gruesome investigation would continue.

...

I had to leave the men's club open. It had to look like business as usual for us to nab other patrons who we might have missed the night of the raid. We put two large cops in civilian attire at the front door to carry on the charade.

*Anyone* showing up with a membership card would be arrested as soon as they entered the building.

We searched the seventy-odd cars for weapons and contraband. We towed half to the police pound and left the rest as decoys. We even had a man inside to answer the telephone. This should be easy. It would produce overtime for some of our officers too.

That damned bartender died. He turned out to be the owner. Thank God that I had friends in high places because my five witnesses gave me a bad report card. One had even claimed that I shot the guy. That obvious lie actually helped my case. Their credibility as witnesses was lost when their mugs each showed up in various snuff movies. Tough guys they were not, liars, yes.

We found their body dump in a forest preserve pond. We dredged almost forty bodies, all female, some pre-teen according to the coroner. Their favorite subjects were illegal aliens who didn't have a paper trail. I planned on charging each of our prisoners with every murder. That was bound to loosen some tongues.

On weeknights, we averaged nine arrests per night. On weekends, it was more like thirty per night. We finally closed up shop when we failed to have a single member show up one weekend. We finally found the clubs method for recruiting membership. Besides the usual word of mouth among peers, there was a short ad in a mercenary magazine. The ad suggested that a man needn't travel abroad to satisfy his base hungers. We got that information from one of the doormen. He was singing like a lark. Both of the doormen passed polygraphs on their lack of involvement with the behavior behind the closed doors. They claimed to be hired muscle only. They claimed that the occasional screams that filtered to the street were assumed to be from movies shown inside. They didn't know that any movies were being made at the club.

We decided to open a club of our own at a more remote location. We already knew how to make it real in appearance. We had experienced girls willing to help us out with the sham. It would be a sting to bring the roaches out of the cracks. If we only caught one man, it would be one less. Since these activities were federal crimes, we brought Schultz in on it.

He was more than happy to participate. He was also insistent on taking over as the highest- ranking Federal Agent in the area. I had no problem since the new club was out in the county and not in the middle of my town anymore. Those snuff people made me sick. I'd let Schultz deal with them while my men and I tended to town business. I told him that SWAT would be at his disposal if necessary.

Once again I found myself shaking my head at the amount of evil drawn to the metropolitan area. It's not like any police force in the area was easy on, or tolerated crime. The exact opposite was true. We earned our reputation of gun and Bible toting rednecks and I was proud to be a member of this group.

...

It was nice to be eating dinner at home with the family again. My oldest son was due for a thirty-day leave before his overseas duty assignment. We were expecting him from Fort Polk this weekend. He took basic and advanced Infantry training there, just like his dad. I hadn't been able to talk him out of the infantry. That was a bull that he was determined to ride. He wanted to go to jump school and be a Paratrooper. That was a step that I never took. They shipped me to the 101st in Vietnam because that was where they needed live ones to replace the dead ones. Combat jumps were out anyway. Everything was helicopter insertion or rappelling from the same. So, Travis was going to go one up on his dad, good for him.

...

Travis used a charter bus to get home, calling me from the bus station after supper. Annie and I went to pick him up in my white van. He was full of a lot of familiar sounding stories. It sounded like he made all the same mistakes that his old man did, visiting all the off limits places in Leesville, Lousiana. The main thing was that he looked and acted like a man beyond his years. He had a personal body count before entering the service. That was something that many career soldiers never get. He said that this fact gave him some celebrity. His reputation had followed him. His familiarity with the M-16 helped too. He was already a private first class or E-3.

He had banked most of his pay to use for a down payment on a car. He wanted me to take him to my friend, the Chevy dealer. He was after a recent model van of his own with low mileage. The black van that he wound up with was a conversion van with a sun-roof and a tape deck. The tinted windows gave a small measure of privacy. He looked happy with his find and the price was right. Six months of payments and it was his. He wasn't going to drive it to Fort Benning, in case he was sent overseas right after jump school. I suggested that he go to non-commissioned officers school. He had brains and leadership qualities. He said that he'd already made up his mind to go there. That's my boy!

Travis and I discussed the possible duty stations where he might be sent. I told him that the DMZ in Korea was always a hot spot. "Bosnia may be in the news, but you're almost as likely to see action in Korea. I certainly hope that you don't put Korea on your dream sheet."

"Too late Pop, you've just confirmed what I've been hearing all along. I already volunteered for Korea after NCO school," he said.

Now I knew how my folks felt when I got orders for Vietnam. I didn't remind him, but it was probably already too late. I expected him to walk point as I had. The thought made me feel old and tired. He must have been reading my mind as he said that he would walk point at every available opportunity. He told me not to worry. The Lord would see him safely home as He had with me.

That is when I tried to explain PTSD to him in words that he could understand. "Killing is only one of the ingredients of that psychological disorder. The worst part is the constant threat of close combat, maybe even hand to hand. You will be facing older, more experienced men who feel that they are defending their home and will therefore be motivated to fight harder. To make matters worse, you will be serving with untested young men who may not even be able to shoot at another man. You could be with a platoon and discover that only a half dozen men can actually perform under fire. Let's say that you lived through your first gunfight and you knew that seventy-five per cent of your men were useless when the chips were down. Now that you have this knowledge, how do you face the rest of your tour with any confidence in your survival?"

I couldn't discourage him. He said, "The same way that you did Pop. I'll just pray a lot and hope that my family is doing the same."

Tell me that he wasn't a chip off the old block. Like he said, his family had a lot of praying and worrying to do. I didn't want to make him over-confident, but I already felt that he could handle whatever he had to. He had so far. He stood up under fire five years ago and he had vanquished his foes.

It seemed like his thirty-day leave was over in the wink of an eye. Now the worrying began. I drove him to the bus station while keeping a stiff upper lip. He still had a lot of training to do before he went overseas. I like excitement, but I'm glad that my army days were over. I was speaking firsthand about the constant dread of close combat and men who couldn't be depended upon.

. . .

Schultz borrowed the other five members of SWAT to play the part of customers in his bogus club. The town's police could handle everything short of a riot, and in that event, the County and State Police plus the National Guard were only a phone call away. It was summer vacation again and the biggest problem that we had to deal with so far was teen drinking and driving. Kids will be kids, so we stepped up patrols. I wanted the town's teens to have their fun safely.

They had a favorite place to drink that they didn't think I knew about. It was the dump by the old bridge on the south side of the West Fork of the San Jacinto River. That was the same dump that the biker gang first became acquainted with the new cop in town. Since then, it had been avoided for a long time, but after nearly seven years, the blood and reputation had all but washed away.

The kids felt pretty safe in their secret place, but from my experience, secret places were usually the most dangerous. Those were the places on the fringes of civilization which were magnets for the stuff that bad dreams are made of. The bogeymen that everyone hoped weren't real eventually surfaced at the secret places. Those girls that had willingly gone out there with the bikers were fixin' to meet the bogeyman and didn't even know it.

The dump had become a popular place once again. That meant that the meat-eaters in society would smell the prey and move in like sharks. It was during the second week of summer vacation that disaster struck hard. Beer makes people pee, that's no secret. The woods provide the privacy to relieve ones needs. They also provide cover for the bogeyman.

Two girls walked away from the group of twenty-some teens who were all drinking beer and having a good time. They left with the purpose of relieving themselves. They weren't missed until nearly dark when the party was breaking up. The woods were searched by all until it was too dark to see, but the two were never found. At least they weren't found on that evening.

A person was supposed to be missing for forty-eight hours to be listed as officially missing. When I got the anonymous call that night from a concerned friend(s) and the third and fourth call from frightened parents,

I threw the forty-eight hour rule out the window. I knew from experience that the colder trails were harder to follow than fresh ones.

I took Sinbad along with my M-16 and a five-cell flashlight out to the secret place and went out into the woods where my anonymous caller saw them last. I let Sinbad roam at will and just watched him cast about. He finally picked up on a scent that made his fur bristle and he trotted off west to a bend in the river where I could see tracks in the mud heading into the water. It was too dark to see much at all, but the tracks were of a booted man with bigger boots than my military size tens.

I took a chance with the snakes and alligators and gar and my fear of water. I knew that Sinbad would follow me if I went into the water. I walked up to my armpits and the current was pushing me along. Then I swam as far as I could and felt for the bottom with my feet. I stood up in about four feet of water with a diminished current. Sinbad was right with me but he looked tired. I caught his collar and pulled him to shallow water so he could walk. He wasn't a pup anymore by any stretch of imagination.

He and I walked up and down the shore until we found the footprints that made him bristle again. I hoped that his keen eyes and nose could get the job done since I couldn't see much and didn't want to flash the light unless necessary. I was able to see crushed vegetation and an occasional boot print, but Sinbad walked on confidently.

It must have been well past midnight when we ran out of trail. We had reached a mud and rock wall that our quarry must have climbed. It looked like a job for a ladder or at least a rope. Since I had neither, we walked west along the base looking for an easier place to climb. I finally found a rain gully that was deep and rough enough for us to make it to the top. The Lord was with us and we didn't run into any snakes.

When we reached the top, we walked east until Sinbad picked up the trail again. It kept going uphill towards a thicket that looked as black as the water. My dog was bristling again. We must be nearing whoever made the tracks. We were very near the embankment for the Southwest Loop 336. Whatever we sought was in the thicket in front of us.

Sinbad was reluctant to go in there. That made it my job. With the flashlight in my left hand and my right hand on the pistol grip of the M-16, I crept forward into the blackness. There was a man made trail leading into the heart of the thicket. A man had to crawl in here, but the knife or machete marks were visible anywhere a bush blocked progress. Give me an M-16 any day over a machete.

I found the two girls wet and bound with strips of their own clothes. They were gagged, but very much alive. I put my finger to my lips in the classic gesture for silence. I removed their gags and bindings and asked in a whisper where their captor went. The older looking girl said that he went to hide the ladder and was coming right back.

He must have seen us coming and taken his ladder elsewhere, like to the 'Loop" embankment to thumb a ride or escape on foot. The girls didn't want to be left alone and we still had a hard trip back. The kidnapper had escaped for the time being.

The girls stayed close to me as we made our way to the erosion gully and back to the river. The girls knew a better place to cross for which Sinbad and I were grateful beyond words. They sure were glad to see a badge and a gun. We got back to the van and I radioed dispatch to call the parents to put their minds at ease. The girls were real troopers and seemed intelligent. They also seemed sober, which surprised me. I was sure that they could provide enough information to bring this animal down. Tonight they could go home to worried parents. Tomorrow I would get their stories.

...

Most cops would have called it a night. That's what set me apart from most cops. I dropped the girls at home and went back to the Loop 336 just north of the thicket. I hid the van on the north side of the highway, crossed to the south side and began looking for the ladder that I expected to find. The ladder was lying down, that might mean that my man was back in the thicket. Sinbad and I clambered down the steep embankment as quietly as we could.

We approached the thicket from the blind side and quietly walked around to the open end. My dog took the lead and dashed into the thicket. I was hoping that he would flush my man and I could wrap this up tonight. Sinbad came out as quickly as he went in. Now I went in looking for clues. My flashlight didn't expose anything new. I would have to search better in the daytime.

We walked back to the river and looked around. When we got back to the embankment, the ladder was back up. Somehow the kidnapper had given us the slip. We scrambled up the ladder and crossed the loop to the van more than a little discouraged. I had this guy pegged as homeless and living in the surrounding woods. I may have scared him enough to make him leave the area, in which case he might never be captured. I had to track him tonight.

I took Sinbad back to the ladder and had him sniff it, then I said, "Go get him!" He surprised me by scrambling back down the steep slope and trotting towards the woods on the south side of the loop. I was able to keep up his pace while he was using his nose. When he actually spotted his prey, he would take off running. Then I wouldn't be able to keep up, nor could his prey escape.

It finally happened, Sinbad broke into a dead run and I took off after him. I heard the man screaming as Sinbad did what he did best, fight. I hollered at Sinbad to halt, which means, "Quit trying to kill whatever is in your teeth at the moment."

When I got there, he had a large man face down with his hands over his head trying to protect his head and neck. I cuffed the guy and pulled him to his feet. He was going to need an ambulance. My belt radio was wrecked in the river so we walked to the van to make the call. After I called the ambulance, I called for a uniform to meet the ambulance at the hospital. I left Sinbad in my van and rode to the hospital with the prisoner. I read him his rights and he kept his mouth shut. Maybe it was all the bandages that made it hard to talk.

They stitched and dressed his wounds. Then we carted him off to jail. I got a ride back to my van. Finally, I could go home. Forty-eight hours my rear end! Go after the hot trail, period.

...

In the morning, I called the homes of the two girls who had been kidnapped. It would be no problem for them to come down and identify the prisoner.

When all the concerned parties were at the station, I had the prisoner put in the mirror room. The girls both agreed that it could be the man, but he was wearing a mask last night. One of the girls said that she scratched the man's arm when they were first grabbed. I had the officer behind the mirror inspect the man for scratches and he had none.

I asked to see the fingernails of the girl who scratched her assailant. They were damaged as if she had indeed scratched someone. I had fingernail scrapings taken for a DNA check before letting the families go. I entered the mirror room to see the man's arms for myself. He didn't appear to be scratched. I felt sure that I had my man, but I couldn't hold him without evidence.

I told him that he would be released as speedily as possible. This was the time for an innocent man to be indignant and file charges for false arrest and injuries from the dog attack. This man expressed no such wishes. He just appeared greatly relieved that he was being released.

I felt like I was making a mistake when I watched him walk out the door. About a half of an hour later, the lab called to say that the scrapings were from latex rubber disposable gloves. Now it was time to visit the site, and hopefully catch my man walking out of town. I put out an all points on the newly released prisoner and drove out to last night's crime scene. I parked well off the shoulder.

Crossing the road, I looked for the familiar wooden ladder. It was missing. Sinbad and I scrambled and slid down the steep embankment to approach the thicket. I had brought along a cloth bag for collection of evidence as well as a box of zip lock plastic bags. The dog and I combed the area between the embankment and the thicket, ensuring that it was empty before circling to check the east- side for clues or evidence. I found the gloves on that side complete with the scratched holes in them. I entered the thicket looking for anything that might help connect my recently released prisoner with the crime.

I bagged up all the bindings from the girls' clothing and I also found the huge knife that was used to hack the little den in the center of the thicket. I also found empty wrappers from all manner of junk food.

After completing my search of the den, I went to the little bluff and there I found the ladder. I chose to use the erosion gully to facilitate the dog's descent and to look for clues there too. I couldn't picture the bound girls climbing the ladder, yet the criminal used it religiously, even moving it from place to place. There were no new discoveries at the gully. I walked over to the base of the ladder. The tracks there were fresh and easily read in the daylight. My man must have thumbed a ride to have beaten me here. Why hadn't he taken the time to pick up the knife and gloves at least? There must have been something even more important that he had to retrieve to have risked returning to the scene of the crime, yet leave such damning evidence.

I followed his trail towards the woods where I caught him last night. Sinbad trotted ahead like he knew what was expected of him. This patch of forest was of considerable size. We were on a regular trail now, not just crashing brush.

That hollow in the thicket must have been just a way station. This well trodden trail probably led to his headquarters. I halted Sinbad when I saw the outline of a shack only thirty yards distant. We left the trail and circled south to approach from a blind side. I dropped to a crouching walk with Sinbad now at my heel. The place buzzed with conversation so the man with the mask wasn't alone.

When I called it a shack, I meant that it was a 'shack'. If the trees didn't block the wind, it would have blown over. I was able to creep up to the rear wall and look through a split board. The man who I had freed only this morning was talking to four girls who were literally a captive audience. They were all bound and gagged. He was trying to justify why he had to kill them. "You've all seen my face too much. It would mean the death penalty for me if I let you live," he said.

The girls all looked dirty and underfed as if he'd had them for a while. He started to strangle the closest one to him. I was around front and inside before even the dog knew I was gone. A hammer blow from my fist to the back of his neck brought him crumpling down over his intended victim. That blow either killed or paralyzed the tough guy. The girls' eyes all lit with hope when they saw the badge.

I checked him for a pulse but it was too late. I must have damaged his spinal cord. I had to be more careful of my temper. The girls' testimony would bail me out. I untied them and removed their gags. I asked if they would be able to walk once their circulation returned. They all agreed that it would be a pleasure to walk out of there.

I would have to carry the tough guy. He was the only one who couldn't walk. I had to put the bum over my shoulder and carry him out of the woods, at least to the gully where he could be found. When we got to the mud and rock wall, I still had enough energy to carry him up the ladder. That was as far as I felt like carrying him. I dragged the ladder up to make it easier to negotiate the embankment by the loop. We crossed over and got in the van and drove to the station.

None of the girls were from town. They were canoeing on the river and stopped for a picnic when the masked man came out of nowhere brandishing a huge knife. He talked of selling them to some men's club to make movies. It looked like I had struck gold. They were all hungry and thirsty, so I cruised through a drive in diner on the way to the station. Some parents would be celebrating tonight.

I sent an ambulance back to pick up the body. I asked the girls to sign written statements to justify the accidental death of their captor. They were more than happy to take the extra time.

Now I had to set up a sting at the thicket to capture the buyers unless Schultz wanted to run that too.

...

Schultz did as I hoped and took over the second sting after I briefed him. I hoped that he didn't feel affronted. He always came in late and stayed after to clean up. I realized that not even the FBI could be everywhere at once. The first two girls weren't due for the missing persons' list until tonight. The other four were in danger of dying even before the masked man decided to speed it up.

I always got more work done by moving around and snooping. If Schultz liked the waiting game, good for him, someone had to do it. Me? I was a man of action. Right now I was spending that action being a father and a husband. Tomorrow it was back to being Police Chief in Conroe. Tonight, hopefully, there wouldn't be any phone calls that the regular staff couldn't handle.

This night was a night to sit on the screened porch and watch twinkling fireflies wondering if they were the spirits of all the infants sacrificed and tossed into the weeds like trash discarded by some careless litterbug. It was a night to contemplate all the evil men that my friends, my son, and I had killed. Were they in Limbo or already in Hell? It was a night to rejoice all the lives that I had saved directly or inadvertently.

I had the feeling that my life was granted to be Satan's worst nightmare. That feeling started long before I became a cop in Conroe. I taught my children that the devil doesn't care if you believe or not as long as you do his work. I told them that they either put bricks in the house of the Lord or in the house of the devil.

On this quiet night, we sat together in the screen house wondering how Travis was doing, and if Rebecca and her new husband were getting along. Ryan idolized his brother and two sisters. They were so much older that it was like having three moms and two dads. It was a diverse learning opportunity for any child. Soon Annie would be going to visit her mom in West Memphis, Arkansas. She would be back here one week before school started. She would be a senior in the fall. It wouldn't be long before she would be making adult decisions of her own.

It was getting to be bedtime for all of us. Sinbad would scratch at the door when he wanted in. Tucking in Ryan was always a time to wrestle. Annie was content with a hug. Margaret and I were still newly weds. Morning always came too soon.

. . .

The phone woke me at four AM next morning. Only wrong numbers and bad news come at four AM. I snapped to full alert as I snatched the phone from its cradle. Night dispatch called to inform me that a body had been dumped in front of the station just moments ago. It had been pushed out the back of a dark, older model van. She wasn't able get a license number. I asked if any of our prowl cars were on the way. She said that a squad was just pulling up now. I told her that I'd be there in twenty minutes or less.

The coroner was already there when I arrived. There was a blanket over the body. The coroner was sitting on the curb, visibly shaken. That worried me. I went to sit by him as I listened to the sound of the approaching ambulance. I asked the coroner what the cause of death was. He just nodded wordlessly at the blanket.

I went over and raised the blanket to view the body. The man's face was gone. I felt for identification, it was Schultz. I remembered the big bartender threatening to rip my face off. I always thought it was just a figure of speech, yet here lay my friend with his face literally ripped off. Now I went to the coroner to ask if his face had been recovered.

"It's in a bag in the front seat of my truck," he said, still not looking up.

"Is there a chance that it can be sewn on for the funeral?" I asked.

"It's too soon to tell. We'll refrigerate it for the mortician," he said.

"When the ambulance is gone, I'll buy you a drink," I told him. "Let's go out to the sting club and maybe get some answers."

I helped load Schultz into the ambulance and the coroner gave them the bag to keep cool. He said that massive trauma and blood loss were the probable causes of death. Then he surprised me by asking what we were up against. I took the 'we' to mean all of us in town. He might have been referring to every Christian in the world for all I knew. He was several years older than I was.

"We are facing the glamour that the devil cloaks evil deeds in. He rewards in currency that fools are attracted to. Money, power in the form of intimidation like we just witnessed, sex, and more. To summarize, we are facing a very determined, and very evil foe. One who is organized better than any of us thought was possible. This organization is able to provide all the vile needs that only the worst in society crave. They cater to individual preferences meeting specific desires. We in this town are evidently at war with a group of evil people who have chosen our town to make their stand. I thought that we were winning because it was so peaceful for so long. Their organization has evidently recovered from the wounds that the good men in our society have inflicted. Now they are flexing their muscles once again as they test our determination and strength."

I told him that we had to take the fight to the enemy. They must have a leader or a headquarters that can be destroyed before we chase all the fleeing rats and roaches and destroy them too.

Just like I zeroed in on the kidnappings and found them in the town of Spring, I would have to coordinate with all the police departments in the metropolitan area. We could put all of our red pins on the same map. I had an idea that the nucleus of our crime wave would be as calm as the eye of a hurricane. That practice goes under the general heading of "Don't crap where you eat!"

As soon as the ambulance left, we drove to the sting club for that drink. The doormen let me in on sight. Something was wrong. As soon as the door closed, I steered the coroner to the men's room. I gave him my .38 special to put in his pocket and told him to expect trouble or leave if he didn't like loud noises. He returned my spare revolver and excused himself. I came out first to draw attention and the coroner left like he had urgent business elsewhere.

I bumped my way through the crowd and squeezed a place at the bar. My badge wasn't too popular there. I was looking for a familiar face but there were none to be seen. It looked like Schultz' advertisement worked too well. I was wondering where the rest of my men's bodies were. None of the men in the bar crowd looked friendly. The bartender was an uglier clone of the guy I killed before. Without a doubt, Schultz' sting backfired royally. This blatant show of force was another version of the message that Schultz' body was supposed to deliver. I had eleven bullets loaded and ready to go, plus a belt full of .357 ammunition. There was a lot more than eleven people here. That meant that I would have to take their weapons before they could be used against me.

I was at the far end of the bar from the bartender. Once again I hopped onto the bar and yelled, "Freeze!" The bartender drew a shotgun making him my first victim. That first shot changed the atmosphere. I was no longer just a pain in the butt with a badge, I was the center of attention with a pistol in each hand and a dead gorilla behind the bar.

The coroner proved to be good for something. I heard several car doors slam as only a cop slams them. He had sent for a silent alarm that would save my life. The doors burst open and the bar filled with the beautiful sight of Conroe's finest. Now that the bar was in good hands, I jumped down behind the bar and searched the gorilla's body for the keys.

This joint only had three back rooms to check out. The same ugly scenes were visible with different faces this time. They must have experienced a shortage of young girls, too bad.

Tomorrow seemed like a good day for that meeting of Police Chiefs. This had to stop.

. . .

We found the bodies of the other agents in the walk in cooler along with the body of a dead girl. Maybe these monsters planned to go back into the meat business.

They hurt us badly by killing Schultz and his men, but we won this battle. God if only it could be the last, I'd never whine about being bored again. Schultz was a family man, as were most of his men. Then there was the matter of the girl in the cooler and forty-some bodies in the pond.

This morning I would call the Mayor of Houston to get assistance in contacting all the Police Chiefs so we could get busy with that map of crime in the area. I felt sure that once all the pins were on the map, we would have a good idea of where the source of our problems lie hidden. I could only hope that the Chiefs weren't corrupted by all of the oil money in the metro area. There were bound to be some who were crooked. Hopefully they would see the benefits of uniting and working together.

I decided to meet my old friend Mayor Walker Archer of Conroe for breakfast and solicit his help. It was just after 6 AM and he went to the Kettle about now. He had been awake almost as long as I had. The Police Dispatcher had called the Mayor and the Coroner after she had called me. The restaurant was packed. The crowd was hushed like they just found out the truth about Santa Claus. People were stunned that the 'all powerful' FBI could be manhandled in such a manner. David was sitting with the mayor and the coroner. They had saved a spot for me.

Every ear in the joint was trained on our table. I broke the silence by voicing my plan of uniting every police department in the metropolitan area. I reminded them of my method of pinpointing the earlier kidnapper to Howlzworth Road and how it could work for us again.

There were no strange faces in the room. All these men took and passed polygraphs and drug tests. This was only a small part of Conroe's finest, but they were family.

I asked Walker if he could get our ball rolling. We could make life easier and safer in this part of Texas and the sooner, the better. It was my voiced plan to work from Katy to Beaumont and from Galveston to Huntsville. That encompassed several million people.

Psychologists claim that two per cent of the populace do most of the killing. In five million people locally, that gave us about one hundred thousand homicidal maniacs. Keeping track of that many actuals and their wannabee friends required the help of the general populace in the form of neighborhood watch and community policing.

The Mayor assured me that he would get on the phone as soon as he got to his office. He said that he would need about forty-eight hours or so to arrange the meeting. I decided to go home after breakfast to reassure Margaret and the kids before the news of the raid hit the TV.

After I brought the sleepyheads up to date, I ventured the guess that Kingwood would turn out to be the headquarters of most of the area's trouble. It had central location as well as being an unusually quiet neighborhood. Kingwood reported virtually no crime. Where was their two per cent busy?

I called my SWAT team together for a fishing expedition. I told them to wear civilian clothes and body armor was a good idea. By 8 AM, everyone was assembled. We got in my van, complete with M-16's. Sinbad was in the way-back of the van. That dog was my divining rod for evil. I couldn't wait for forty-eight hours. I wanted to test my theory now. We were riding the tail of rush hour traffic, not really knowing what we were looking for but sure that we would recognize it when we saw it.

Kingwood had really filled in since I used to work on roofs there in 1982. I told my partners that I half expected our target to be a church. We stopped at a store in a strip mall and bought a disposable camera and a map of the area. I circled all the churches then gave the map to Steve to be the navigator. On a weekday, most all the churches would be deserted. We found one that was all hustle and bustle. Sinbad was growling as we watched the familiar bald headed monks moving about.

I was out of my jurisdiction here, but I took a few pictures before we drove back to Conroe. We jotted down directions before we left. That place sure looked like the vortex that I was looking for.

...

That was a very impressive church that we spied on. It looked as big as the opera in Sydney. It takes a lot of dough to put up a palace like that. Half was probably counterfeit according to my experience. That fact pointed to bank complicity or a lot of cash deals. Now, to share my find with the proper jurisdiction.

I started at Mayor Walker Archer's house and had to backtrack to city hall where I should have looked first. He was still on the phone.

"The boys and I went hunting and found something," I said. "There was a church the size of two horse barns and it had those baldheaded monks crawling all over it on a weekday morning."

Walker said, "Let me guess, it's in Kingwood. That's the only place that reports no crime and their mayor doesn't want to get involved with our effort."

"Now I may have wasted gas to confirm what you think you know, but I know what I know, and I know where what I know is." I thought that should hold him for awhile.

Walker was busy with his political arrangements for the meeting. I hated to interrupt him, but this situation seemed immediate. He said that the meeting was still a good idea for tomorrow. "Today you can meet with the new FBI Chief in the area and raid that place if circumstances warrant it." He gave me a phone number and pointed to a vacant telephone.

The ball was in my court and I wasted no time. Introducing myself to Agent Jason Sprague seemed to be a magic key. He wanted to meet with me ASAP and discuss today's find.

I dropped my friends at the restaurant by their cars and met him at a makeshift office in a vacant suite in one of the new office buildings in town. There would be few distractions in a place like this. I brought Sinbad in with me to get his valued opinion early in the game. This man was the TV stereotype of the typical FBI agent. He didn't mind the dog at all. He said that he expected the dog treatment. He was a firm believer himself.

"According to the files, you're the best thing to hit law enforcement since fingerprints were discovered," he praised.

"Flattery will get you," I told him. "Now, just in case haste is as important as I think it is, we have movement at the object of tomorrow's search. It looks like one day of waiting is all the time the bad guys need to evaporate. We need four men in one car to follow the monks to their new place. We'll need twelve plainclothes besides SWAT, you, and me. The undercover can be state troopers if the Kingwood Chief is stingy with his manpower. You can squeeze in my van."

This new man was a doer, not the hesitant or stationary type. He already had body armor and an M-16 at his desk. "There is one thing that you need to get straight," he said to me, "The FBI is in charge here."

I spoke up, "Now here is something that you need to remember, you are the third Bureau Chief here. I killed the first one. The second one tried squeezing me out. They ripped his face off while he was alive, and filmed the whole thing. I killed the man who did it. I've killed more people than the plague and I'm still here. The place that we are about to raid is a place that I discovered before the investigation got under way and the investigation was MY idea. Now, Mr. "I'm in charge", take your cues from me and my men and you may live to head up another investigation!" That was my reply.

Sinbad had been watching him carefully since I started my speech perked up his ears. He still wasn't showing any signs of animosity. He was used to hearing me talk like that. The new man of action didn't like what he heard. Hell, I expected him to take over. I just didn't like the way that he put it. There were no lies in the speech I just made. The worst that he would do is prohibit my participation in 'my' operation.

It sure was quiet in there as we sat staring at each other. He broke the ice by saying that he meant no disrespect for my years of effort in this ongoing battle, he only wanted to establish his role as Bureau Chief.

I told him that my main concern was eliminating the vermin and I didn't care whose name made the paper. Then I laid out my plan for his input and approval. It looked like we could still work together.

We used his office for a staging area. He called the State Police rather than risking the use of Kingwood's forces, which was a good idea. The Bureau would put surveillance on the Mayor and the Chief of Police of Kingwood. My call was simple. I called SWAT at the Kettle where they were chomping at the bit. I told them to bring flares in case the operation went beyond dark along with five- cell flashlights for seven.

Within the hour we were underway. Traffic this time of day was light, that meant that we were at ground zero in just over an hour of our phone calls. The State Patrol, as usual, was right with the program. Those guys were as good as Paratroopers.

We met and passed out assignments in a shopping center parking lot two blocks away. All vehicles were fully gassed up and unmarked. Everyone had body armor, torches and flares. Our team had M-16's and the State Patrol had riot guns loaded with deer slugs alternating with double-ought buckshot.

Now to creep into position and observe for a while to establish the enemies' pattern. As far as Kingwood's Mayor and Chief of Police, we had squads on the way to watch their houses. Those two didn't expect anything until after tomorrow's meeting, the one that they had planned on boycotting. They must have planes to catch.

The radio frequency that we were on was scrambled. We slid quietly into place with our very inconspicuous vehicles. The pedestrian traffic near the church was moderate. Every vehicle that was loaded at the church had a shadow when it left.

We couldn't afford to have any more load and leave. I wanted the battleground to be right here where the birth of our miseries was. After that last car left, Sprague, the Bureau Chief agreed with me that it was time to move. The signal was "Converge" and it was given now. The State Cops took care of the arrests and security outside. SWAT and Sprague were the internal commandos.

We borrowed seven robes before entering. Our common denominators were our combat boots and our hair. We walked in upon a very busy scene. Box upon box was frantically filled and stacked waiting to be loaded as empty vehicles became available. The place was so busy that we went unnoticed as we made our way onto the stage and spread out on line, dropping our robes to reveal badges and weapons.

"FBI, Freeze!" hollered Sprague like he practiced it for just this moment. It sure worked no matter what the case. We had twenty-some men inside to cover. Steve, Al, and Sprague stayed on stage providing security as the rest of us moved through the crowd disarming the monks. There were two men in the 'peanut gallery' that were quite obviously major players, since they were giving orders and had hairdos like ours. Sprague made them as the Mayor and Police Chief that we were looking for. It was time for an interim election in Kingwood.

As soon as we disarmed a man, he was sent outside for a more thorough search by the State Troopers. They were put in nylon handcuffs and marched out of sight. When we had the auditorium empty, I got Sinbad to lend us his nose and ears. Letting him run loose worked best as a general rule. He lead us to eleven more monks hiding in back offices and bathrooms.

We had to hurry to assist the crew that was following the cavalcade of monks on the move. A quick call on the radio informed us that the monks were pulling into a house that looked like a castle about two miles away, still in Kingwood.

We followed their directions and slid inconspicuously into place. This house was as big as the church. Someone was making money, probably literally. We left a skeleton crew at the church and had the paddy wagons take out the trash. We radioed instructions to the church and notified the shadows of our presence. They informed us that no new vehicles had come since they had arrived. We had to move quickly before they figured out that their supply line had been interrupted.

As soon as the State Troopers came on the scene, we pulled the same operation. The State took care of external security and arrests while those of us with less intelligence went inside. I'll tell you what, though. Those State Cops looked like the Marine Corps. I pity the fools that got on the bad side of those dudes.

"Sprague, let me show you what Sinbad does best," I said. I walked to the door that was blocked open and told Sinbad to go get 'em. In less than two minutes, a full dozen men had run out the door into the arms of the officers. Now we went inside to see which closed doors were hiding bad guys. Sinbad led us to four more.

A thorough search of the house and garage produced nothing but cash, funny money and printing plates, guns and videos but no more bad guys. It was time for me and mine to leave before someone found out that we were outside our jurisdiction. Sprague thanked us and cut us loose. He said that he'd bum a ride back with one of the State Troopers.

...

The trip to Conroe was a happy one. The operation was a huge success and not a shot was fired. We decided to get the families together for a picnic at the beach. We worked well together and enjoyed each other's company. Our kids got along well together too.

I wondered how the organization could survive the blow dealt to it today. The answer was, "It couldn't." It took money to start a ball like that rolling, brains to run it, gorillas to keep order and stooges to do the light work. Between the arrests and the previous killings and confiscation's we shouldn't hear a peep out of that organization ever again.

Players in the snuff videos would get the death penalty. Accessories would get thirty years to life. Then there were the drugs and counterfeiting to keep the rest in the shade.

Tomorrow's meeting of the mayors and police chiefs would almost be a moot point, unless there were some factions of the organization in one of the other jurisdictions. The meeting would be interesting if only to see who had been doing their job and who was asleep at the wheel. At any rate, tomorrow would take care of itself. Today was for fun.

# Part Three

Today was the day of the big meeting when all the Chiefs of Police got together to compare notes on serious and unusual crimes. The town of Kingwood sent an acting chief since we arrested their regular one yesterday along with their mayor.

Jason Sprague, the new FBI chief in the area presided over the meeting. He had all the crime statistics from the last ten years.

Homemade name and town placards served as introductions until such time as a Chief felt the need to speak. Most everyone there knew me on sight from news broadcasts or the Chevy commercials.

Sprague used *my* town's police force to illustrate the successful results of aggressive police work. He said that we displayed good detective-work and follow up, along with frequent coordinating of county and state resources and the FBI.

The microphone was passed around the room as all did their best to summarize their unsolved crimes. Sprague and I took notes to look for similarities or overlapping situations. I took special note when any Chief insisted that he had no problems that his force couldn't handle alone.

Today's meeting was supposed to create an information bank to assist all of us in performing our jobs. Sinbad was leashed to my chair with a muzzle on for safety. This many opportunities for corruption in one room was bound to have some bad apples. I'd let those people think that they had us fooled.

The meeting went on through lunch. We survived on the classic favorite, coffee and donuts. It looked like supper was going to be very late. The only ones leaving early, were already suspect in my book. As the early departures each came over to shake Jason's and my hand, Sinbad growled as expected. We honest cops who took the welfare of our communities more seriously were much later in leaving.

Once the last con artist was gone, I really stuck my neck out. I told the remaining men that the ones who left early were already suspected as players in the grander scheme of things. I went so far as to remove Sinbad's muzzle and let him roam. He wandered freely through the crowd as docilely as if moving among family.

"So you all see for yourselves that my large, hairy friend is not a bad dog so much as an excellent judge of character," I told the crowd.

Later, after Sprague and I said farewell to the last of our guests, he and I literally compared notes. It was an amazing parallel.

"Let's do breakfast at the Kettle at your earliest convenience," I suggested.

"Six O'clock tomorrow is fine with me," was his reply.

...

The next morning found Jason and me seated by our selves in a corner booth. We had last night's notes spread out on the table. We were in a debate over similar crimes in neighboring communities. I suggested U.S. Marshals and State Police to sew up jurisdictional problems. I said that we needed to keep the bad guys off balance and on the defensive.

Agent Sprague and I fully agreed to put pressure on the rogue cops who left our meeting early. We decided to set out bait for our greedy friends. First we had to find their weakness or favorite vice. We could make an accurate profile from their unsolved-crimes list. We needed a computer hacker to give us this information. Any college campus had two or three.

For now, that was the unpolished plan. I could go back to being a regular cop and he would call me when things started rolling. I reminded him that a hidden camera could be worth its weight in gold. I stopped at the station to see if I was needed. Washington made a better Police Chief than I did. At least he didn't mind the routine and structured part of the job. If I ever ran for County Sheriff, and I probably would, he'd be a shoe in for Chief. He sure as hell had *my* endorsement. I signed a few papers and told him I would go home and stay out of his way.

It was a good feeling to leave the office and not worry about anything.

I'd rather pursue my role as head of SWAT. It gave me a lot of free time to play detective as well as family man. SWAT earned their time off by sometimes being away from the family for days or even weeks.

Home was my next stop and there was plenty of time to do something with the family. We opted for a picnic in the yard. We let Ryan and Annie invite some friends and asked Rebecca to come by too. By noon, the place was a zoo of kids and teenagers. Pizza was the sensible remedy to feed the masses.

Annie and her friends disappeared in the movie chamber. Ryan's noisy bunch filled the playground equipment and ran around like rats in a rainstorm. Sinbad presided over activities, dodging children good-naturedly.

We shooed everyone out early enough to go home and wash up for his own supper. Ryan was so full of sand that he had to be swept clean before he could go in the house.

The phone rang during supper. It was my friend Washington at the station. He said that a hitchhiker had shot at the officer who stopped to question him. The fugitive took to the woods by Kroger and was surrounded by as tight of a cordon as manpower would allow. I told him to radio the other SWAT members to meet me at the scene.

Sinbad and I jumped in the van. I listened on the radio as the other team members were rounded up. I said a silent prayer that no one would be hurt. If the Lord charged me for prayers like the telephone companies billed for calls, I'd be broke. No, I'd be in the hole!

The first cop to stop the hitchhiker had his armor on. That was all that saved his life. The patch of woods was small and bordered by homes and apartments. None of the officers had entered the woods. When the rest of SWAT arrived, I spaced them out among the cordon. The man must have been lying down because no one had him in sight. Hopefully he hadn't already escaped.

I used the bullhorn to order him to surrender. After two such warnings with no response, I put Sinbad to work. My dog had the man up and running, pistol still firmly in his grasp. "Drop your weapon!" I ordered. He kept running at Steve who was trying to draw a bead on him. Stack dropped him with a shot to the head.

Now I would never know why this man was so intent on going out feet first. His ID gave him a Houston address. We ran his name and Drivers

License. He had several major priors and an outstanding warrant for manslaughter. He didn't want to go back to prison and this was his way of committing suicide. It was always a shame for a man to throw his life away. This man was a career criminal who graduated to murder.

I walked over to Stack and asked him if he was all right. Stack said that he probably saved more than one life by taking this one. He said that he could live with that. His attitude told me that we had the right man as sniper.

Sprague called me that same evening for another breakfast appointment. I took that as an extreme compliment. It was probably due to the similarity of our notes from the big meeting. One thing that stood out significantly when listening to the unsolved crime lists was the number of missing teenagers that were assumed to be runaways but were still listed as missing. So far, and happily so, none of their bodies showed up. The towns and suburbs northwest of Houston seemed to be the focal point of this phenomenon.

The missing teens were of both sexes and between the ages of thirteen and seventeen. If we were to count the missing eighteen-year olds, the number nearly doubled. This epidemic had gone unnoticed since it was spread evenly over several communities. The cases seemed to have a common starting point from approximately six months ago and continuing through the present.

I considered solving this to be our single most important task. It reminded me of the days of the meat locker and I prayed that this wasn't the case now. These were the thoughts that I fell asleep with.

Jason greeted me warmly at the restaurant next morning. He confirmed my guess as to the topic of conversation over breakfast. He had a map of the area in question with every disappearance plotted. We found it amazing that no bodies ever turned up and none of the children ever returned alive. They just vanished.

I did a lot of tossing and turning last night and came up with a few ideas of my own. In the center of our mysterious land of missing persons was a large wilderness. It was bordered on the north by FM-1488, on the south by Spring Creek, and lay west of the town of Pinehurst.

Agent Sprague said that he had ideas of his own, but he wanted to hear mine first.

I pointed to the large wilderness area and said that all our answers would be in there somewhere. "Either we'll find their remains or they're still alive and living out there."

He said that he suspected the wilderness area too. He also pointed out that the three Chiefs who left early were from Tomball, Pinehurst, and Magnolia. Those are the three nearest towns to the woods in question. "This information should give us a head start on the three musketeers."

I suggested a fly over and photo-reconnaissance. He jumped on that idea. He was as anxious as I was to lower the boom on the corrupt cops. He rolled up the map and went to make a phone call. When he came back, he was smiling and said, "We have a plane available. It will be ready by the time we get to the airport."

Now I was smiling too. I hate to waste time once I get started on something.

The plane was a tiny thing, but it had some sophisticated equipment on board. It had a viewing screen that allowed us to zoom in on any area we wanted. We could then use the computer to locate exactly where each photo was taken using a transparent overlay with a grid. This system was accurate to within a few feet. I suggested that we note all the dry areas and look for trails.

Without the viewing screen, it all looked the same. 1488 was visible and parts of Spring Creek shone in the sun. The rest was just green. When viewed via the screen, Details leapt out as if we were flying at treetop level. There were a few areas that looked unnatural as if man made camouflage was utilized. We both agreed that these were probably what we were after.

Back on the ground, we dropped the film at a specialty lab to be developed. Jason said that it was a secure lab. We wasted an hour at a local coffee shop while we waited for our photos. After we retrieved the photos, we went to his office suite to devise a plan.

Jason and I would go in the woods along with the rest of SWAT. We'd all be in camouflaged clothing and have our faithful M-16's. Sinbad had to stay home. We would use Spike for his quieter, bird dog type alerts. We would go in tomorrow before sunup and thread our way to the areas in question. We would have one day's chow, two canteens of water and cameras with telescopic lenses. Sprague's office was our staging area. We would meet at 3:30 AM tomorrow.

...

In the morning, we were saddled up and moving out at 3:45 AM. One of Sprague's men drove us out 1488 about a mile past Pinehurst. We unloaded speedily before any headlights were in sight. I walked first with Spike at my heel. He would go first as soon as I found a trail. My job was to get us under cover away from the highway and out of sight of cars. The roads were virtually dead this time of morning. The absolute last thing that we wanted to see was a squad car. It felt strange to be hiding from police, but we didn't know who our friends were.

I came across a small clearing large enough for us to group up and discuss the order of march until it grew brighter. Sprague would walk behind me. Stack would bring up the rear. Steve and Al at left flank, then Joe and Eddie at right flank. If we could avoid snakes and fire ants until sunup, I would consider it a successful insertion.

The dew was forming and the humidity added to that had us all pretty wet before we even started out. I was grateful for the chance to move when the sky got brighter. I used a compass to head us towards the nearest area under suspicion.

Steve and Al found a trail going our way. We all moved onto it, drawing in the flanks. Spike took the lead and we proceeded cautiously with one eye on the compass. The trail never veered except to dodge a wet spot or a patch of thorns. This was a well beaten-trail that probably led from Pinehurst to our first destination. If we weren't so early, we would probably have run into other foot traffic. As we neared our objective, we would have to move off the trail to avoid this very thing. The dog never alerted and we were able to make good time.

We had plotted seven camouflaged areas. Initially we were to reconnoiter the three on this side of the wilderness and try to get a peek at the larger area in the center of the woods. I already had my suspicions about the status of the missing teens. I had a feeling that they were used as forced labor for some illegal dealings, the most obvious being a marijuana plantation. Another might be prostitution. I shuddered at that thought.

Very soon I could see the false ceiling made by camouflage netting strung in the trees. When we reached the clearing, the first piece of the puzzle was evident. The clearing was full of opium poppies and marijuana. There were no guards or workers, but the plants all looked well tended.

We photographed our find and moved out towards our next target area. All we had to do was follow the trail.

When we reached the second deserted field, we paused only long enough to take pictures before moving on. Once again there were no guards. They must have been very confident of their safety.

Spike alerted shortly before we reached our third objective. We moved cautiously ahead and could soon hear voices. Some of the voices were loud and authoritative. There were three uniformed policemen in this clearing. They were big, beefy men with the cruel faces of bullies. The rest of the people were all teenagers who looked underfed and stoned. They were tending the plants and pulling weeds while the cops verbally abused them. These children were just as much prisoners to the heroin refined from the poppies as they were to the cops. No physical restraints were needed. The kids were probably lured in by the offer of free pot and the junk was introduced later as the glamour wore off and they expressed the desire to leave. I imagine that threats of incarceration were another tool to keep the teens in line.

We got photos aplenty here and melted back out of earshot. We had a group meeting and unanimously agreed that there had to be a barracks and a mess hall, probably in the center camp. I pointed out that we hadn't seen any females yet even though our information indicated equal amounts of missing girls. Sprague said that they probably had other duties at the center camp. Our next objective was about fifteen minutes away.

We skirted the work detail quietly and walked to the center camp. Once again, Spike alerted before we heard the voices. This was a large camp with tents everywhere. Most of the sides of the tents were tied up to allow a breeze, making our photographing easier.

Some of the tents were storage for harvested pot. The plants were hung upside down in bunches. One tent was obviously a lab for processing the poppies into heroin and opium. There were several girls working in that tent under the supervision of some men in civilian clothes. Once again, the girls all looked stoned and underfed. There were tents for cooking and dining. It was a very elaborate setup. There were a few uniformed police walking about, but they seemed to be mostly flirting with the girls. One of the tents had the sides down and the flaps closed. We had to find out that tent's secret.

Jason insisted that he be the one to enter it and take the necessary photos. It was the head man syndrome. No problem, we had the cops at this camp out gunned. Luckily for him, the mystery tent bordered on the woods.

While Sprague did his illegal entry, I contemplated the location of the inevitable parking lot for our criminal's vehicles. It was bound to be near 1488 with a double layer of netting over the top to shut off reflections.

Jason came crawling out of the tent with the camera. He said that he couldn't take any pictures because of the flash. He said that the tent had been full of cots. Many of the cots had sleeping or stoned girls in them. A few had cops taking advantage of them. He wanted to bust the place now, but we had a manpower shortage.

I told him about the inevitable parking lot that we had to find. "We could muster additional forces to enter at that location using the scrambled radio," I said. "We could locate the road in and mark it for arriving forces. If there are only three guards at each plantation, one cop with an automatic weapon should be able to contain them or kill them if necessary. We have the right number of men to do that now. We'll have to coordinate the raid on the center camp with the arrival of our other men at the outer camps."

"What about all the kids on the work details?" asked Jason.

"The SWAT members can offer them immunity from prosecution in exchange for their testimonies against the crooked cops. Social services can assist them with the recovery from their addictions," I suggested.

He accepted my plan. Sprague would take care of finding the parking lot and marking the road that led in while the rest of us covered the outer camps. I would take the extreme western camp. All of us had belt radios that connected us to Agent Sprague's main scrambler. By the time that we had to use our radios, the backup should be ready at the parking lot.

The six of us split off on our own objectives. I estimated about forty minutes for us to get in place. That was forty more minutes for the boys on the work gangs and forty more minutes for the girls in the tents. It couldn't be helped. We wanted to do this with no more harm coming to the teenagers. As for the rogue cops, that would be up to them.

My team passed the first two plantations west only to find them deserted. That made sense, three guards, and one work crew. They moved from plantation to plantation and returned to the central camp at night. I hoped that the other half of SWAT found the same pattern, all of our jobs would be easier. As we neared the westernmost camp, the bully cops' voices could be plainly heard. "Hurry up or there'll be no supper for you!"

The bully cops were so careless and confident that we were able to walk right up to the clearing and spread out to give us individual targets if it came to that.

"Freeze! Sheriff's Police!" I hollered. That got their attention. Our automatic weapons made freezing their menu choice eclipsing others such as "Die!" for instance. The workers looked happy to see some real police, especially after we told them about the immunity we offered.

Steve moved among them, stripping them of their weapons and handcuffing them.

"West all clear," I sent over the radio. Now we would move closer to central and wait for word to bring them in. While we were hiking in I heard, "East clear," over the horn. Good men, not a shot fired and everything under control.

We walked to the plantation nearest central and gave the hungry looking kids a break. The bad cops looked positively suicidal as they contemplated their futures. The teens were buoyant, like their lives were taking a turn for the better. Police work can be rewarding.

Soon we heard, "Center clear." That should put the cork in the bottle for my men and me. The work to follow would be in other hands.

We marched our troop in. There were a total of nine cops in handcuffs plus the chemists who had been processing the heroin. The slime buckets in the tent raping the girls had turned out to be our three rogue Police Chiefs. There must be some good men left on their forces to democratically produce three new chiefs. Once again, law and order would flourish.

Now that we'd done a good days work, we could think of food. Even the LRRP rations sounded good. We couldn't leave yet, so we heated up some water and made the dehydrated meals. The kids went out in the first wave of paddy wagons to their respective towns. The next wave was for the prisoners. The three towns were notified to pick up their squads and appoint acting Police Chiefs.

One of Sprague's men came out in my van. He and Jason stayed to finish the details. The rest of us went to Sprague's office to pick up our vehicles. We all needed showers and time with our families.

. . . . . . .
. . . . . .
. . . . .
. . . .
. . .
. .

Approximately five years have passed since we put a stop to the 'exploitation plantation' as it later came to be known. The three new Chiefs of Police appointed were retained and worked out fine. Montgomery County had become one big community as far as Police work was concerned. It was like a giant neighborhood watch. A suspicious vehicle couldn't pass through without being reported to the next jurisdiction along its route of travel.

Margaret and I were still virtual newly weds. Travis was out of the Army and married. He was now a member of SWAT since Eddie died of a heart attack. He built his home across the street from his sister, Becky. Annie had married a soldier. She was living at Ft. Benning. Her husband would be getting out of the Army soon. Ryan was a sturdy eleven-year old. He was studying Tae Kwon Do while managing to stay on the honor roll at school. He wanted to be on SWAT with his older brother when he grew up. I was slowing down enough to know that I'd need to be replaced on SWAT by the time Ryan was ready.

Traffic violations and the occasional domestic disturbance were our only noteworthy crimes. Oh, of course, there were the usual problems among the teenagers in the area, just psychological growing pains. It never went beyond their first offense. Community service, fines and a probationary period straightened them out. Just the threat of a year at Navasota or hard time in Huntsville was enough of a deterrent. I hadn't had to send any of our locals off to either place in many years. Drug usage was virtually non-existent after the nightmare of the marijuana and Heroin plantation was made known. The youngsters who survived that mess were my best advertising against drug use.

There was a new religious school being built north of town. Priests from there who came to Conroe to shop seemed like a quiet lot. They kept to themselves, never engaging in conversation with the locals. My experience as a kid in Chicago and its suburbs was that the priests were very outgoing, relying on the community to build their church or school.

Maybe it was only because they were "teachers" of other priests, but they were definitely different from what I'd expect. They never smiled and they spoke only when necessary.

Their aloof behavior told me to keep a close eye on them. They never declared which faith they were affiliated with. Upon completion of the school, the glaring absence of a cross on top, or anywhere on the grounds, struck me as peculiar. They were obviously not endorsing any of the Christian faiths.

This was still America, land of religious freedom. As long as the school's members broke no laws, they had a right to their faith. As long as I was Chief of such a peaceful town, any disturbance to the tranquility would bring scrutiny to the newcomers. They had some awfully hard faces for priests. There wasn't the usual Christian light in their eyes. They had northern New England accents. It was customary for Easterners to settle in Florida for a climate change, not Texas. Everything about these men seemed out of place.

So far, we'd only seen the half dozen teachers. The students hadn't started arriving yet. I decided to get on the Internet to see what I could find out about any religious sects from the northeast that were migrating. My search would be made easier by the fact that these guys were non-denominational. I found something very interesting in links to a Vermont cult that had recently closed its doors.

According to the news story, a school with no conventional religious affiliations had closed without any notification. There was nothing in the story to hint at where all the teachers and "students" had gone. It went on to say that authorities were suspicious due to the multitude of disappearances of young and middle aged women in the area beginning at the same time the school had opened its doors. Upon examining the abandoned school, a crematorium was discovered inside. Everyone involved from the head master to the students was being sought for questioning.

I immediately sent a fax to the Vermont State Police. In no time, my phone was ringing. Some human teeth had been found at the crematorium. I was to apprehend any and all at the school immediately. U.S. Marshals would come for the prisoners. The men at the school were to be considered dangerous and probably armed.

My first thoughts were to collect SWAT and go to the school in plain clothes. Before I did, I put an all points bulletin out on the school's van with instructions just to keep an eye on it. I didn't want anyone to escape if they got wind of the raid on the school while they were in town. "Do not apprehend without backup and wait until all were in the vehicle. If it is parked somewhere, you'll know everyone is inside when it pulls away." Next, I radioed the SWAT team to meet at my office in civilian clothes ASAP.

I got a call almost immediately. The suspect van had been located. Soon, my SWAT team was arriving at the office, eager to know what was up. When all were assembled, I briefed them. "The school van with the Vermont plates has been spotted in the Kroger parking lot. It just pulled in a few minutes ago."

Armed with M-16's, Stack's having a scope, we loaded into my van and sped to the Kroger. The regular patrolmen had an almost invisible perimeter around the van at a respectable distance, only perceptible from the view we were afforded as we approached, looking down on the parking lot. When my van was spotted, the police on the scene exited their vehicles and made their way toward the school van on foot among the vehicles in the crowded parking lot. I was so proud of their quiet professionalism. This force could never be compared to the Keystone Cops. I drove past the school van and parked several spaces away. The van was empty.

A long twenty minutes later, all four of the "teachers" came out of the store pushing carts full of groceries. It looked like they were shopping for a lot of people. There was an awful lot of beer and hard liquor. Some priests!

We let them load their cargo before I motioned all the men to move in. They were definitely surprised to find out that they were completely surrounded. They probably thought that they were safely lost in small town America with Barney Fife in charge of the police. The liquor loving priests were handcuffed without incident.

Having secured those four, my men and I got into the cult's van and drove to the school. I backed the van to the front door. Two men came out of the church to help unload. They knew the game was over when they opened the back doors to the van. Two of my men hopped out with their M-16's at the ready. They were handcuffed and left for Stack to watch.

Travis and I headed up a search of the school. There were only four main rooms inside. I had Joe wait inside the front door to back up Stack or us, whichever was needed. Each of us remaining team members took a room apiece to search. Mine came up empty, as did Steve's. Al found the crematorium. My son, Travis, found two very frightened ladies who were bound and gagged.

After inspecting the crematorium, Al said, "It appeared unused so far, thank God."

It turned out that the two ladies had been kidnapped from Huntsville this very morning. Talk about good timing. My suspicious nature saved some more lives.

The US Marshals arrived after the fact. They were glad to get their men even though they missed what they referred to as the "fun" of the capture. I assured them that the County was happy to be rid of them.

Our current chore was to auction off the empty school with the human incinerator. The crematorium would have to be demolished. Profit from the sale could help with the town budget. Mayor Archer could decide the terms of the sale. If those priests would have been more open and friendly, they might have gotten away with their evil deeds for a while. Their behavior drew my almost immediate scrutiny. As far as most men in law enforcement are concerned, newcomers are always checked out.

The Governor gave our department an award for out standing police work. It was our first in five years. The Police Station had a wall full of impressive citations and awards. Every one of them had been earned and was well deserved. No manner of misbehavior was tolerated. Speeders were dealt with as criminals. Safe streets were another ingredient of a happy community.

...

I was happy but bored with my safe community. Things were so placid that it felt like I was retired. I wasn't ready for that yet. I was toying with the idea of becoming a skip tracer or bounty hunter. The problem with either occupation would be the time spent away from home.

At any rate, I needed something to get my adrenaline coursing through my veins again. I decided to get Sinbad and go over the recently built style at the back fence. That swamp was always an exciting place. Every time I'd gone out there, it was the beginning of another adventure. This time would just be for old time's sake. The tunnels had been blown up and were probably full of water. The smokehouse had been burned to the ground.

Only the tree fort where Tiny hung out had been left intact. It was so well constructed that we'd have had to cut down the tree to destroy it.

I told Margaret that I was going camping with Sinbad for one night. My son, Travis, wanted to come with me. No finer company could be had. He and I hadn't talked much about his time in the Army. I was curious as to how much "The Green Machine" had changed since I'd worn a uniform. I called the station to inform Detective Washington that he was in charge until further notice. Travis and I loaded our backpacks and brought our M-16's to back up our side arms. Sinbad seemed happy to be doing something too.

Before noon, we were going over the style that my dog had learned to use like regular stairs. It hadn't rained in a week. We were treated to a fairly dry and sandy hike. We walked as straight as we could toward the tree fort, hoping our memories hadn't rusted. We were going to pitch our tents in the small clearing near the tree. We had a shaky moment when Sinbad scared up a small bear. Our dog's 120 ferocious pounds was more than the small bear wanted to deal with so he moved on. I hadn't been out here in a long time. It was as primal and creepy as ever. This swamp would never change.

We waded across the shallow creek and managed to find the clearing with the tree fort. There was a small, brackish pond where the smokehouse had been. The tunnels were evidenced only by a nasty looking trench with puddles of murky water scattered along its length. The trench disappeared out of sight to the west. Nature had reclaimed the unclean ground that man had defiled. The pond had some doomed fish from the last flood. They would fall prey to water birds during the day or snakes and raccoons at night. The cacophony from birds and insects was a symphony that only outdoorsmen could enjoy. We pitched our tents and gathered firewood for the evening.

Sinbad had been sniffing around the base of the tree that held the fort. It was past time to check it out. The knotted rope was still hanging in the same place. Travis volunteered to climb up and look it over.

"Holy cow! There's a body up here!" he exclaimed.

I climbed up next to see what he'd found. The body looked like it had been up there for years. The ants were done with it. There wasn't much left but bones. The coroner would have his hands full. Thank God teeth were present and they looked like they had professional dental care.

I was shaking my head. Thinking out loud, I said, "I have never come out here without finding trouble."

It looked like the skeleton of a white male about six feet tall. That was the extent of my forensic knowledge.

Thinking about the grief that this discovery would bring another family made me tired. Another missing person that loved ones were praying would return safely. Now, this man was just a shell to provide sad news.

Who was this man? What was the cause of death? If this was a homicide, who murdered him? If it was a suicide, what drove him to it? My cop's mind was already at work. There were no outward signs of violence to the remains. Did he climb up here, or had he been carried? A six-foot tall man would be very difficult to carry up here, even with a ladder. Still, roofers, carpenters, laborers, and firemen can perform some amazing feats of strength. Therefore, it was a possibility. It made more sense to start with the premise that the victim had climbed up under his own power.

Next question being cause of death. It could be snakebite, disease, hypothermia, heart failure, poison, drug overdose, or murder. I searched the head for bullet holes and found none. Another question to consider, were there other bodies nearby?

Our camping trip was not to be. At least we weren't lying dead in the tree fort. That man's problems were over. We had a fresh batch. I radioed the Coroner, telling him to bring boots and a camera and meet me at my house.

I left Sinbad with my son while I went to fetch the Coroner. The walk back to my house was a trip down a haunted memory lane. The bear that Sinbad frightened was long gone. I was glad because I really don't like to kill animals. Shortly after I arrived home, the Coroner pulled in. I had just enough time to explain developments to Margaret before he and I struck out for Travis' location. I fully expected to be a pall- bearer with my son on the return trip.

Sinbad came to greet us as we drew near the water. The Coroner grumbled about wading across the creek, but crossed without hesitation. He knew that it went with the job. Once across, I led him to the tree fort.

"Where's the body?" he asked.

Travis called down; "It's up here." That scared the daylights out of the Coroner.

As I expected, the aging coroner couldn't negotiate the climb, hence the camera. I climbed up to Travis and photographed the deceased from every angle possible. We wrapped the skeletal remains in a poncho and lowered it as gently as we could. My son and I climbed down as soon as the coroner freed the rope. Now we'd see what the professional's early diagnosis would be. His surmise mirrored my earlier thoughts. No signs of violence, the dead man's cause of death would probably hypothermia or heart failure.

Since we had no reports of locals missing, identifying the body might take a while. Travis and I cut a couple of poles and made a stretcher out of the poncho for easiest transport of the departed. Getting the litter over the style was no chore for two strong men, much to the Coroner's amazement. He allowed us to slide the remains into his station wagon, rather than wait for an ambulance.

As the coroner was about to drive away, I said, "Let me know what you come up with right away so I can get started." I planned on starting anyway just with the information I already observed. Adult white male, medium build, 5' 11" to 6' 1" early middle age with a full head of sandy hair, no visible tattoos.

"Let's pray that it was natural causes," I told him as he drove away.

. . .

After a week, the coroner was still calling Travis' find "John Doe". That meant that he probably wasn't a local man. The possibility still existed that it was some bachelor who told his neighbors that he was moving out of town. His travels could have been interrupted by whoever was the last to see him alive. We would have to fax his dental records to every State Police Department in America who had an unsolved missing person fitting our John Doe's description.

The cause of death appeared to be hypothermia. Succumbing to the elements is an easy mistake to make to inexperienced interlopers into the wilderness. If John Doe had been ill prior to seeking refuge in the tree fort, the elements would have had an easier time of doing him in. A hasty diagnosis of this incident was that he climbed up under his own power and perished in his sleep. My cop's mind didn't entirely accept that simple solution.

Travis was disappointed that the body's discovery didn't lead to an immediate investigation. We were both glad to know that it wasn't anyone local.

Our search of the area the next day didn't turn up any more bodies. We cut down Tiny's tree before we left. My best guess was that the dead man was some straggler or lone wolf who was connected to the criminal element that had operated in the swamp for so long.

So, here I was, bored again. Travis and I still hadn't had time to compare notes on today's Army and the Green Machine that I served in. I wanted him to bring it up. He already knew my negative feelings about integrating the sexes in the military. It was a bad idea, period. Nurses, WACS and WAVES had their part and performed admirably. Combat is a biological thing that requires brutality, not nurturing. It's all about speed, strength, and violence. Yes, there were some rare women comfortable in that setting. Too, there were men more gentle than others were. Those men did not perform well in combat situations. Still, the odds for success and victory favor an all-male combat force. The military's primary mission is victory, not social experimenting. Social experiments should be saved for sissy campuses where no one gets killed. Please don't dredge up Kent State or bring up freak incidents where some loony tries to break the last mass murderer's record. Concealed carry by qualified people would reduce and maybe eliminate campus and mall shootings.

To be fair to Detective Washington, I should give up my job as Chief and run for County Sheriff. He was already doing the job well and had all the qualifications. I liked the freedom and excitement of SWAT. I would maintain my status in that role. I could probably run unopposed since the current Sheriff was ready to retire and no one enjoyed as much popularity as I. Decisions as Sheriff could easily be made over the phone. The county already had a good force since Walker and I ferreted out the bad apples long ago.

Speaking of Mayor Walker Archer, I was sure to have his endorsement as well as the approval of the current Sheriff and all the Chiefs in the county. The American Legion and VFW would be in my corner too. It was about time that Washington got paid for the job he was already doing. He deserved the prestige and pay raise.

...

That was the psychological birth of the Derrick Johnson for Sheriff campaign. I was soon to find out that the county was 100% behind me. Within the year, I was the new Sheriff. Margaret was as proud as I was. It seemed like I'd been fated to have this job since I arrived back here in Conroe.

Margaret and I still had the same small circle of close friends. I had no further political ambitions. I preferred a quiet life out of the political spotlight. This position suited me just fine. I could keep an eye on the entire county from were I sat and share information with Sheriffs from the neighboring counties. It wouldn't hurt to get to know each of the neighboring sheriffs a little bit better than I already did and on a more personal level. It should be as simple as dinner and cards at my house so our respective wives could meet too. One couple at a time to keep it more personal and have less distractions. It was my hope to have our county be a model for all Texas and perhaps the nation.

Gaining the reputation of being a safe place to raise a family would lead to an influx of new residents. This would be good for real estate and retail businesses. Local industries could expand and new industries would be encouraged to locate here to absorb the growing workforce. I didn't want my neighbors out of work or having to commute long distances to find work. With all these thoughts running through my head, I could see that I'd be earning my new salary. It would be necessary to meet with the County Supervisor to alert him to these almost certain developments. He could get a head start on attracting new businesses and factories.

I hoped all this wouldn't lead to high-density housing and loss of country style living. It was time for me to roll up my own sleeves and rise to my new part time roll as managing advisor to the County Supervisor.

It might be nice to be a plain old cop again, but those days were over.

...

Montgomery County in general and Conroe in particular did indeed become magnets. Some 'California money' people came to town. They were extremely impatient with our meticulous way of doing business.

I called it legal and orderly. They accused us of living in the past. They started out by attempting bribery. Next, they tried intimidation. That resulted in their tough guys getting some Texas style butt whuppin's. Having hit the proverbial stone wall, they took their crooked nickels and dimes elsewhere.

One of their boys must have held a grudge because someone took a shot at me. My aim was better. His funeral was not held locally for all the obvious reasons. If they hadn't left, they'd have been run off anyway. Building codes were for everyone and compromises weren't for sale. They tried their baloney in Harris County never thinking I'd call ahead. They were run out of there too in short order thanks to my warning.

Building and developing went on anyway, by the rules of course. Local developers followed the rules. The trades were kept busy. Everyone prospered. Life went on without the California money and the shenanigans they brought with them. Churches were added onto and new ones were built. The 336 Loop was completed. Crime was virtually nonexistent.

Locally, our racial makeup mirrored the national average, quite by accident. Folks just settled wherever they felt comfortable. There was very little neighborhood polarization that caused street gangs to be formed. We were constantly running off illegal aliens to keep our own sons and daughters working for respectable wages.

Children enjoyed their youth without guns being brought to school. There were hunting rifles in the trunks of some cars during deer season. I never thought of that as a security breach. Some of those lads would grow up to be Policemen. Some of the hunter's families depended on the meat to balance their grocery budgets.

Kids were more worried about their grades or their after school jobs to worry about who was what color. Unless I was missing something, racial tension didn't seem to be a problem.

Something in the back of my mind was telling me that I *was* missing something. On a whim, call it premonition, I decided to check parole dates on that bunch of bikers that I'd rounded up years ago. With haircuts and jobs, they could keep a low profile while recruiting new members until strong enough to cause trouble again. A few hours on the computer told me that they wouldn't be a problem in my lifetime. So why was I so uneasy? Time to check on the latest about the body we found in Tiny's tree fort. A message to fifty states and the patience of a saint still brought no results. I guess it was possible that the man was a foreigner here illegally. For my next move, I called all the Police Chiefs in my county to ask if any of their residents were from abroad. It seemed as if Willis was getting a large influx of men from South Africa. The Chief in Willis said that he hadn't seen any signs of Arian activity, but he'd keep eyes and ears open.

The problem that finally surfaced came from left field. Overseas interests were 'buying' guards at Huntsville State Prison. They were being made offers that they couldn't refuse. The threats to their families coupled with substantial monetary reward procured the services of enough guards to create a large hole in security. The worst case scenario became reality. The maximum-security module cracked like an egg, spilling the contents in a torrent that no one expected. Death Row and life sentence inmates poured onto the streets of Huntsville. Some of the escapees never looked back. Many wound up in hostage situations.

The list of escapees who fled the area was turned over to U.S. Marshals for their dangerous roundup. The SWAT team and I were engaged in resolving the hostage situations. Stack and his sniper capabilities would be a very valuable asset. The hostage takers' demands were so uniform as to sound like movie scripts. They all wanted large sums of cash plus a car or helicopter. Most of them got paid in lead guided by Stack's deadly aim.

The few holdouts were coming out on their own with their hands up. They had televisions on in their hostages' homes and the news wasn't encouraging.

Patching up the hole in security at the prison was going to be a challenge. Tracking down the cause was going to be tougher. Evidently, the financial backer had considerable funds to draw upon as well as political connections inside the prison system. This entity must already have a network of muscle in place for intimidation purposes. Not all the escapees were accounted for. Finding out who those men and their connections to each other would be vital to busting the source of this calamity. My hunch was that they were *expecting* to be freed *and* there was a pre-planned specific purpose requiring the particular talents these men possessed.

I couldn't take over because this was a Walker County problem, out of my jurisdiction. My SWAT team had only been on loan. I feared that the Walker County Sheriff might have been made an offer he couldn't refuse. The State Police were in my corner. We'd worked well together before. I hoped that they could be the bridge between jurisdictions. I'd speak to the State Troopers assigned to Walker County and suggest that they keep an eye on both the Huntsville Police Chief and the Walker County Sheriff.

Now, I'd start looking for trouble in my own back yard where I was used to it showing up. I started a program of neighbors watching neighbors. All it took was a three-minute segment on the evening news on top of all the expected coverage that an event this size would receive.

Hopefully the bad guys wanted out of the country and not revenge on the folks who put them behind bars. Men in the business of being 'bad' sometimes worried too much about saving face. They felt the need to make an example out of the brave men who stood in their way. The reason that they'd wound up on the losing end was that they underestimated the local police forces. Now, they might feel like they owed us a sound thrashing.

They'd be easier to deal with if we didn't have our families to worry about. Loved ones could be used as weapons against us. The escapees who fought it out and died or surrendered turned out to be the local bikers. The ones who got away were affiliated with the creeps who dealt in flesh or live human sex slaves who wound up dead.

The massive jailbreak was obviously a smoke screen. It was designed to camouflage the escape of those entities, foreign and domestic, belonging to the cult. I wondered if they'd quietly slip out of the country or be foolish enough to stick around and seek revenge. I never got the impression that they were fools, just evil. They might have thought us to be the fools. Cops in general get underestimated frequently.

I wish I knew if that bunch in Willis from South Africa had anything to do with the escape. I figured that they would be a good place to start the investigation.

I checked with the chief up in Willis on the status of his newest citizens. He told me that they kept to themselves and didn't show any concern one way or the other when that escape in Huntsville took place. I told him that we'd keep a close eye on them all the same. They were the only unknowns in the equation, therefore most likely to be involved.

As quickly as possible, I set up 'round the clock surveillance using plain-clothes county cops in unmarked vehicles. First, we got a census of the residents of the enclave with photos or at least descriptions of every member.

I wasn't surprised to learn from our surveillance teams that the population of the enclave had grown by six. I was certain that it was no coincidence that there were six escapees as yet unaccounted for. Next step was acquiring telephoto pictures of all and sundry to compare to the mug shots of the Huntsville escapees.

...

After scrutinizing the photos, we established that our Huntsville Dirty 'Half' Dozen were among their number. I arranged for a visit from Immigration to see who of them were here legally and which ones might be wanted by INTERPOL. It was decided that an armed, pre-dawn raid would be safest to pave the way for Immigration authorities.

Using both Willis City Police and Montgomery County Police in body armor and black fatigues, we served our warrants at 4 AM. They were as arrogant as ever and had no one on guard. It was a bloodless arrest. We took our six back to the newly improved Huntsville Prison to finish their sentences plus time added for escape. Immigration led the larger group off to face federal sentences. Many would be deported.

Prosecuting the guards involved with aiding and abetting the escape would be complicated. There were mitigating circumstances. I defy anyone who has seen someone's family, including children, wiped out in a snuff film, to refuse cooperation with people capable of carrying out such a heinous act. I know that I couldn't. If anyone harmed my family, I doubt if I could limit my response to the confines of the law.

...

Jason Sprague was disappointed that I didn't involve him in that last minor adventure. I suggested that he turn over the dental records of our John Doe to the South African Embassy to see if he was one of theirs. I promised him dinner one way or the other if he would clear up that one hunch for me.

He seemed to accept this as my best apology for snubbing him on that last shindig. Praise The Lord, we were still friends. He managed to get me to agree to dinner in advance, making it a family affair. The isolation of my house made it the natural choice of locations for dinner. With Sinbad loose in the yard, we weren't likely to be interrupted by man or beast, at least not without a warning.

...

Jason was still operating out of that suite downtown. I asked him when he would settle into something less formal, like buying one of David's last lots and building a home. He was reluctant to take that discussion any further and I didn't pursue the matter. He probably had a divorce in his recent past that made nest building low on his list of priorities.

I changed the subject to my youngest son's progress in Tae Kwon Do. That's when he opened up a little and said that he had a son in Karate too. He also had a daughter in ninth grade. They lived in Virginia. He hoped to rent here a house so they could visit in the summer. His marriage lasted 12 years before his wife got tired of the empty spot at the dinner table.

After dinner, we went to the underground theater to watch a movie on the big screen TV. He was noticeably impressed at my personal movie theater and even more impressed with the story behind it. He had been briefed on the Conroe situation but was eager to hear a first hand account and missing details. He said that he finally realized why we mistrusted any and all strangers. I reminded him that truth was stranger than fiction. All he did was shake his head soberly.

Travis left for home after the movie and history lesson. Before Jason left, he promised quick results on the dental records from John Doe. Sinbad walked him to his car like family. That dog had been an asset since I got him. I'd always gotten good vibrations from Jason too. Sinbad was a very important part of the security at my secluded outpost.

Margaret and I planned on turning in early. I had nothing on the front burner for tomorrow. She and I could spend some quality time together. Sinbad and I walked the property line before turning in. It was a ritual that we'd adopted. I doubt if either of us could have slept had we not done it. Once we were back inside, he took up his place on the rug by the front door, curling up for the night.

I called the barracks while Margaret took her shower. All was well at the office. I was grateful for a quiet night. I mused about the prison break.

That had been a close call. Horror movies are made from the deeds such evil men perpetrate on innocents.

...

In the morning, Margaret and I went to The Kettle for the social factor. I missed having breakfast with my friends and ribbing the waitresses. It was the best source of local news too. If you wanted to know what was going on within ten miles of Conroe, just ask a waitress at this particular restaurant. Chief Washington was here too. Knowing him, he'd probably already been at the office a couple of hours prior to coming here. The next person through the door turned out to be Jason. It was old home week at The Kettle.

While we were discussing the positive impact of that immigration roundup, Jason's cell phone went off. When he hung up, he informed me that John Doe was not from South Africa. I asked him to try Belgium next since they had contributed players to our original and worst fiasco. He blackmailed me out of another dinner. This time I invited the Chief and Mrs. Washington too. As long as Mayor Archer and his wife were there, I went to their table and invited them too. We'd go out this time since the KP on that many people would be a monumental task. Everyone agreed on tonight.

...

We went to a fancy spot that Eleanor and Margaret liked so well. Margaret had grown up in a more austere environment. Fancy places had always been for other people. I was proud to be earning enough to give her the better things in life. Chief Washington had been raised poor from what I heard. I think that he felt as I did and was happy to show his wife a good time.

I picked up the tab despite others reaching for the check. I explained to them that I was still flush on reward money so no one would feel insulted.

I said, "As far as I'm concerned, we all ate for free tonight."

The ladies kept the table buzzing, so the four of us men carried our drinks to the bar for our own conversation. That allowed them to tattle secrets on us when they ran out of small talk.

I'm sure that Jason was feeling lonesome for the married life he used to have and the rest of us were enjoying. At the bar, it was less of an issue. I figured that one of our local girls would catch his eye before too long. There were plenty available and he was a pretty good catch. If he got his children for the summer, a mother figure would be an invaluable asset. That was his business to be taken care of at his own pace. Choosing a lifetime mate was serious stuff that required both time and caution.

Time flew, but it was still early enough for honest folks to get a good night's sleep. We broke up the group therapy session at the ladies table to regain our spouses and go our separate ways. I could tell from Margaret's conversation on the way home that Jason's eligibility was discussed thoroughly. They'd already come up with a lady that they thought would be perfect for him. Jason was fixin' to meet this girl soon, one way or another, no matter what scheme they had to resort to.

It seemed like it was my duty to warn Jason. He would either like the girl or he wouldn't. At any rate, he'd be happier with another woman. Loneliness will eventually kill a man. (Don't tell the ladies I said that!)

...

The next morning, Jason called with news on John Doe's dental records. Belgium was the ticket. The deceased was mixed up in all manner of diabolical mischief. Belgian authorities said that all humanity could breathe a sigh of relief with that man in the ground. If only that could be the last of our problems along those lines.

I called my son, Travis to tell him the news. His response was almost verbatim what mine had been. Those men weren't human. They were God-less demons in the flesh.

He and I decided on a father and son breakfast at The Kettle. Our topic of discussion after John Doe was Annie's return to the family group with her new husband. He was likeable enough and expressed interest in police work. To me, he seemed more the detective type than SWAT material, but the Army can change a man. The expression is, "You can't tell a book by its cover." I wasn't going to be guilty of any hasty decisions. I was hoping that he'd go along with putting up a house on one of my lots.

It has always been my hope to keep the family close. Her homecoming was only a week away. They could stay with Margaret and me until their house was built if that was what they wanted.

...

In three months, Annie and her husband Sam were moved into their new home on Derrick Place. Jason was hitting it off well with the girl our wives led him to. When I'd warned him, he just smiled and shrugged his shoulders. She, in turn, got along well with his two children. Sam had put on a lot of muscle since I'd seen him last. He said that he didn't want to look scrawny next to the other members of SWAT.

All this peace and harmony was getting on my nerves. I missed sharing adventures with my Army friends. As crazy as they were, we were like brothers. I sincerely wasn't hoping for anything bad to happen in our community, but I was bored to tears. As it turned out, I didn't have long to wait. One thing remains constant on Earth. There will be evil until the Second Coming of Christ.

The vacuum created when the biker element was killed or incarcerated had gone unfilled as long as organized crime could stand it. They tried using the same tactics as the South Africans used on the guards at Huntsville. Intimidation can work both ways. Our response to them was to shower their contacts with photos not only of thirty-odd bikers in various positions of death, but the myriad other photos of cultists cut down in a two month period. We left the guards the photos to show these new comers who were trying to gain a foothold in the local world of organized crime. Our tactics proved effective. The attempts were ceased without bloodshed. We'd shown that bigger and 'badder' fish had already been fried. The new fish swam off after learning that this water was too hot.

Back to boredom. I was hoping that Jason's wedding would break the monotony. The bash planned would rival Cinderella's Ball. There were to be State, Local, and County Policemen, FBI, and SWAT. It would unwise for anyone to crash this event. The reception was to be held outdoors at my home. It would provide entertainment for everyone's children too. There would be cartoons on the big screen TV, games in the yard, and all the playground equipment that I'd accumulated. Sinbad would patrol the fence line like a shepherd. He had grown to love children. I'd even invited my Army friends to add a little color, if not class to the event. They already knew some of the guests from that two month shared operation. Barry was recently married. I invited their wives too. None of them had ever met Margaret. I was really looking forward to the wedding, almost as much as Jason and his bride to be. The wedding was planned around a three-day weekend this summer. That way, very few of the guests had to miss any work.

It gave my Army friends time for traveling too. I'm sure that they missed being in a bunch like old times. My hair was getting grayer by the day. Barry's was practically non-existent. Ed's was pure white. Travis' hair was pretty gray too. We needed some group photos before we looked like old men. So far, everyone still had square shoulders and straight postures. Travis could still fight up a storm. As for myself, I was healthy as a horse and darn near as strong. Still, time waits for no man. No one gets out alive. It was nearing the time to pass the torch to our sons and younger teammates. Despite being strong as a horse, there was no denying that I couldn't run like I used to.

The war in Vietnam kind of froze the four of us at 20 or 21 years old mentally. None of us thought of ourselves as old. I was still a cop geared for action. The other three still had steel in their eyes the last time I saw them.

...

I picked Barry up at the airport in Houston. Ed and Big Travis were driving. They expected to be here before nightfall. Barry hadn't changed much since I last saw him. He gave me some good-natured kidding about my graying hair. I kidded him back about his lack of hair. Thank The Lord that we get a new body in Heaven.

Travis and Ed made good time. They had time to shower before supper. We'd all gotten grayer and a little heavier. All of their wives decided to stay home so their hubbies could go play with their friend in Texas. We were like a bunch of kids when we got together.

Big Travis wanted to say hello to his namesake to see how young Travis was growing up. We stopped over with his permission, but only for a few minutes. It was getting late and my son had his own life. Tomorrow was Saturday, D-Day for Agent Jason Sprague. He seemed so happy. I doubt if he was nervous. The four of us had tents and canopies to erect in the morning. We also had to buy beer and fireworks.

Saturday came and went. Jason and his new bride looked so happy together, like they were meant for each other. I hope those feelings never wore off. Cleanup was a major task. Everyone but the newly weds pitched in. Even the kids performed little tasks. By 6 PM, it looked like none of it ever happened. I could clean the underground theater or bribe Ryan and his friends to do it.

Now it was time for some peaceful conversation with my three Army friends. Ed had bought a new pickup. That is what he and Travis drove to Texas. Travis was too busy buying vehicles for his daughters and wife to get anything fancy for himself. As long as his Harley ran, he was happy. It rained too much around here this time of year for them to bring their bikes up. Barry and I were strictly cage drivers. It was trucks or vans for us most of our lives.

The conversation went from our vehicles to the adventures we shared along Peach Creek chasing that abominable headhunter. Inevitably, we got around to talking about the war. Ed was the most fortunate because he remembered the least despite having been in Vietnam more than twice as long as Barry or me and 9 months longer than Travis.

Even though Ed was in a different platoon, the whole company was used whenever we'd tackle a hill. The four of us would always have Hills 882 and 714 in common. A lot of blood was spilled on and around both. John DelVecchio mentions both in his book, The Thirteenth Valley. Keith Nolan mentions Hill 882 in his book, The Siege of Fire Base Ripcord. Fire Support Base Ripcord overshadowed our battles on 882 because it involved a lot more troops *and*, bad as we had it, their fighting was worse. We felt bad at the time for not being able to go help them. We couldn't abandon our own mission. There just weren't enough troops to go around in 1970. There certainly wasn't a shortage of enemy. The 101st Airborne Division, *alone,* suffered 50 more KIA than the 30,000 troops involved in the Cambodian Incursion and *they* had it rough. Try to find that in your school books kiddies.

War talk gets old fast. We were all getting heebie-jeebies, like we were back in that damned jungle. It was time for a good night's sleep, hopefully free of nightmares after our grim conversation.

In the morning, it was evident that we'd all tossed and turned. The nightmares were in everyone's eyes. A guy asked me one time to name two things that reminded me of Vietnam. I told him the backs of my eyelids and a mirror. He quit asking after that. Take two salt tablets and drive on. It don't mean nothin'.

We had the day to ourselves without any plans. A few phone calls placed my workload on willing and ample shoulders. The county pretty much ran itself. Besides, I was never more than a phone call away.

We stretched our late breakfast 'til almost noon. There were a lot of familiar faces coming and going. We decided to spend the day at The Gulf as the beach at Galveston was usually referred to. My legs needed a tan.

It only took a few minutes to run home for our swimsuits. In that brief time, the radio was awash with news that couldn't be ignored. All available units were called to cordon the hospital. Six men in lab coats had converged on the pharmacy. They had produced automatic weapons, demanding entry, and were in the process of cleaning it out. They had over a dozen hostages in the pharmacy waiting area. The remainder of the floor was being evacuated and the rest of the building sealed by security and Conroe's finest. SWAT was to meet at the main entrance.

By the time I'd armed my three friends and myself, and driven to the hospital, the rest of SWAT was in place. My first order was to scramble a helicopter and have it hover at a high altitude. If we had to let these guys drive away, I wanted to keep track of them.

So far, there hadn't been any violence. I was hoping to keep it that way. We were advised that the thieves were young. They were obviously strangers to try anything in this town. My son and the other members were dispatched to rooftops nearby to await targets of opportunity should there be no peaceful alternative. Barry and Travis boosted Ed and me onto the canopy roof over the front door. Then they raced up the stairs to the second floor, each one manning a window on either side of the canopy. We'd have clean, clear shots from behind if it became necessary. All of our weapons were laser sighted. Our sunglasses enabled us to see the red dots in the bright sunlight.

Before long, our inexperienced drug thieves came out the front door holding their human shields in front of them. We had the usual show of force in place in the form of several squad cars and a like amount of uniformed Policemen. The robbers' attention was focused on the police barricade. They directed their demands at the cops in front of them. After their speech was over, naming all of the things on the little creeps' wish list, I made a speech of my own.

"Don't turn around! Look at the red dots on the foreheads of your friends. Now, think of four more automatic rifles behind you. This is your one brief opportunity to live through this adventure. Lay down your weapons now or die where you stand! Next, step over your weapons and walk toward the police cars with your fingers laced together on top of your heads."

The noise of AK-47's and Uzi's hitting the ground was a welcome sound. The uniforms swarmed the robbers like wolves in a herd of sheep. In a matter of minutes, everything was under control. News cameras were just arriving, moments after the fact.

Now, where were we? Oh yeah, going to Galveston to get some suntans.

...

We were determined to go to the beach despite the interruption. Thank God that I was there to orchestrate a swift solution. It made me wonder how another man would have handled the situation. One thought leading to another had me contemplating the politics of my inevitable retirement. Would I be content to sit on the sidelines watching others protect my safe, happy community in their own fashion?

The warm beach soon dispelled these deep thoughts as the four of us frolicked in the waves like teenagers. Despite the subtle signs of aging, gray hair, thicker waistlines, there was still a lot of muscle on our little patch of beach. Even unarmed, the four of us had a lot of obvious firepower. No one came around to kick sand in our faces anyway.

After the beach, it was a steak dinner in Houston before heading back to town. Conroe, Texas still looked like home to me despite the obvious signs of expansion that didn't exist twenty years ago when I first came here.

My property at the dead end would never change. It was backed up to a swamp, which was part of Sam Houston State Forest. I had a bad moment as I remembered living there alone next to a cemetery. Those days were gone. There'd be nothing but happy times from here on out at this end of Derrick Place.

That evening, as the four of us walked the property line with Sinbad in the lead, I voiced my thoughts. "We all need another adventure before we lose our edge altogether."

Their responses varied little. All were in sync with that thought. Sinbad picked up the pace a little too, joining in the lament of all aging warriors, dying with our boots on and a weapon in our hand. Musing aloud again, I said, "The Good Lord will provide for our needs. That might mean a peaceful ride into old age. I'm going to trust His assessment of our needs and abilities."

That thought was denied so vehemently by my three friends in unison that I felt embarrassed to have voiced it. Damn fire breathing dragons to a man. The apology on my lips was stifled by the awesome growling of Sinbad as he dashed ahead barking so furiously that I thought he'd caught someone. We all ran to the dog's location at the back fence where we could hear the tread of many feet running off into the wilderness. Sinbad went for the style to go over the fence, but Ed grabbed his collar. I gave Ed my pistol before the rest of us ran to the house to get rifles for everyone. Margaret unlocked the gun safe while I called my son Travis and Annie's husband Sam telling them to join us in full gear with extra ammunition and extra flashlights.

The Lord certainly hadn't taken long to dump another adventure on us. Ask and you shall receive. My adrenaline was starting to flow. My friends were grinning too. They knew this was 'it'. We all felt alive again. My last call was to the station. I had Chief Washington send four uniformed Policemen to protect the house so the rest of us could give chase.

The preparations took less than ten minutes. Sam and Travis pulled up just then, followed by a police cruiser, then a second one practically on the first one's tail.

Our hastily formed army numbered six, plus we had Sinbad. He had a lot of energy for a twelve-year-old dog. We let him trot ahead, following cautiously at a swift pace. We didn't want to run headlong into an ambush.

Three of us had belt radios and everyone had a cell phone. Calling for backup and staying in touch wouldn't be a problem if we had to split up. We caught up with Sinbad just before sundown. He was waiting at the river. There were marks in the mud from a flat-bottomed boat. It was almost a guarantee that they headed for the lake. The river, actually just a creek, got narrow and shallow real fast as it meandered west. There was nowhere to launch a boat from in that direction. I got on the radio to muster a Water Patrol craft to block the creek where it went under the bridge to the lake. I warned them to have plenty of back up, because there were multiple unknown individuals headed their way. I suggested that they call for a squad to park on the bridge.

Thank God that Travis and Sam had thought to bring mosquito repellant. We'd have been miserable without it. The little bloodsuckers had descended in a cloud as soon as we stopped running.

Sinbad's attention was all aimed to the east. If that boat got past the bridge before the blockade, we might never solve the mystery about our evening visitors.

It was seven miles on foot to the bridge. We'd never get there in time to be any help. However, if the fugitives spotted the blockade and pulled a U-turn, we might be back in the game. They could opt to go back west to where the creek split only two miles to our west. Overland, it wasn't too far to get to a highway. That is the direction that I moved our miniature army in.

At the first place that the creek looked shallow enough, I took my son Travis and Big Travis with me, wading across, praying that there were no alligators between us and the other shore. I told the rest of the men to walk west parallel to us and respond as the situation dictated. It was just on the brink of full darkness now. Soon the woods would be alive with more than just mosquitoes. The chorus frogs were starting to sing. We could hear the deep moans of bullfrogs scattered around as well.

Water levels must have been lower than usual because the creek had become too shallow for a boat with more than one passenger well before we reached the fork. I radioed a halt with instructions to find some kind of cover where they were. My last words were, "Watch out for snakes." There were both Cottonmouths and Timber Rattlers out here. The clouds of mosquitoes caught up to us again the moment we stopped. Gotta love that bug juice!

In a minute or so, the sound of gunfire drifted towards us from the east. It sounded like AK-47's initially. Almost immediately we could pick out the boom of the Water Patrol's deck mounted 50-Caliber machine gun.

The creek formed a tunnel through the woods that made it possible to hear sounds many miles away, despite the all the twists and turns. The chase was swiftly moving in our direction. Everyone flattened out not wanting to be struck by the 50. A round in the thigh could take your leg off. When the noise of the two boats drew near enough so that we could hear two distinct engines, I requested a cease-fire from Water Patrol informing them of our danger. I also warned them of the shallow water that their larger boat would definitely run aground in. Grudgingly, they abandoned their chase to our ambush.

Abruptly, their quarry's flat-bottomed boat came in sight. There were six men aboard. All were armed with AK-47's. They ran their boat aground on the land that divided the stream. They were practically in our laps. Their nonchalance told me that they thought that they were alone. I radioed to Sam to holler "Sheriff's Police" as soon as he heard me shout, "Freeze!" My hope was for a peaceful surrender once they learned that both banks had men on them. I could only hope that Ed had control of Sinbad so he wouldn't burst forth and get shot.

My shout was echoed by shouts from Sam's group. Also, as hoped, all six men surrendered. They must have assumed that they were surrounded and had nowhere to run. That was a wise move. Besides, I didn't want to clean my M-16.

We only had three pair of handcuffs between us. We cuffed four men together. Barry and Big Travis took the men's belts and looped them around their necks like leashes. The prisoners could use their free hand to hold their pants up. It would keep them out of mischief.

Five of us walked the prisoners downstream to where the Water Patrol waited. Big Travis was familiar with every kind of watercraft, so he followed in their flat-bottomed boat. We borrowed more handcuffs from Water Patrol so the prisoners could be cuffed singly making it easier to get on and off the big boat. The rest of us followed in the flat-bottomed boat. When we got to the bridge, there was a paddy wagon waiting.

Our prisoners were just peeping Toms until they shot at the well-marked police boat. Now we had something serious to hold them on. It would give us time to find out who they were and what their intentions were. The six prisoners looked familiar. All were about the ages of my sons and son-in-law. That mystery could wait for morning.

I personally thanked the men with Water Patrol for their prompt and timely response and their brave and persistent pursuit of six armed men. I made a mental note to see that they were recognized for their actions. There were only three men on their boat against six bad guys. I'd be sure that there was a piece in the paper too. They and their families had reason to be proud. After we loaded the prisoners in the paddy wagon, we bummed rides from the two idle squads on the bridge.

...

I let my guests sleep in the next morning. My curiosity had me at the county jail at 7 AM. None of last night's prisoners were talking. We already had positive ID on all of them. Some of their names were hauntingly familiar, as were several of their faces. Before long, it hit me. These were the sons of the thirty-odd bikers that were killed in my yard many years ago. They'd held their grudge all these years. Too, there must have been more sons and daughters of those bikers out there somewhere. Each one would blame the deaths of their daddies on me. Never mind the fact that I didn't go to their homes and shoot them. They were killed in my yard trying to murder me.

Those thoughts had me contemplating the possibility that these six men were the vanguard of a much larger operation. I needed to take this personally and proceed with all caution. The first thing I did was call Margaret to tell her of my suspicions. I recommended that she pack up some things and stay with her sister for a while.

Next, I put detectives to work looking up the names of all the men killed in my yard that night. Once that list was complete, I had them trace family members. While they were working on that, I called the members of SWAT to let them in on my hunch and asked them to meet at my home. Now, I could go home to tell Big Travis, Ed and Barry what was likely to be going on.

I had a full house when I got home. My army friends were grateful for the extra sleep. They'd already been filled in by SWAT as to my theory about a revenge attempt in the works. Barry, Big Travis and Ed had five days left to waste. They wanted in.

We moved our group to The Kettle for seating and the availability of coffee. When I called the station for a progress report, they warned me that a complete list was probably not possible since most of the children were born out of wedlock.

Our best hope was to try to learn where the group was congregating. That would mean squeezing it out of the six we already had with promises of the long prison terms each would get for three counts each of attempted murder of a police officer. One or more was bound to crack under that kind of pressure.

We remained at the restaurant drowning ourselves in coffee, getting more wired by the minute. We were trying to imagine the scenarios that might pop up, then work out a solution for every possibility.

A little after 10 AM, we got a call. One of our prisoners had caved in. I told them to hook him to a polygraph before we bought into his story. He could be setting us up for an ambush. We had to assume that these guys were as ruthless as their fathers were and maybe even smarter. They'd had a lot of years to work out a plan.

The rat's story didn't hold up under the lie detector. A second one said that he had some information that might help if we went easier on his sentence by reducing the charges. He turned out to be a liar too. This was a tough, determined bunch of youngsters. It was a good thing that we'd had Sinbad at the fence with us or we might have been killed on the spot.

Since none were cooperating, we scheduled their indictment and put them back in jail. I'd ask the judge if he'd allow us to hold them without bail until their trials. I instructed the guards to keep them in cells separate from each other. General population might change their minds about jail. That would come later. Now we needed a man inside with a wire, moving about their cells. This could take a while and time might not be on our side. I told my Florida friends to try for an extended leave of absence from their jobs. All were happy to do that and all got permission.

We got what we wanted later the same day. Young men like to brag in jail to elevate their prestige. The bits and pieces that our inside snitch was able to glean from his spying mission provided the name of a favorite hangout in Cleveland beyond Cut'n'Shoot. That was sure to be where the rest of this large group of hate-mongers frequented. At least it was a starting point.

Our first subtle infiltration was a female police officer. She got a job as a barmaid there. She was a crack shot and tough for a 140-pound black belt. She was pretty enough to draw customers too.

Next, Big Travis got a job working the door. He was a muscular 230 pounds and 6' tall. He looked the part. His face had more scars than an entire hockey team put together. He'd been punched in the face with too many beer mugs. So far, he'd never lost a fight. A keg might slow him down, but a beer mug just makes him mad.

Edwin got a job, tending bar. He'd done that more than once in Florida and Indiana. At 6' 2" and with his rough face, he was a pretty convincing bartender. When he smiled, he looked more like a hungry wolf than a happy camper. He had experience as an MP besides his time in the Infantry.

Barry volunteered to be a new customer. It was a tough job (yeah, right) but he sacrificed for us. What a guy! He, too, was big enough to be dangerous at 6' 2" and a solid 190 pounds.

My son Travis had some pretty big arms and a couple of tattoos. He, too was a customer. His role was that of an unaffiliated biker who kept to himself.

Sam arrived next as another patron playing a wannabe role. He dressed like a biker but didn't look like one. Truth be known, that wholesome looking ex-GI could kick some serious butt.

My job was to sit across the street in a junky old van that ran like a raped ape, but who would guess? Darn thing had a Chevy 454 engine. I monitored everyone's wire and tried to recognize the patrons who came and went. By and by, we'd sneaked enough undercover people in there to have an even chance in an unarmed bar fight. Trust me when I say that none of us were unarmed. I'm sure that most men in that bar were armed too, as far as that went. This was going to be interesting.

The owner of the joint wasn't let in on our operation because he was a suspect too. He readily hired our people. I guess there was quite a turnabout in personnel there. The help wanted sign never left the window. Another thing he didn't seem to notice was the rise in clientele, all of them strangers to this neck of the woods. The poor man must have been as dumb as he looked.

At this current stage, with all the bugs in the men's and ladies rooms and by the pool table, I needed help deciphering and keeping track of all the information. My Army friends asked for and got the extra time off. They too, had some leverage as minor celebrities.

After three weeks, we learned that the six men we caught by Peach Creek in the dark had been a hit squad. Again I thanked The Lord for my dog. We had finally identified the rest of the patrons in the place. All had prior arrests. Some had major priors. It was time to make our move.

I would come through the front door leading several plainclothes men. All of us would be wearing ski masks with guns drawn. We'd declare a robbery. I hoped to disarm the customers without firing a shot. All were guilty of two counts of conspiracy since they were already planning their next attempt on my life.

Our people inside would don ski masks too to avoid accident. The bad guys wouldn't know that it was a bust until they were all disarmed. As we hoped for, all known suspects were on the scene this particular Friday evening. Tonight would be the night.

The sting went off successfully without a shot being fired. Forty-five bad guys tonight plus the six in custody with no casualties equals good police work. I think that even my old Math teacher would agree.

The sting was over, so my army friends were out of excuses to stick around. It was back to their homes and jobs. I hated to see those guys leave. Together, we *were* an army. Apart, we were just lonesome. Family and friends are wonderful, but combat soldiers have a special bond.

...

As enjoyable as that last adventure had been, it didn't quite live up to the excitement that my friends and I craved. I wasn't actually hoping for something bad to happen in my community, but I needed a shot of adrenaline and that last operation did *not* give it to me. The first six guys were definitely the worst we were up against. Their arrest was kind of a non-event. War is a pretty tough act to follow. The only thing like it is another war. Like all old soldiers, I didn't want to simply fade away and be forgotten.

I needed to get used to the placid life our tamed town provided and a normal man would be grateful for. I gave up on feeling normal the second or third time that my adrenaline came out back in 1970, early in my tour in Vietnam. Back then, adrenaline floods had become normal for us. The stuff might really be addictive. It sure was exciting at the very least. I can only speak for myself, but I truly enjoyed feeling like Superman. One day, and regrettably soon, all that I would be was a walking library unfit for active police work, suitable only to train other cops.

I wouldn't even consider becoming a mercenary. Half are wannabes, the other half are murderers with a hero complex. I asked Jesus to be my personal savior a long time ago. I had a clear shot at heaven. I didn't want to mess that up. If The Lord wanted me to retire here in peace, I wouldn't question His will.

I was a grandpa now. I had the responsibility to set a good example for my grandchildren. The truth is that I loved to see them having fun. Their smiles and laughter were a comfort to a bored old man. There I go again. Who was I kidding? How many "old men" did their pushups fifty at a time? I still have a lot of good years left in me. What I needed was patience. Trouble had always beaten a path to my door. Sooner or later, it would come knocking. Besides, my body would tell me when it was time to roll over and play dead.

...

I was playing Frisbee with Sinbad. It was just after sunup. We both needed the vigorous exercise. At the moment, he and I were in a very familiar tug of war. As smart as he was, he would never fetch properly. I'd throw it. He'd run and get it. Then the tug of war began. He'd never just drop it at my feet. He'd make me work to get it away from him. His game was hell on Frisbees, but good exercise for both of us.

This time, when I got it away from him, I deliberately hooked it around the corner of the house. I was surprised when he didn't come right back. After about thirty seconds, I knew that he'd found something. It was probably a snake or a turtle looking for a place to lay eggs. I thought it a good idea to see what he'd found in case it was a bad snake. I sure didn't want him to get bit.

When I turned the corner, I saw Sinbad at the fence. He was licking the hand of a small child who was on the other side of the fence trying to pet him. The poor waif was just out of diapers and into training pants. He was barefoot. He was covered in mosquito bites with cloud of the critters flying around him. I reached over the fence and picked him up to rescue him from the mosquitoes. I carried him into the sun. He seemed quite comfortable with my dog and me. My guess was that he came from a home with a large dog.

I called out a few times in case some adult was wandering around the woods looking for the little guy. No one answered my shouting except Margaret.

"Who have you got there, Derrick?" she asked. "Did the stork bring you another grandchild?"

I filled her in briefly and asked her to take the boy into the house. Sinbad and I went over the style and walked to where the child had been standing. When we got there, I told him, "Find!" He picked up the trail and led me along the fence back toward the main road and the rest of our neighborhood. He followed the trail nearly to the beginning of Derrick Place, right up to an open patio door. It was one of the first homes built on the street when David had started developing it.

We went inside to find the grizzly beginning of my next adventure. There was a fairly large dead man on the kitchen floor on the other side of the table. I'd guess him to be in his mid-twenties. He had multiple stab wounds including in both eyes. It looked like the wounds were made from a large knife. I drew one of my revolvers and walked cautiously through the rest of the house with Sinbad at my heel.

I found a dead woman approximately the same age as the man and a dead infant. Again, both had multiple stab wounds and their eyes had been stabbed too. The woman's clothes were mostly gone. What was left was torn and useless.

The toddler must have slipped out unnoticed, probably through the patio door that the killer entered through and left open.

Searching further, I found a dead dog in the nursery. It too, had multiple stab wounds including to its eyes. The dog was a golden retriever mix, about eighty-five pounds.

There was blood on the doorknob inside the room. That meant that our killer would need treatment for bite wounds. It also meant that the killer was strong, fast, fearless, and methodical. The dead man in the kitchen was over six feet and looked like a construction worker in good shape. I was pretty certain that only one perpetrator was involved. I was also quite sure that he would strike again.

I'd let the forensic team and the Coroner tell me for sure, but I had a hunch that the baby was killed in here and tossed onto the bed next to the woman whom I assumed was its mother. I hope that she was already dead at that point.

The phone line was dead. That explains why 911 hadn't been called. Other than on the telephone on the wall in the kitchen, I'd left no fingerprints. I was careful not to have stepped in any blood. By nature, my dog sniffed the blood but didn't walk in it. Sinbad and I left by the same door that we'd entered, leaving it open.

Sinbad and I walked to the house directly across the street to borrow a telephone. My cell phone was at my house being charged.

The man in the front yard shut off his lawnmower and told me to help myself. I dialed 911 and advised dispatch to send the coroner as well as an ambulance.

I walked back to the scene of the crimes and sat on the front porch petting Sinbad. While I waited, I was running the visual evidence through my head. I contemplated the importance to the killer of stabbing their eyes. I pictured a man who wore glasses with thick lenses. I wondered if there was a motive. I wondered too, if this family had been a specific target, or just a random spree to satisfy some maniac's needs. Maybe the psycho had 20/20 vision and just liked this kind of mutilation. In the Army, we were taught to go for the eyes immediately in hand to hand combat. Those poor people could have been alive when he stabbed out their eyes. Murdering the adults that way was horrible. Brutalizing and killing that infant was diabolical. He deserved the death penalty if he made it as far as court.

I pictured the father getting it first, out of necessity. The dog would be next for safety reasons. Too, it had to be silenced. I shook my head in revulsion again at the thought of someone putting out the eyes of a dog and an infant. I had to stop this guy, no matter what, ASAP. It was my main priority now.

I wandered outside and found where he'd cut the phone line at a weep hole in the brick that it had been fed through. I wondered if the killer knew before hand that no cell phones or CB radios were inside. If not, he took a mighty big risk. Maybe he'd been incarcerated a long time and missed the advent of cell phones. The fact that no CB antenna was outside the home might have removed that worry from his head.

Upon the arrival of the crime scene investigators and the Coroner, I went back inside, standing out of the way near the front door. I wanted to hear their comments to see if their findings and hunches matched my thoughts. I fully expected them to. Soon, they were confirming my analysis. Blood tests and fingerprints would give me more information as the reports became available.

Before I left, I reminded them that this guy was still out there. "Killers like this will strike again when the 'high' wears off. Please put all other cases on the back burner and help me catch this guy.

Sinbad and I walked the mile to my house. As I filled Margaret in, I could read the horror in her eyes. She asked, "How could a beast such as this even exist in our community? Worse that it should happen practically on our doorstep. He mustn't be from around here."

"That is something I'd already made up my mind about. He has to be an outsider." I told her. "Psychos like this show signs as they progress toward murder and mutilation. I'd have been aware of it if someone in town was torturing animals and terrorizing his neighbors."

...

Before I'd left the crime scene, I asked the detectives to keep me informed. My cell phone still hadn't rung in the forty-some minutes since I'd left. I decided to put on my uniform and drive back there. Before I left my house, I arranged for a news team to meet me at the scene. Everyone had to be warned. Most folks in town never locked their doors during the day. Some left them unlocked at night. That practice had to change.

I recounted everything I knew to the reporters, but didn't allow any cameras or unauthorized people inside. I spoke to the people through the camera, telling them not to ignore barking dogs and to keep their doors locked and yard lights on.

The yard had been taped off. There were two uniformed members of Conroe's finest there to enforce my wishes. During the brief news conference, I stood so that the cameras could capture the Policemen behind me. Their wives and children would get a kick out of seeing them on the news tonight.

The next door neighbors put me in touch with next of kin of the deceased. I had the crummy job of telling them about the slayings of their family members. The only good news I had to share was the survival of the toddler who had shown up at my fence. The mother's parents lived in town. They came to pick up our little guest at my house right away.

The child's name was Everett. While I was gone, Margaret had soon found out that he could talk. We had a female child psychologist who could interview the toddler at the grandparents' house today. I impressed on everyone involved the urgency of capturing the killer right away. All I had to say was that monsters like this kill over and over until caught or destroyed.

Details about this crime were whirling around inside my head, all pointing to this, my hypothesis; The killer was brave, strong, ruthless, a stranger to this area, taunting me personally *and* he would strike again very soon, probably on this same street. He seemed to be a bold, confident killer who had won all his fights. His crime was thorough to the point of slaying the infant, therefore he did not know about the toddler slipping out the open patio door. This meant that despite his confidence, he wasn't infallible. I could capture or kill this guy. I had to think like him, but try to stay a step ahead of him. Organization was the key, a hasty block watch meeting was organized to get my new plan in motion today.

These feelings were so strong that I kept this as my main focus while adhering to what my experience dictates. I must keep an open mind and consider all possibilities. If some bit of stray evidence or information deviated from my theory, but seemed likely, I'd assign someone to look into that also, keeping it separate from the main investigation.

I wasn't very good at waiting, but some things take time. There were many things occurring to me that I could be doing simultaneous to the investigators' and lab's efforts. One thing to check out aside from my main plan was if the murderer was a person from the past of one of the dead parents. The bigger motorcycle gangs had long memories. If you owed them, they got paid or you died. There was only one warning. Skipping out doesn't work. Sooner or later, they will find you. When they do, pray that they kill you quickly. That has not always been the case.

The grandparents would be a wealth of information. Usually, it was the male spouse with a dark past, but both parents had to be considered. Women who owed money weren't exempt from their brutal form of gang justice.

...

The crime scene investigators confirmed that the baby was killed in the nursery and carried to the master bedroom. The father had been the first to die, right where he was found in the kitchen. He might have been checking out what had the dog barking and growling, being the first to encounter the killer. They thought that the dog was closed in the nursery with the infant. After dispatching the man in all haste, his next move was to silence the dog. That must have been when he discovered the baby, whose crying had to be silenced too. The mother had been the last to die. This was proven by the fact that her wounds had trace amounts of blood from the other victims including the animal. Both the front and back doors had been unlocked, just like most doors in town. There were strange fingerprints on every door in the house except for the door from the kitchen to the garage. Those prints were still being run through their database. Bloody footprints indicated a large, heavy man exited through the front door. I thought that was strange to do in daylight when the neighbors were home. Maybe the crimes were committed in the pre-dawn hours. He might have been looking for witnesses since the drapes were open and the blinds up. I wondered about a disguise to make the intruder seem harmless. He could have been dressed as a cop, a priest, or a utility worker. Their best guess was that he'd come through the unlocked patio door at the rear of the home.

They placed the time of death of all the victims at around 4 A.M. Air conditioners might have provided enough noise in neighbors' houses to mask the screams and barking. Still, I had to ask all the neighbors if they'd seen anything.

If our man was out and about in the wee hours, nearby convenient stores or the 24-hour gas stations might have tape of this guy on their security cameras. I wanted to check on that personally. If he hadn't been treated at the emergency room for bite wounds, he might be in another nearby home performing his own first aid. Many times today, I wished that I could clone myself so I could be in several places at once.

I asked Chief Washington to send men to look for blood on doorknobs on both sides of the street from the highway to my gate.

The 7/11 store's night manager said that an unusual looking man with his shirt wrapped around his arm came in a little after four A M. He had purchased some first aid cream and bandages. He'd claimed that he burned his arm trying to wire up his muffler. I was given the videotape from the night before which I played in the back room of the store. The manager let me burn a C D to keep.

The man on the tape looked like a bona fide gorilla to include a protruding brow and bushy eyebrows grown together. He was so muscular as to appear hunch backed. I had never seen this man before. He certainly didn't live on our street. I was 99% sure that this was our man.

Armed with a description of who we were looking for, I went back to Derrick Place to assist in what turned out to be a door to door search. I called the local TV station to come and pick up the C D so the segment showing our suspect could be aired on the evening news. Someone had to remember seeing this remarkable looking man in the area. A remote possibility was that it was just some drifter committing a random act of violence. I still had the feeling that he would strike again and he would strike on our street. Something told me that he was teasing me, that I was his main target.

After the newscast, we received a phone call informing us that the man on the tape was staying at a nearby 'high end' motel. I had the place surrounded immediately and drove out there. When we didn't get an answer to our repeated knocks, I had the manager unlock the door. The room was empty except for a bloody shirt carelessly left lying in the bathtub. This motel required picture ID and a major credit card to get a room. Now, we had positive ID on our suspect and a blood sample.

The motel was too pricey for most. That meant that our suspect was one of two things; Affluent or well paid to assassinate me.

We put out an all points bulletin and contacted the Huntsville Police. The man's ID named that as his town of residence. I was told that the address on his Drivers License was just another motel, but it had weekly rates. It wasn't nearly as fancy as his temporary digs in Conroe. The man had kept to himself. He'd not so much as even jay walked. On the rental application, there were no names in the section for nearest living relatives.

So, our man was a loner who kept to him self. Prison will do that to a man. It was past time to inform and involve the FBI. It would be good to work with Jason again. His resources made my County Force look like we operated on Barney Fife's budget. I asked him to check all recent prison releases in Texas. If that search was fruitless, he agreed to expand the search first to neighboring states, then nationwide if necessary.

Currently, it appeared as if our man had left he area. I'm sure that is only what he wanted us to believe. Savages like him were like man-eating tigers. Once they get a taste of human blood, nothing else tastes good.

We asked neighbors to look after neighbors and report anything suspicious or out of the ordinary. I hated the thought that he would do this again. It was inevitable. If he was indeed hired to kill me, or at least make me look incompetent, his next strike would be in my neighborhood, closer to my house.

. . .

So, I had to find one solitary man eating tiger that looked like a gorilla. Bigger fish had been fried in this town. The challenge would be in getting this particular fish in the frying pan before he struck again.

The videotape from the convenient store was my best piece of evidence. I studied it well over and over. My suspect was about 5' 10" and 230 pounds of muscle with little sign of fat. He had such a rough face that it was hard to guess his age with any accuracy. He looked anywhere from 30 to 40 years old. He must have been right handed since he fed the dog his left arm and stabbed it with his right.

Advanced martial artists and Military Police are taught the tactic of feeding their weaker arm to the animal, using their stronger arm to dispatch it. If unarmed, they are instructed to drop a hammer blow to the dog's snout. Turning the arm will bring the jaw vertical pulling the dog's nose upward. Both participants in that fight get hurt, but the dog loses. Smaller dogs can be taken out of the fight with a kick.

This guy was a loner. That would make him harder to locate. He adhered to the same street wisdom that all smart criminals do. A partner is a witness. If you're going to pull something stupid, do it alone and keep your mouth shut.

Another glaring truth is that our killer could be anywhere in the country. Dying his hair or shaving his head or growing a full beard would make him hard to spot. He could put lifts inside big-heeled boots to dramatically alter his height. He could have left town on a freight train the same way that I left Wisconsin all those years ago.

He could disguise everything but his gorilla like appearance. I already had some still photographs pulled from the videotape to circulate far and wide. As long as he didn't leave the planet, he'd get caught sooner or later.

If he wasn't holed up in someone's house, he might just take to the woods and try to live off the land. His casual attitude toward killing and his skillful use of the knife, coupled with the way that he handled a fairly large dog, gave me an idea. The killer could have been in one of the branches of Special Forces. I couldn't rule out Green Beret, but I was leaning toward him being a Navy SEAL. Green Beret usually train and lead indigenous forces. SEALs are all about killing. Special Forces like the two mentioned and Recondo Marines attracted the 2% of society who have no natural aversion to taking a human life. Not all were psychos. It's just that their kind of work attracted some evil men. When they were found out, they were discharged and even prosecuted sometimes. These thoughts were like a light going on in my head. Somehow, I knew that I'd need the help of Agent Jason Sprague to pry the necessary information from the Department of Defense.

...

With Jason working on that angle, I felt like I'd done all that I could in advance of physical preparations to protect my neighborhood. I had the creepy feeling that he'd chosen Montgomery County and Conroe in particular because of our nationally famous and very competent police personnel. The monster even had the boldness to strike on my street with three cops living at the dead end. That made it personal. If only he'd just called me out instead of murdering that family. I'd meet his challenge and he won't like the results of our battle. All he could put in the fight was him self. I had God on my side. There was no way that he could win.

I had the impression that he enjoyed killing since he hadn't come straight for me. I felt like I was experiencing divine inspiration. I was comfortable with all of my assumptions, like The Lord was steering my thoughts in the direction that I was taking. In my mind, I pictured this fellow planning to strike on my street again and again until he drew me into a face to face confrontation. I was going to make his consummation of those plans as difficult as earthly possible.

...

I asked for volunteers from both the city police and county police to pitch tents in every single back yard on Derrick Place from the highway up to the dead end with the exceptions of where my sons and I lived. Of course we'd be the ones camping there. There were more than enough volunteers. I distributed manpower and dogs as evenly as possible. Every husband on the street except for one elderly gentleman pitched a tent as well to help split up guard hours. If this turned out to be a waiting game, we couldn't afford to doze off.

We literally had a U-shaped perimeter with security front and back. I also staggered cops front and back to avoid a cluster of untrained men, thereby creating a weak spot. Every other position had a Policeman. Approximately every other tent had one or more dogs. Every other position would be awake at all times. I synchronized the shifts to ensure that no two adjacent positions would be asleep at the same time.

All this was organized by the evening of the day we discovered the bodies. It had been a long and hectic day. I was alternating between exhaustion and moments of being completely alert. Lab results weren't even complete. The extended parts of the investigation were still works in progress. The immediate defense of what I was sure that the murderer had chosen for a kill zone was taken care of. I felt much better for that fact. It was almost as good as a one-hour nap.

It was fast approaching sundown. The street was quiet. No one was taking this as a lark. Everyone's families were in danger. Everyone's life was in danger too.

I had the largest part of the perimeter to cover. This worried me more than I cared to admit. The killer was bigger and younger than I. He was more ruthless too. In my favor, God was on my side. That is the second time today that I was comforted by that thought. It really was a comfort too.

After I had driven the length of my street and surveyed the preparations, I felt better. I arrived only minutes before nightfall. Since I couldn't be home to look after her, I called Margaret earlier in the day and told her to back to her sister's for safety. She was only too happy to get out of there, knowing what might happen. She was smart enough to have left lights on throughout the house.

After I parked, I went inside, letting Sinbad lead the way. His relaxed demeanor told me that all was well. Still, I checked every nook and cranny just for peace of mind. Next, I fed my dog and made myself a sandwich. I grabbed a bottle of water out of the fridge to wash it down. It was too dark outside to sit at the table like a target, so I turned on the outside lights and killed the ones inside. Sinbad sat quietly by my chair at the table while I wolfed the sandwich down. Now, I killed the outside light at the back of the house and went out that door.

I had pitched my tent in a part of the yard that I knew would be very dark. The house shadowed it and no light from the front invaded this corner of the yard. I'd left my sleeping bag rolled up. Unzipping the tent slowly, I pulled out a five-gallon bucket that I put there to use as a stool. I sat outside the tent listening to the woods and letting my eyes adjust to the dark. I felt like I was operating on about a 50/50 mix of adrenaline to blood. I was as wide-awake as a man could be, thank God, because I'd forgotten to make arrangements for someone to help me pull guard.

...

After a while, Sinbad laid himself down next to me and went to sleep. I spent the next few hours with my natural radar locked on insect noises all around me, remembering countless nights spent in the jungle in Vietnam doing this very thing. It was much darker over there. There were no lights whatsoever where we operated. Visibility was virtually non-existent on cloudy nights. It was still pretty dark on moonlit nights due to the triple canopy jungle. Here, though relatively dark by normal standards, I could see much better than I could in that damn jungle.

Hours crawled slowly by in this manner. Every now and then, some night time predator would interrupt a portion of the insect noises. Almost as quickly, they'd start right back up. It was in one of those longer moments of silence that Sinbad sat up with his fur bristling. I too, felt that we were no longer alone out here. I put my hand on the dog and whispered for him to be quiet. After all these years together, it was like he could read my mind. He'd seen me kill enough men over the years to know that no matter what we were up against, he and I would live to see another sunrise. It hurt to see his obvious signs of age. No better friend could be found.

A large swath of the woods was dead silent around the area of the fence where the style was located. Soon, a bulky, shadowy figure could be seen moving very slowly toward the style. It was creepy to watch this big man moving so quietly and stealthily. I wondered, only for a moment, if he had a demon inside of him. No matter, he was mine to deal with and God would see me through this. It was a good thing that I acted quickly today or we'd have been caught off guard.

I was surprised to see that he made no move to approach my house. I moved quietly behind the tent, putting it between us. Sinbad, of course, came with me. I could feel his energy. His adrenaline gave him the attitude of a much younger dog. It looked like the intruder was going to pass my house on the West Side and go to my son's house. His pant legs were wrapped close and tied around his calves in military fashion to keep out bugs and prevent snagging in thorns. There was a short barreled assault rifle in a sling draped across his chest and he was carrying a large, pointed knife. It looked like it had been customized from a military machete to suit the man carrying it.

Sinbad and I crept to the southwest corner and lay down so as not to show a silhouette. He was definitely going to Travis' house. I'd viewed the convenient store video enough times to memorize every detail of the suspect. Even in the dark, fifty feet away, there was no mistaking that it was the same gorilla like man creeping toward my son's house.

At first I crawled after him until he was far enough past me so I was comfortable standing up to follow. He was in the outer edges of my front porch light's glow. He was as ugly in person as he was on the store video. I was now entering the part of the yard illuminated by my front light. If he looked over his shoulder, he was bound to see me. His automatic weapon was in a ready sling, not casually slung over his shoulder. This man had combat training and maybe even combat experience. He looked like he was very comfortable working alone at night.

Sinbad's hair was still bristling and he finally lost control and growled aloud. The suspect whirled to face the dog. He looked surprised to see me at all, and even a little afraid to see me so close. The gunfight started as soon as our eyes connected. He wasn't the type to be frozen by fear. He fired a short burst in my direction. Three of his slugs hit me. I had opened up at the same time. I had a little training and combat experience of my own. I had a thirty round clip in my M-16 and fired off an eight round burst. All of my shots hit their target and he fell backwards, kicking out his death throes violently.

The lights were still on in his eyes when I got up to him and looked down into his ugly face. Travis got there in time to see the man jerking out the last of his life. He looked at me and said, "Pop, you're bleeding a lot!"

I must have fainted from blood loss because I woke up in the hospital to a room full of smiling faces. I didn't feel much like sitting up. I hurt a lot. Travis told me that I was in intensive care for two days before they moved me to this room. He said that they removed three 9mm slugs. I had fuzzy memories of them bandaging me. That must have been after they removed the bullets. I learned that two were in my guts and one in my upper left thigh. I'm glad that I was unconscious when they were sewing my intestines up. I guess that I was closer to death than I had ever been. I can honestly say that I was glad that night was over and we got our man.

My son Travis said, "You saved my life pop. I didn't have a dog and I was sawing logs big time." Then he asked the nurse if he could hug me.

"Of course not!" she said forcefully. We did sort of shake hands. Margaret was in tears of happiness when she leaned down and kissed me. I was a bit misty myself. She said that a Pastor had read my last rites to me the night I was shot.

I found out that everybody and his brother was donating blood and praying for me. It was a good feeling to be loved like that.

The nurse eventually shooed everyone out of the room so I could take a nap. Over the course of the next week, I slept most of the time. One time I awoke soaked with sweat. I'd been having a nightmare about North Vietnamese Special Forces. If that was what dreamland was serving up, I thought it best to stay awake for a while. I fell asleep shortly after that thought. When I woke up next, Barry was in the room. He was grinning happily.

He said, "Big Travis and Ed are outside having a smoke. They got bored listening to you snore. I figured that I'd stay here looking sad in case some good looking nurse wanted to comfort me."

I should have known that they'd show up as soon as they heard the news. "How did you three find out?"

Barry said that my wife called everyone to tell us that you'd live. "She thought that we'd panic if we saw on television that you'd taken two bullets."

I corrected him, "Three bullets, not two, one in the left thigh and two in the stomach. Don't leave any out. They all hurt."

Barry said that they were here for the party in case I died. That SOB was always good for a laugh. "I'm sorry to disappoint you. The joke will be on you wiseacre! I'll be dancing on your grave some day."

Ed and Big Travis walked in just then. The first thing that Travis said was, "Damn! No party! I even brought a suit along."

Ed said, "I was going to ask your wife out after the funeral." Who could ask for more loyal or sympathetic friends?

Now that cordiality's had been exchanged, they actually expressed concern as to how I would heal and if there would be lingering effects.

I said, "Not to worry friends, I have always taken a lot of vitamins. I'll be out of here in a week." It turned out that I did go home a week later. My Army friends were already gone. They could only stay that one weekend that I saw them. They did visit twice each day that they were here. They'd felt left out having missed the camp out and said so.

I said, "You guys must love mosquitoes." I was shaking my head when I said that.

. . .

They kept me in the hospital for two weeks after I got out of ICU. Even then I was very sore. I guess that I should have been grateful to be alive and did remember to thank The Lord for that. The truth is that I was so mad that I would have killed the guy who shot me if he wasn't already dead. It's too bad that the gorilla had gone down the wrong path. He was a one-man army and might have been a good soldier had he not been a psychopath.

It was months before I felt like myself again. It's a creepy feeling to have stitches in your intestines. I was worried that they might burst and they'd have to open me up again and re-stitch me.

I hadn't run the whole time and I didn't walk too fast. I put the weight back on that I'd lost in the hospital. I started lifting weights again and doing calisthenics. We finally had to call all the neighbors and tell them, "No more pies, cakes, or cookies please!"

Every house on Derrick Place had at least one dog now. Fewer homes were without a gun. Most folks kept a shotgun *and* a pistol at their house. People had learned their lesson.

...

It was a blessing that things remained quiet for several months while I mended. I could still shoot, but a physical altercation would have had to be handled by the other members of SWAT. Those guys were plenty scary without me. Most of the time I was just the planner and the one who made decisions. There is something about combat in the Infantry that inspires a man to being good at making swift decisions. In civilian life, he who hesitates is lost. In the Infantry, hesitation resulted in being wounded or killed.

Currently, the biggest problem that my team and I had was feeling useful. When we weren't called up to be used as SWAT, we earned our salaries as regular County Patrolmen. On the bright side, we finally had time to attend school functions, parades, and Little League games. That didn't mean that we weren't bored to distraction. When we got together, it was generally agreed that life was boring lately.

There are three reasons for a man to become a cop. Two in particular are the biggest motivators. It was a toss up as to which of the two was the greater attraction. Excitement was one reason. The other was the desire to be one of the good guys, a knight in shining armor, a hero, and a role model. The third is the steady employment and retirement. That was low on incentive. Working for the City or County in Maintenance or becoming a Mail Carrier supply a steady income with a retirement package down the road. Men of action want to be soldiers, cops, or Firemen.

To break up the boredom, I decided to have a carnival at the unused fair grounds. We'd have competitions in physical fitness, boxing, and wrestling. I wanted no shooting events or tough man contests. Insurance for the carnival would be much more affordable without those two. It would give all these Spartans a chance to burn off some energy. I thought it wise to leave the competition open to everyone in the county who wanted to participate. My hope was to have regular citizens mingle with and grow to like the folks charged with enforcing the law. Cops are human, and not all citizens are criminals.

There would be trophies for every event broken down into weight classes with no special events separating age groups. Entrants could enter as many as but no more than three events. There would be only two weeks for participants to prepare. Excitement and anticipation among the population would have time enough to build in that two weeks.

I knew better than to enter any long distance running events, but I did enter the 440-yard dash. I didn't expect to win, just finish in a time that didn't embarrass me. I thought that I could be of some use in the tug of war and entered that event. I also put my name down for the push-up contest.

. . .

The long, two-week wait was finally over. This was the big day. Most of the contestants that signed up were cops. There were port-a-potties scattered around the fair grounds. Food and beverage sales would cover them and leave enough to pay for event insurance. Anything above and beyond cost would be divided between Fisher House and Ronald McDonald House equally.

There was an ambulance standing by and an EMT team. Police patrols today were broken into two-hour shifts. County and city security wouldn't be a problem. With the exception of boxing and wrestling, all events would be repeated. In most cases, contestants raced the clock rather than each other. The results would be posted in tomorrow's newspapers. Volunteers would pass out awards and trophies tomorrow.

My 58 push-ups were only good for a 4th place overall. In my defense, the competition was half my age. I was proud anyway. Our man in the boxing event lost in a 10th round split decision. He vowed to win next year. We did take the heavyweight wrestling trophy. The winners of those two events were local celebrities for the next several weeks.

All in all, it was a huge success. Everyone was talking about training for next year. The excitement and enthusiasm was obvious and genuine. My people were happy, so was I. That carnival was the best idea I'd had in a long time.

. . .

The fervor over the carnival finally faded away. Boredom, like rigor mortis set in once again. Autumn was here and it looked to be a rainy one. The days were still warm. Nights grew increasingly cooler. A cold winter was predicted to include the occasional snow flurries. Snow was pretty rare around here. I have seen it in Conroe before, but that was a long time ago. I hadn't had a white Christmas since I left Wisconsin. I hadn't frozen to death either. It was a trade off. I'll take warm weather any day. I preferred Texas even if I still hadn't quite mastered the language.

Speaking of dialect, I'd still never had chicken fried steak. I planned on remedying that little shortcoming tonight. I promised to take Margaret to dinner where I would be ordering, you guessed it, the elusive but ever popular (drum roll please) Chicken Fried Steak!

Call it force of habit, we went to The Kettle. There was bound to be at least one familiar face there this time of day. Nor were we disappointed. Jason Sprague and his new wife Courtney were there by themselves. Of course we joined them. Of course they were having Chicken Fried Steak. Jason, like me, had never tasted it.

Most of our conversation was about the carnival. He was miffed that no one from the agency had been invited. I told him that we did that to avoid embarrassing him and his unit in the competitions. We both knew that he and his men couldn't attend without the possibility of being exposed. Much of their success depended on operating anonymously with a low profile.

Jason said, "I was going to call you tonight to set up a breakfast appointment. There is something that I wanted to talk to you about. We can discuss it tonight after dinner. Now you will have one more night to mull it over."

Maybe my palate was burned out. The meal was no big deal. It certainly wasn't something to write home about. That doesn't mean that I'd never order it again. I was just expecting something special after all the years of not trying it.

After dinner, Jason and I took our coffee to a different table in an empty corner of the restaurant to talk. He started his end of the conversation by saying, "Things in Conroe and Montgomery County might take a turn for the worse over the next month. You might get lucky and this trouble might bypass you like the wind." He continued, "There has been a rash of murders along Interstate 45 moving in this direction. All the signs of a serial killer are present. The perpetrator has been cutting the victim's limbs off and tying them to the torso to create a more condensed package, which he then wraps in a plastic drop cloth. Evidently, the killer finds this package easier to dispose of quickly. So far, he's made no attempt that we're aware of to hide the bodies. If he has, there are more victims that we haven't found." Pausing long enough to take a sip of his coffee, Jason went on. "Everyone that has been found has been within plain sight of the freeway that passes through the middle of Conroe, I-45. All the victims have been traced to the town just north of where their body was found. He, and we think that it is a solitary, strong male, has left no fingerprints on the plastic. We are pretty sure that he dumps his victims at night to avoid detection. We think that he originated in Dallas since his first victim was found just south of there. So far, all of his victims have been women in the 25 to 40 year age bracket."

As soon as I thought he'd completed the briefing, I said, "Let me guess, traces of alcohol have been found in all the bodies, leading the FBI to think that he's picking up his victims in bars. Besides being muscular, you think that he has better than average looks because his victims have been attractive, younger women. Your investigation has been complicated by the fact that Texas is full of strong, good looking young men. However, his modus operandi makes you think that his capture is imminent because he leaves such an obvious trail. He seems insatiable in his hunt for new victims and you'd like it if I helped."

"Next thing, you'll want my job," Jason kidded. "You've pretty much summed it up. Can you help and do you want to?"

"Anything to stop this beast," I said. "It will give us something to do besides watch the rain."

We rejoined our wives and said goodbye to each other. Tomorrow would be long, busy, and hopefully successful.

...

So, that was the beginning of another bit of excitement. Where do all these psychos come from? It was like hell was full and sending them back. I didn't get much sleep that night thinking that this animal could very well be coaxing some poor woman to her worst nightmare and certain death at this very moment. I was lying there wondering if Jason's plans would parallel mine. I pictured eight of us with radios and cell phones in eight different locations looking for an unknown suspect. He'd be in charge. I was confident that he'd come up with a good plan and it would be organized, coordinated, and successful. I quit looking at the clock at 1:35 AM and finally fell asleep after praying for tomorrow's task.

The next morning, we all met at Jason's office with our suitcases. There was Steve, Al, Joseph, Stack, my son Travis, Sam, Jason and myself. He said that we'd be spending a lot of time in bars. (I hate smoky bars) Alcohol consumption was out. We'd be using our private vehicles. Everyone had to wear body armor. Damn if it didn't make me look fatter than I was already getting. Oh well, it's not like I was trying to pick up a chick.

Our first stop was the town of Rice. We were hoping that he hadn't gotten past here yet. The town was so small that we left Stack in charge of a four-man team. The rest of us went north to Alma. Alma only had one bar near the Interstate. It also only had one gas station. We fueled our vehicles, never letting on that we knew each other. We spaced our departure by a few minutes. Every vehicle eventually wound up at the bar. It was still early enough for the bar to be dead. I entered after Jason and sat at the bar. He was seated at a tall table in a cheap suit with a cheap briefcase open, pretending to be reading some papers. Travis and Sam came in together and headed for the pool table after getting two sodas.

The bartender was half-asleep and seemed to resent the intrusion on his afternoon nap. He was obviously not the owner. At least none of us were in danger of drowning in our nonalcoholic beer or Shirley Temples. This bartender wasn't the type to keep checking our bottles and glasses to sell us our next drink.

Shortly after 4:30 PM, people started coming in a few at a time. Some local industry must have gotten out for the day. In no time, there were about twenty-five people inside. Ten were females in the age group that appealed to the killer. Maybe I was too healthy, but they all looked pretty good to me.

A little after 5 PM, a big man in a Stetson and western cut suit walked in. Everyone looked up but no one greeted the man. Either he was a stranger or he wasn't well liked. I looked over at Jason and caught his eye. He nodded. This might be our man. He was tanned and had a set of shoulders that were probably manufactured in a gym somewhere. He'd be a handful in a fistfight. None of the ladies in here could resist enough to get away if he got rough. The big cowboy had a bottle of beer and hit the road. He didn't seem to notice all the looks the girls were giving him. He was probably used to it. At any rate, he was gone and we awaited the next stranger.

About an hour later, Stack called my cell phone. He said that a big stranger in a Stetson just walked in and sat next to the only woman in the bar. He said that Joseph was inside with him at the other end of the bar. I relayed his message to Jason. He said that he had a feeling about the cowboy. He asked me to tell our men at the pool table to sit tight and call us if they got bad vibrations.

We sped to Rice at over 100 miles per hour, making it there in twenty minutes. All that we could do was stand by. If we went inside, we might be recognized. I called Stack to let him know of our arrival. I told them to sit tight if the cowboy left with the lady while Jason and I followed. Get on the phone and send Steve and Al over to the motel while you and Joe hold down the fort. Tell them not to check in until the cowboy does if it turns out that he heads that way with the woman.

I was still 'up' from driving all that way at mach five give or take a few miles per hour. Jason and I were parked at the gas station where we could see the bar and the only motel at the same time. Minutes later, the big cowboy and the woman walked out and got in separate vehicles. I was in front of Jason, right behind our suspect's pickup truck. I called in his plates on the police radio. When first the woman, then the suspect pulled into the motel, I kept going and watched Jason in my mirror. He turned in, behind the pickup truck by several car lengths. After only a few blocks, I pulled a U-turn and went back toward the motel. I drove past in time to see Steve and Al entering different rooms at opposite ends of the strip motel.

I parked out of sight of the motel but where I could see the bar that the cowboy left as well as the gas station. I called Stack and told him to leave Joe there, but he should go to the other bar that Steve and Al left unguarded. Jason called me to say that he was checked into a room next to and on the East Side of the suspect. He said that he was setting up a listening device. I drove back to the motel and checked into the room on the other side. I opened my drapes and turned on the television.

A few minutes later, the cowboy came out and got in his truck. I called Jason to tell him. He said that he could hear water running in the shower and the lady humming. I called Joe and Stack next. I told them to remain nonchalant if the cowboy showed up. "We still aren't sure if he is the killer. Hold your positions."

I watched the suspect drive to the bar that he'd just left. I wasn't surprised to see him get back in his truck carrying a bottle. I closed my drapes before the cowboy pulled in. When I heard the door to his room close, I called Steve and Al, sending Al to Jason's room and having Steve join me. One fearful sound from the room in between and Jason would say, "Red" which would send the four of us crashing into the room with our suspect, through the window if necessary.

Just under an hour later, Joe called me to say that a large, middle aged man with the eyes of a predator just walked in. He sat at the bar, which was still almost empty, watching the door. I told him to stay put. "Play pool, watch TV, do anything to look natural. If a lady comes in, ignore her completely. Let the predator be the Romeo."

So far, the room between us had been quiet. Our next surprise came when the two lovebirds came out. They got in their vehicles and drove away in opposite directions. Jason and Al joined us to discuss our dilemma. We decided to split up our forces.

Jason took his cheap briefcase to join Joseph with the middle-aged predator. I joined Stack at his empty bar. We were looking across the street at the other bar when our bartender, a rather large fellow, walked past us. He was carrying a large and apparently heavy bundle wrapped in black plastic. He put it in the back of a pickup truck, got behind the wheel, and drove away. Neither one of us noticed his flesh toned surgical gloves until he put the cumbersome package in the truck. Our man had been right under our noses! We ran to our cars and took up pursuit. I radioed the others to explain the new situation.

Agent Jason Sprague was in his unmarked FBI vehicle with an Interceptor engine. He whizzed by Stack and me. The man in the pickup truck wouldn't stop for us. We could hear Jason on the horn with State Police. He was trying to order a road- block, but it sounded like it would take too long to organize. In desperation, Jason zoomed ahead of the pickup truck and slammed on his brakes. Stack had pulled alongside with his gun pointed at the open passenger's side window. I was right behind the killer with my gun out. He had no choice but to surrender.

His radiator blew when he rear-ended Jason's car. It was a scary moment for poor Jason. The suspect finally braked to a stop, putting both of his hands on the dash- board of his vehicle like he'd done it before. There was indeed a woman's body inside the package, mutilated like the others. Later, we found out that she was the lady bartender who normally worked there.

Soon, my son Travis and my son-in-law Sam joined us. We all drove back to the motel to retrieve our belongings before starting the long trip home.

We weren't quick enough to save that poor bartender's life, but we did stop the monster the same day that we sought to do so. Hopefully, the courts wouldn't be overly kind to the killer.

...

Jason had been riding with me. His vehicle had to be towed. We were of mixed emotions. There was elation at such a swift resolution to what everyone thought would be a much longer ordeal. Then there was the tragic disappointment at having lost another innocent life at such a tender age. We got back to Conroe so late that we didn't even stop for coffee. Jason switched over to Joseph's car since they lived in the same neighborhood. We said our good-byes and promised to meet for breakfast in the morning. It was a good feeling to drive down Derrick Place with two sets of headlights in my mirror, knowing my son and my daughter's husband were safe. Cops never know if they're coming home when they go out the door.

...

Breakfast the next morning was a magnified version of what Jason and I already felt on the trip home last night. Conversation started on a high note but quickly turned to anger and disappointment. That wasn't just a bundle of meat in that guy's truck. It was somebody's daughter, sister, friend, wife, girlfriend or mother. Times like this, I felt like Satan was winning here on Earth. I wasn't very proud about the way that turned out. Still, I don't question The Lord's Will anymore than I underestimate Satan's power on Earth.

Due to the swift end to that mass murderer's career, Jason said that he'd talk to the Governor about forming a state task force for similar operations. He got an across the board consent to volunteer all of our names. Saving lives and fighting crime is every bit the calling as some men get to be priests or pastors.

With the breakfast meeting out of the way, everyone left for home with hopes of having a day off. I say, "Hope" because police work gets an awful lot of stimulation from a scary place referred to as "left field". Murphy's Law usually set the rules and today was no exception. Before many of us could even get home, a massive explosion could be heard and felt. It seemed to be centered just west of the city limits. It was impossible to tell how far away, but it got the same eight-man team headed west on Highway 105. I had just dropped Jason off and naturally pulled a U-turn to pick him up. No matter if he had jurisdiction, I was sure that he'd want to be on the scene. I liked how he analyzed situations and respected his intellect.

The blast came from west of the northernmost expansion of The Woodlands. I remember when that fancy subdivision had just started out. Now, it was a sizeable city. It was easy enough to zero in on the tall pillar of smoke. The Fire Department was right on my heels and I was driving fast with my lights flashing.

The eight of us performed crowd control. We let the Fire Department do what they got paid for, extinguish fires, analyze and investigate them.

A large pole barn had exploded. My initial thought was that the fire and explosion were connected to something illegal. There were no licensed facilities around that dealt in explosives. I suspected that drugs were involved. Before long, it was a steamy ruin. All the sight-seers drifted back to their cars and left. My men and I converged on Jason to hear his thoughts on the explosion.

He said that drug laboratories sometimes blew up like this. We just nodded our heads at this bit of common knowledge waiting for him to go on. He said that oil money built most of The Woodlands, but bad apples turn up frequently in affluent societies.

I suggested that we do a quick deed search for the owners of this property. It was the most logical place to start. I got on the radio to set that in motion.

Before we left, the fire chief joined our group. He said that human remains were found in the fire. He said that there were several adults but didn't have an exact count yet because they were still going through the rubble. He said that my crime scene investigators were welcome at the site effective immediately. I thanked him and sent for detectives. We were in the county now. Our coroner and his men never let me down. They were thorough and professional.

I turned the rest of my men loose to go home and waited outside the yellow tape for the coroner and his crew. Jason caught a ride with Joseph again. When they arrived, I reminded them that they were here early on invitation. "Be polite and respectful to the Chief and firemen still here."

Still outside the tape, I watched the experts work like archaeologists at a dig. I was mystified that something so explosive would be this close to town. This pole barn had been here ever since I could remember. I'd driven past it many times. I hope that didn't mean that something illegal had been going on for a long time yet escaped my notice. The barn had been part of a farming operation for so long that I accepted it as part of the landscape. Most of the farm had been sold to accommodate the expanding Woodlands. The barn had been left unmolested.

The bodies found in the fire were a mystery. They could have been workers or captives. They might have just been some illegal aliens hiding out. Fire damage might keep that knowledge secret for a long time. I wasn't good at being a spectator, so I let the specialists do their job without my useless presence. I figured that I could go home now to await the results of the deed search.

The phone was ringing when I got to the door. Margaret let me answer it, knowing that it was probably for me. My cell phone had been in my pocket and I didn't hear it ring. The barn still belonged to the same family, but it was leased to someone who lived in the older part of The Woodlands. I jotted down the address and went to pay an unannounced visit.

My son Travis was in his yard when I was driving by. I invited him to come along as backup. He grinned and he joined me happily. My son was eager as I to stay in the game. Neither of us wanted to miss a chance at some more excitement.

When we got to the address, there was a late model, very expensive crew cab pickup truck in the driveway. It looked like someone was packing to move. I parked so the driveway was blocked. Travis and I split up to make two armed targets in case things took a violent turn. As we neared the front door, a man with two large suitcases came walking out. Like contestants in a quick draw event, Travis and I pulled our guns. The man grasped the situation, dropped his suitcases, and raised his hands. Travis motioned him down on his belly and cuffed him as I walked past to check the house.

Before I could enter, a lady with two equally large suitcases struggled out the door. Travis used my cuffs to corral her and I went inside. I stepped through the door and stood motionless for a moment, listening to the house. That action probably saved my life. A man with a machine pistol was coming down the stairs. He, too, had a very large suitcase in his empty hand. Had I been moving, he'd have seen me first and things might have turned out worse. As it was, I was able to surprise him. I arrested him without firing a shot. He was so distracted that he practically bumped into me in his haste to get out the door. I took his weapon and put him face down in the driveway. I secured his hands with a nylon fastener.

I asked Travis to watch our prisoners while I searched the mansion, all 3000 square feet of it. The house was silent as only an empty house can be. It turned out to be empty. Now I could call for a paddy wagon.

My detainees wouldn't talk without an attorney. We arrested them on suspicion of explosive's charges and homicide. I called my favorite judge and had a search warrant delivered within 30 minutes so we could search their suitcases and whatever else they'd put in the cargo area of the fancy truck.

They were traveling light, toothbrushes, socks, underwear, hundreds of packets of fifty and one hundred-dollar bills, plus some crack cocaine along with two weapons. One of the guns was being carried concealed by the first man out the door. Now, we had something serious to hold them on, without bail of course, since they were captured in the act of flight.

It took over a week to get the reports and lab results from the scene of the fire and explosion. Ether was determined to be the catalyst in the explosion. Other than 'Hispanic males', the bodies couldn't be identified. Assuming them to be here illegally, we shipped the bodies to Mexico for identification. Their families could at least have the closure of memorial services.

Eighteen charges of manslaughter were added to manufacture of a controlled substance with the intent to sell. They must have been selling their product outside of our area to avoid detection. The men would each wind up with twenty plus years. The lease had been in the woman's name. She would probably get thirty years. It is never worth it.

. . .

Our policing efforts worked like a well-oiled machine. I attribute that to the total lack of apathy among our law enforcement personnel, in town as well as the deputies. Every crime was hit by our attack-dog attitude until we put an end to whatever bit of evil that we were up against. We took our jobs seriously and loved our jobs.

For anyone who thinks that tacking on the manslaughter and accessory charges was too harsh, remember this: That wasn't aspirin that they were selling. Crack ruins lives and kills people on a regular basis. Harsh penalties discourage copycats, and prevent repeat offenders. We weren't in the business of slapping wrists except with handcuffs.

Back to serene little Montgomery County, this time with no loud noises or dead bodies. For the first time in my life, that thought appealed to me. Either I was getting old, or I'd finally grown up. You pick.....

## The End